VISUAL QUICKSTART GUID

FIREWORKS 3

FOR WINDOWS AND MACINTOSH

Sandee Cohen

Peachpit Press

macromedia®
PRESS

Visual QuickStart Guide
Fireworks 3 for Windows and Macintosh
Copyright © 2000 by Sandee Cohen

Peachpit Press

1249 Eighth Street
Berkeley, CA 94710
800 283-9444 • 510 524 2178
fax 510 524 2221
Find us on the Web at http://www.peachpit.com

Published by Peachpit Press in association with Macromedia Press
Peachpit Press is a division of Addison Wesley Longman

Cover Design: The Visual Group
Interior Design: Sandee Cohen
Production: Sandee Cohen
Illustrations: Sandee Cohen
Page 4 artwork: © 1999, Ray Villarosa

Notice of Liability

Trademarks

ISBN 0-201-70452-8

0 9 8 7 6 5 4 3 2 1

Printed and bound in the United States of America

DEDICATED TO

Everyone who has discovered the power of
being master of your own (web) domain.

THANKS TO

Nancy Ruenzel, publisher of Peachpit Press.

Kelly Ryer, my project editor at Peachpit Press.

Lisa Brazieal, the production coordinator from Peachpit Press.

The staff of Peachpit Press, all of whom make me proud to be a Peachpit author.

Karen Dominey, who provided excellent copy editing.

Steve Rath, who does the best index in the business.

Diana Smedley, of Macromedia.

Dennis Griffin, of Macromedia who did the tech edit.

Mark Haynes of Macromedia, who provides the best support in the Fireworks news-group (http://forums/macromedia.com/ macromedia.fireworks).

Joe Lowery, author of the *Fireworks 3 Bible.* Joe has been a great resource, and I'm thrilled that readers will now have his book to graduate to after they read mine.

Fireworks beta list participants, too numerous to name, who all gave me great insight into features and techniques.

Ray Villarosa, who created special artwork for the Introduction that shows off all of Fireworks' graphics capabilities.

Michael Randasso, and the staff of the New School for Social Research Computer Instruction Center.

Sharon Steuer, author of the *Illustrator 8 Wow! Book,* who helped me during more than one late-night panic attack.

Pixel, my cat, who still thinks chapter 12 is all about her.

Colophon

This book was created using Fireworks for illustrations, QuarkXPress 4 for layout, Ambrosia SW Snapz Pro and Snagit for screen shots. The computers used were a Power Macintosh™ 8500, a PowerBook G3, and a Monorail 166LS. The fonts used were Minion and Futura from Adobe and two specialty fonts created using Macromedia Fontographer.

TABLE OF CONTENTS

Table of Contents

INTRODUCTION

Welcome to Macromedia Fireworks 3. In a very short period of time Fireworks has become an important tool in the creation of graphics for the Web. Using Fireworks, designers have been able to create extremely sophisticated graphics without having to learn complicated code. Now, with this third version of Fireworks, the program is even more powerful and sophisticated.

It has been very exciting to revise this book. Many new features have added more pages to the book. And yet, some of features have been made much simpler and easier to understand. Just as Fireworks has evolved, so has this Visual QuickStart Guide.

What You Can Create with Fireworks

Fireworks was specially designed to create graphics to be used on the World Wide Web. Fireworks gives you one tool that does it all, from start to finish. All your Web graphic elements—text, photos, buttons, banners, animations, and interface elements—can all be created, modified, optimized, and output from one Fireworks file. As the artwork at the end of this introduction shows, Fireworks has all the tools you need to create sophisticated graphics. This makes Fireworks a complete Web graphics solution.

How This Book Is Organized

The first two chapters provide overviews of the program. Most of the other chapters cover all the tools and techniques for creating graphics from within Fireworks. This is where you learn to create artwork and add special effects.

Since exporting, converting file formats, and optimizing Web graphics are so important, you may want to pay special attention to Chapter 14, "Optimizing," and Chapter 19, "Exporting." If all you want to do is put existing images up on a Web site, you can jump to those chapters and get right to work.

Using This Book

If you have used any of the Visual QuickStart Guides, you will find this book very similar. Each of the chapters consists of numbered steps that deal with a specific technique or feature of the program. As you work through the steps, you gain an understanding of the technique or feature. The illustrations help you judge if you are following the steps correctly.

Instructions

Using a book such as this will be easier once you understand the terms I am using. This is especially important since some other computer books use terms differently. Therefore, here are the terms I use in the book and explanations of what they mean.

Click refers to pressing down and releasing the mouse button in the Macintosh, or the left mouse button in Windows. You must release the mouse button, or it is not a click.

Press means to hold down the mouse button or a keyboard key.

Press and drag means to hold the mouse button down and then move the mouse. In later chapters, I use the shorthand term *drag;* just remember that you have to press and hold as you drag the mouse.

Menu Commands

Fireworks has menu commands that you follow to open dialog boxes, change artwork, and initiate certain actions. These menu commands are listed in bold type. The typical direction to choose a menu command might be written as **Modify > Arrange > Bring to Front**. This means that you should first choose the Modify menu, then choose the Arrange submenu, and then choose the Bring to Front command.

Keyboard Shortcuts

Most of the menu commands for Fireworks have keyboard shortcuts that help you work faster. For instance, instead of choosing New from the File menu, it is faster and easier to use the keyboard shortcut.

The modifier keys used in keyboard shortcuts are sometimes listed in different orders by different software companies or authors. I always list the Command or Ctrl keys first, then the Option or Alt key, and then the Shift key. The order that you press those modifier keys is not important. However, it is very important that you always add the last key (the letter or number key) after you are holding the other keys.

Rather than cluttering up the exercises with long keyboard commands, the shortcuts are listed in Appendix B separated by platform.

Learning Keyboard Shortcuts

While keyboard shortcuts help you work faster, you really do not have to start using them right away. In fact, you will most likely learn more about Fireworks by using the menus. As you look for one command, you may see another feature that you would like to explore.

Once you feel comfortable working with Fireworks, you can start adding keyboard shortcuts to your repertoire. My suggestion is to look at which menu commands you use a lot. Then choose one of those shortcuts each day. For instance, if you import a lot of art from other programs, you might decide to learn the shortcut for the Import command. For the rest of that day, use the Import shortcut every time you import art. Even if you have to look at the menu to refresh your memory, still use the keyboard shortcut to actually open the Import dialog box. By the end of the day you will have memorized the Import shortcut. The next day you can learn a new one.

Cross-Platform Issues

One of the great strengths of Fireworks is that it is almost identical on both the Macintosh and Windows platforms. In fact, at first glance it is hard to tell which platform you are working on. However, because there are some differences between the platforms, there are some things you should keep in mind.

Modifier Keys

Modifier keys are always listed with the Macintosh key first and then the Windows key second. So a direction to hold the Command/Ctrl key as you drag means to hold the Command key on the Macintosh platform or the Ctrl key on the Windows platform. When the key is the same on both computers, such as the Shift key, only one is listed.

Generally the Command key on the Macintosh (sometimes called the Apple key) corresponds to the Ctrl key on Windows. The Option key on the Macintosh corresponds to the Alt key on Windows. The Control key on the Macintosh does not have a Windows equivalent. Notice that the Control key for the Macintosh is always spelled out while the Ctrl key for Windows is not.

Platform-Specific Features

A few times in the book, I have written separate exercises for the Macintosh and Windows platforms. These exercises are indicated by (Mac) and (Win).

Most of the time this is because the procedures are so different that they need to be written separately. Some features exist only on one platform. Those features are labeled to reflect this.

Continuing Your Fireworks Education

One of the benefits of the Visual QuickStart Series is that the books are simple and don't weigh you down with a lot of details. However, they were never designed to be a complete reference work. So, if you need the most complete reference book—a bible, let's say—you should look at *The Fireworks Bible* by Joseph W. Lowery. Joe's book goes far beyond the scope of this QuickStart Guide. And since many Fireworks features are designed to work with Macromedia Dreamweaver, you may also want to get Joe's *Dreamweaver 3 Bible*.

If you have been working with Web graphics for some time, then all you need to do is learn the specific features of Fireworks. However, if you are new to the Web, you may need some background information. I have tried to provide references in the chapters.

But however you use Fireworks, don't forget to have fun!

An example of the types of artwork you can create using Fireworks.
(Artwork courtesy of illustrator/designer Ray Villarosa, industrial@earthlink.net)

Sandee Cohen

(Sandee@vectorbabe.com)
December, 1999

FIREWORKS BASICS

When I start learning a new application, I'm always in a rush to get started. When I pick up a book about the application, I never read the first chapter.

I don't want to read about buttons, fields, and controls—especially if I'm already familiar with other programs from the company such as Dreamweaver or FreeHand.

No, I rush right into the middle chapters of the book.

However, after a few hours of slogging helplessly though the book, I realize there are things I don't understand about the program. I recognize I'm a bit confused. So I come back to the first chapter to learn the foundation of the program.

Of course, since you're much more patient than I am, you're already here—reading the first chapter.

System Requirements

There are certain minimum requirements of your computer and operating system you need to have for Fireworks to perform correctly.

❶ *The Macintosh* **Memory** *display.*

Minimum System Requirements (Mac)

- System 8.1 or higher
- Adobe Type Manager 4 or higher to use Type 1 fonts
- Power Macintosh (G3 recommended, G4 for AltiVec performance) processor required (Power Macintosh 604/120 MHz or greater, 603e/180 MHz or greater, or G3 recommended)
- 64 MB of application RAM with virtual memory on (32 MB or more with virtual memory off recommended)
- 64 MB of available hard disk space (100 MB or more recommended)
- CD-ROM drive
- Mouse or digitizing tablet
- 640×480 resolution, 256-color monitor required (1024×768 resolution, millions-of-colors monitor recommended)

❷ *The Macintosh* **Hard Disk space** *display.*

To check memory (Mac):

- ◆ Choose About This Computer from the Apple menu ❶.

To check hard disk space (Mac):

- ◆ Open the hard disk and read the available space at the top of the window ❷.

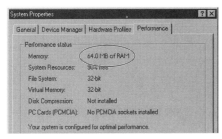

❸ *The Windows* **System Properties** *display.*

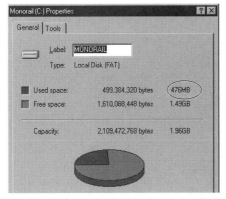

❹ *The Windows* **Hard Disk Properties** *display.*

Minimum System Requirements (Win)

- Windows 95, 98 or Windows NT 4 (with Service Pack 3) or later

- Adobe Type Manager 4 or higher to use Type 1 fonts

- Intel Pentium 120 MHz processor required (Pentium III recommended)

- 64 MB of system RAM

- 60 MB of available hard disk space (100 MB or more recommended)

- CD-ROM drive

- Mouse or digitizing tablet

- 640×480 resolution, 256-color monitor required (1024×768 resolution, millions-of-colors monitor recommended)

To check memory (Win):

Choose System Properties from the Control Panels directory **❸**.

To check hard disk space (Win):

1. Select the hard disk, usually named a letter such as C.

2. Click with the right mouse button and then choose Properties from the contextual menu **❹**.

System Requirements

Installing Fireworks

Once you have confirmed that your system meets the minimum requirements for running Fireworks, you can then install the application.

To install Fireworks (Mac):

1. Disable any virus-protection software.
2. Insert the Fireworks CD-ROM in the CD-ROM drive.
3. Double-click the Fireworks installer ❺.
4. Follow the instructions that appear.
5. After installation, restart the Macintosh.

To install Fireworks (Win):

1. Insert the Fireworks CD-ROM in the CD-ROM drive.
2. Follow the instructions that appear ❻.
3. After installation, restart the computer.

Launching Fireworks

Once you have installed Fireworks, you can then launch the application.

To launch Fireworks (Mac):

Open the folder that contains the Fireworks application and then double-click the Fireworks application icon ❼.

To launch Fireworks (Win):

Use the Start menu ❽ to navigate to the Fireworks folder and then choose the Fireworks application.

❺ *The* Fireworks installer *for the Macintosh.*

❻ *The opening screen for the Fireworks installer for Windows.*

❼ *The* Fireworks application icon.

❽ *The* **Fireworks application** *in the Start menu.*

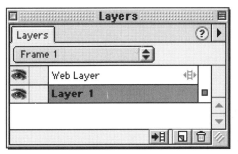

❾ *The* Layers *panel.*

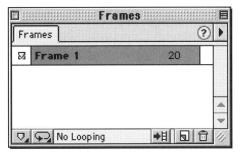

❿ *The* Frames *panel.*

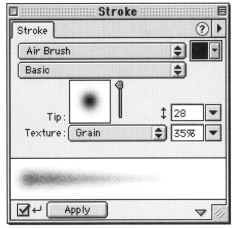

⓫ *The* Stroke *panel.*

Onscreen Panels

Once you have launched Fireworks, you see the various Fireworks onscreen panels. These panels control different aspects of the program. They can be closed, opened, re-sized, or rearranged to suit your own work habits.

The Layers Panel

The Layers panel ❾ allows you to control the order in which objects appear onscreen. *(For more information on the Layers panel, see Chapter 6, "Working with Objects.")*

The Frames Panel

The Frames panel ❿ controls the elements used for creating rollovers and animations. *(For more information on the Frames panel, see Chapter 15, "Animations.")*

The Stroke Panel

The Stroke panel ⓫ controls the look of the stroke that is applied to the edge of an object. *(For more information on strokes, see Chapter 8, "Strokes.")*

TIP The Expand button, found on the Stroke, Fill, and Effect panels lets you show or hide the preview area to create shorter panels.

Onscreen Panels

The Fill Panel

The Fill panel ⓬ controls the effect that is applied to the area inside an object. *(For more information on working with fills, see Chapter 7, "Fills.")*

The Effect Panel

The Effect panel ⓭ controls the additional effects that can be added to an object. *(For more information on effects, see Chapter 9, "Effects.")*

The Color Mixer Panel

The Color Mixer ⓮ allows you to define colors according to five different modes: RGB, Hexadecimal, HSB, CMY, or Grayscale. *(For more information on the color modes, see Chapter 3, "Colors.")*

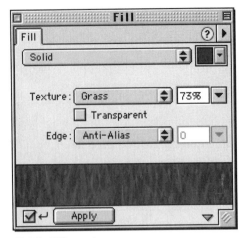

⓬ *The* Fill panel.

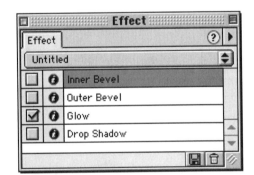

⓭ *The* Effect panel.

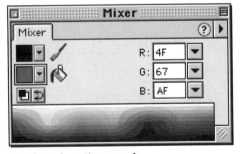

⓮ *The* Color Mixer panel.

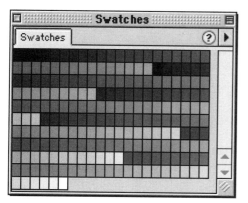

⑮ *The* Swatches panel.

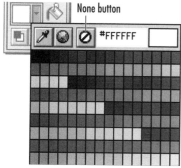

⑯ *The* Color Well Swatches panel.

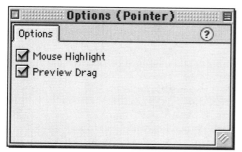

⑰ *The* Options panel.

The Swatches Panel

The Swatches panel **⑮** lets you work with preset palettes of color or store your own sets of colors. *(For more information on the color modes, see Chapter 3, "Colors.")*

The Color Well Swatches Panel

Rather than repeatedly going to the Color Mixer or Swatches panel to apply colors, you can use the Color Well. It is located in the Toolbox and other panels and dialog boxes. When you click on the small control next to the Color Well, the Swatches panel appears **⑯**. This allows you to choose a swatch or access the eyedropper to apply a color. The None button lets you remove a fill or stroke from an object.

The Options Panel

The Options panel **⑰** displays any options for working with the currently selected tool. These options change depending on the tool selected.

Onscreen Panels

The Info Panel

The Info panel **18** provides feedback as to the color and position of selected objects. *(For more information on using the Info panel, see page 50 and 76.)*

The Object Panel

The Object panel **19** controls the opacity of objects and how they interact with other objects on the page. *(For more information on using the Object panel, see page 106, and pages 109–110.)*

The URL Panel

The URL panel **20** allows you to add URL links to areas on the page. *(For more information on adding links to areas of your Web graphics, see Chapter 16, "Hotspots and Links" and Chapter 17, "Slices.")*

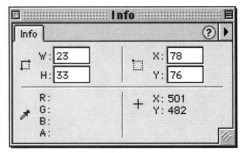

18 *The* Info panel.

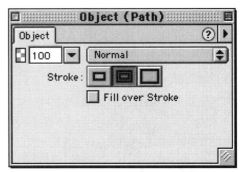

19 *The* Object panel.

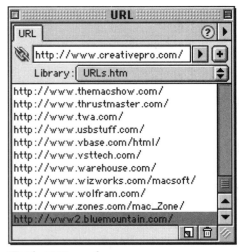

20 *The* URL panel.

㉑ *The* Behaviors panel.

㉒ *The* Find and Replace panel.

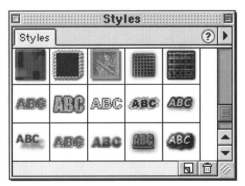

㉓ *The* Styles panel.

The Behaviors Panel

The Behaviors panel **㉑** allows you to assign JavaScript to elements such as rollovers and image maps. *(For more information on working with Behaviors, see Chapter 18, "Behaviors.")*

The Find and Replace Panel

The Find and Replace panel **㉒** allows you to make changes in text and graphic elements. *(For more information on working with the Find and Replace panel, see Chapter 11, "Automation Features.")*

The Styles Panel

The Styles panel **㉓** allows you to save the settings for an object's appearance and then apply them quickly to other objects. *(For more information on working with styles, see Chapter 11, "Automation Features.")*

Onscreen Panels

The Project Log Panel

The Project Log panel ❷❹ allows you to list a series of files you are currently working on and apply find and replace commands to all the files in the list. *(For more information on working with the Project Log, see Chapter 11, "Automation Features.")*

The Color Table Panel

The Color Table panel ❷❺ lets you control the colors used in exporting GIF images. *(For more information on working with the Color Table, see Chapter 3, "Colors.")*

The Optimize Panel

The Optimize panel ❷❻ allows you to control the colors and settings for exporting images. *(For more information on working with the Optimize panel, see Chapter 14, "Optimizing.")*

❷❹ *The* Project Log panel.

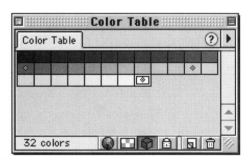

❷❺ *The* Color Table panel.

❷❻ *The* Optimize panel.

Onscreen Panels

❷❼ *The* **History panel** *lets you record actions and save them as scripts.*

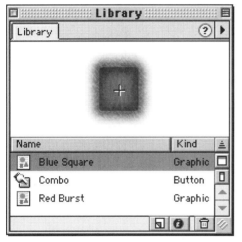

❷❽ *The* **Library panel.**

The History Panel

The History panel **❷❼** records the series of actions and commands you create within Fireworks. You can then play those actions back as part of automatic scripts. *(For more information on working with the History panel, see Chapter 11, "Automation Features.")*

The Library Panel

The Library panel **❷❽** stores the items defined as graphic and button symbols. You can drag items from the Library panel onto your pages. *(For more information on working with the Library panel, see Chapter 15, "Animations.")*

Onscreen Panels

Working with Panels

The panels can all be customized to make it easier for you to work with Fireworks. You can change how panels are grouped, resize them, or quickly minimize or maximize their size.

To group panels:

1. Drag a panel by its tab onto another panel to group the panels together ❷❾.

2. Drag a panel by its tab out of a grouping to separate the panels.

To resize panels:

◆ Drag the resize icon of a panel to change the size of the panel ❸⓿.

To minimize panels (Mac):

1. Click the minimize icon of a panel to display only the title bar of the panel ❸❶.

2. Click the minimize icon to restore the panel to its full size.

To minimize panels (Win):

1. Double-click the title bar of a panel to display only the panel tab panel ❸❷.

2. Double-click the title bar to restore the panel to its full size.

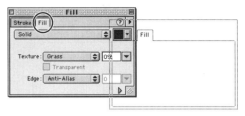

❷❾ Drag the tab of a panel *(circled)* to group or ungroup the panels.

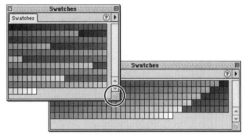

❸⓿ Drag the resize icon of a panel *(circled)* to change the size of a panel.

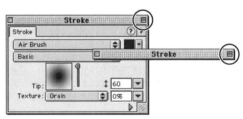

❸❶ (Mac) Click the minimize icon *(circled)* to quickly show and hide the contents of the panel.

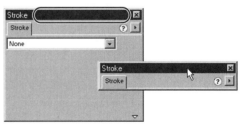

❸❷ (Win) Double-click the title bar of a panel *(circled) to quickly show and hide the contents of a panel.*

③③ *The* **View Controls** (Mac) *control the page display and preview animations.*

③④ *The* **View Controls** (Win) *control the page display.*

③⑤ *The* **Animation Controls** (Win) *let you display animations.*

Window Elements

The Window elements allow you to change the magnification and previews of images, see how images are optimized, and display animations.

The View Controls (Mac)

View Controls **③③** are part of the document window. They let you change the magnification and display of your page. They also let you preview animations within the document window. *(For more information on using the View Controls to change the page display, see page 25. For more information on working with animations see page 216.)*

The View Controls (Win)

The View Controls **③④** let you change the magnification and display of your page. They can either be fixed to the edge of the application window or positioned as a floating panel. *(For more information on using the View Controls, see page 25.)*

The Animation Controls (Win)

The Animation Controls **③⑤** let you preview animations within the document window. They are fixed to the edge of the application window. *(For more information on using the View Controls for animations, see page 216.)*

Window Elements

Using the Text Editor

The Text Editor **36** lets you enter and format text. *(For more information on working with text, see Chapter 10, "Text.")*

Using the Windows Toolbars

The Windows version of Fireworks contains two special toolbars that contain frequently used menu commands.

The Main Toolbar (Win)

The Main Toolbar **37** can be fixed to the top of the screen or dragged into position as a floating panel. It contains commands for working with files and displaying panels.

The Modify Toolbar (Win)

The Modify Toolbar **38** can be fixed to the top of the screen or dragged into position as a floating panel. It contains commands for working with objects. *(For more information on working with the commands in the Modify Toolbar, see Chapter 6, "Working with Objects.")*

36 *The* Text Editor.

37 *Click the icons in the* Main *toolbar (Win) to apply the commands.*

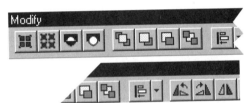

38 *Click the icons in the* Modify *toolbar (Win) to apply the commands.*

39 *Click to select a* Tab.

40 *Enter a value in a* Field.

41 *Click to apply a* Button.

42 *Click to select an* icon.

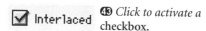

43 *Click to activate a* checkbox.

Using the Interface Elements

All the panels and dialog boxes use similar interface elements.

Tabs

♦ Click to choose a tab **39**. This changes the information displayed.

Fields

♦ Enter a value in a field **40**. This can be either numbers or text.

Buttons

♦ Click to apply a button command **41**.

Icons

♦ Click to select an icon **42**. The selected icon is indicated by a change in its appearance.

Checkbox

♦ Click to activate a checkbox **43**. A check appears to indicate the box is selected.

Pop-up menus

1. Click to reveal a pop-up menu ㊹.

2. Choose from the menu items.

Panel menus

1. Click the triangle in the right corner of a panel ㊺ to open the menu.

2. Choose from the menu items.

Wheels

◆ Drag the wheel handle ㊻ clockwise or counterclockwise to change the value.

Color Ramp

◆ Click anywhere in the color ramp ㊼ to select that color.

Pop-up Sliders

1. Press the triangle to reveal the slider control ㊽.

2. Drag the small pointer to change the amount in the field.

㊹ *Click to open a* **pop-up menu.**

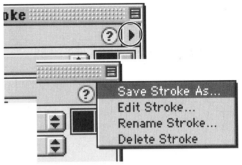

㊺ *Click to open a* **panel menu.**

㊻ *Drag to adjust a* **wheel.**

㊼ *Click to choose a color in a* **color ramp.**

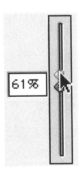

㊽ *Press the triangular arrow to open a* **slider** *and then drag to change the setting.*

Using the Interface Elements

Toolbox and Keyboard Shortcuts

Fireworks has many different tools. You can choose the tools by clicking the tool in the Toolbox **49** or by pressing the group.

You can also access the tools by pressing the keyboard shortcut (shown in parentheses). The tool shortcuts do not need modifiers such as Command or Ctrl.

TIP (Win) The Toolbox can be fixed to the side of the window or positioned as a floating panel.

TIP When tools share the same keyboard shortcut, press the key several times to rotate through the different tools.

Small triangle indicates a group of tools that appear when you press the triangle.

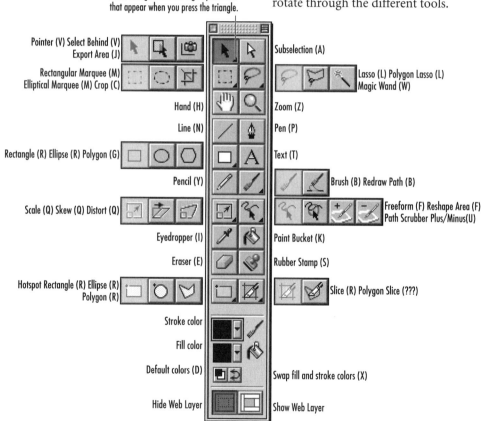

Pointer (V) Select Behind (V) Export Area (J)
Subselection (A)

Rectangular Marquee (M) Elliptical Marquee (M) Crop (C)
Lasso (L) Polygon Lasso (L) Magic Wand (W)

Hand (H)
Zoom (Z)

Line (N)
Pen (P)

Rectangle (R) Ellipse (R) Polygon (G)
Text (T)

Pencil (Y)
Brush (B) Redraw Path (B)

Scale (Q) Skew (Q) Distort (Q)
Freeform (F) Reshape Area (F) Path Scrubber Plus/Minus(U)

Eyedropper (I)
Paint Bucket (K)

Eraser (E)
Rubber Stamp (S)

Hotspot Rectangle (R) Ellipse (R) Polygon (R)
Slice (R) Polygon Slice (???)

Stroke color

Fill color

Default colors (D)
Swap fill and stroke colors (X)

Hide Web Layer
Show Web Layer

49 *The tools in the* **Toolbox** *and their keyboard shortcuts (in parentheses).*

Using the Precision Cursors

Each of the tools can be set for icon cursors or precision cursors **50**. The icon cursor shows the representation of the tool as it appears in the toolbox. The icon cursor shows a cross hair and dot that indicates the center point or active point of the tool.

Choosing icon or precise cursors

◆ Press the Caps Lock key. This switches between the two cursor modes.

or

◆ Choose Precise Cursors from the **Preferences** > **Editing** dialog box.

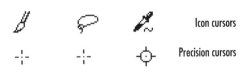

Icon cursors

Precision cursors

50 *The difference between* icon cursors *and* precision cursors.

DOCUMENT SETUP 2

Remember back when you were in the fourth or fifth grade and you were going to the first day of school? Remember how the night before you would carefully lay out all of your new clothes for the next day? Remember how you'd spend extra time to set up your notebook, dividers, paper, pencils, and rulers?

Even then you knew the importance of document setup. You knew that setting things up properly right at the beginning of the term would help you later on in the school year.

That's how it is when you start each new Fireworks document. The document setup helps you organize your work and will help you later on.

Opening Documents

When you start a new document, you must make certain decisions about the document that affect the final output.

To create a new document:

1. Choose **File**>**New**. This opens the New Document dialog box **❶**.

2. Use the height and width fields to set the size of the document.

TIP Use the pop-up lists to change the unit of measurement from pixels to inches or centimeters.

3. Use the resolution field to set the number of points per inch for the graphics of the document.

TIP Most Web graphics are saved at 72 pixels per inch. Print graphics usually need higher resolutions.

4. Set the canvas color of the document by choosing white, transparent, or custom.

5. If you choose custom, click the Color Well to open the color picker, where you can set your color.

6. Click OK to create the new document, which appears in an untitled document window **❷**.

TIP The Original, Preview, 2-Up, and 4-Up tabs at the top of the document window are used as part of the process in optimizing files *(see Chapter 14, "Optimizing").*

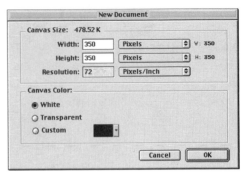

❶ *The* **New Document** *dialog box.*

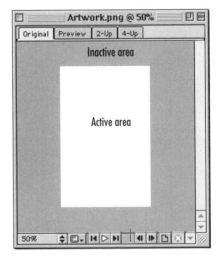

❷ *The* document window.

Mac icon

Windows icon

❸ *The* document info display area icons *for Macintosh and Windows.*

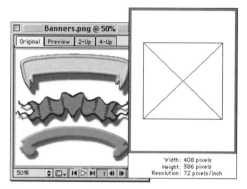

❹ *The* document info display area.

To open previously saved documents:

1. Choose **File**>**Open**.

2. Navigate through your directories and folders to find the file you want to open.

3. Click OK.

When you open a previously saved document, Fireworks lets you protect the original file by opening it as an untitled document.

To open a document as untitled:

1. Choose **File**>**Open** and navigate to find the original version of the file.

2. Click Open as "Untitled" and then click Open. The document opens in an unsaved, untitled version.

3. Make any changes and save the document as you would any other file.

To see the document information:

◆ Press the Document Info Display button ❸ to see a representation of the size of the document as well as a read out of the document's size and resolution ❹.

Altering Documents

Once you have created a document, you can still make changes to it. You can change the size of the image or the size of the canvas. You can also change the color of the background of a document.

To change the image size:

1. Choose **Modify** >**Document** >**Image Size** to open the Image Size dialog box **❺**.

2. Use the Pixel Dimensions height and width fields to change the absolute number of pixels in the document.

TIP The Pixel Dimensions fields are not available if Resample Image is turned off.

3. Use the Print Size height and width fields to change the display size of the image.

TIP Press the pop-up menu to change the size of the document by a percentage.

TIP Select Constrain Proportions to keep the image from being distorted.

4. Use the Resolution field to change the image size by increasing or reducing the number of pixels per inch.

TIP Scanned images may become blurred if the resolution or size of the image is increased by more than 50% **❻**.

5. Use the resampling pop-up menu to choose how the scanned imaged will be changed **❼**. The four choices are Bicubic, Bilinear, Soft, and Nearest Neighbor.

TIP Use Bicubic for scanned images such as photographs. Use Nearest Neighbor for images with straight lines and text such as screen shots. Use Bilinear or Soft only if you do not get acceptable results with the other two methods.

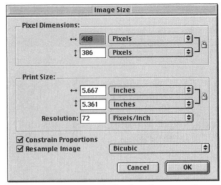

❺ The **Image Size** dialog box lets you change the size of an image.

Original image

Resampled image

❻ The effects of **resampling an image** to increase its size and resolution. Notice the blurry edges in the resampled image.

❼ The **resampling choices** control how scanned images are changed.

Altering Documents

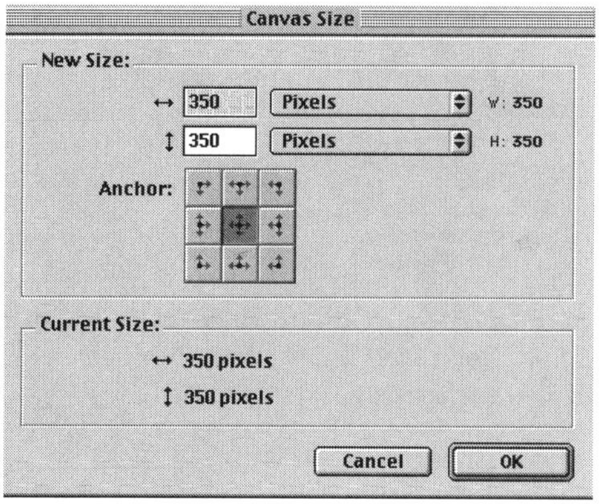

❽ *The* **Canvas size** *dialog box lets you adds space to, or delete space from, the canvas outside the image area.*

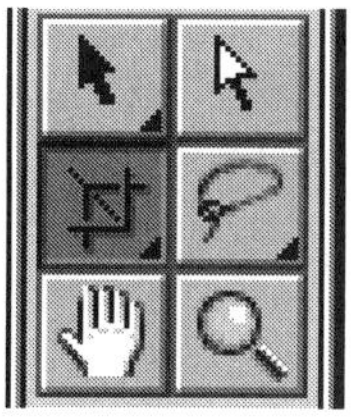

❾ *The* **Crop tool** *in the Toolbox.*

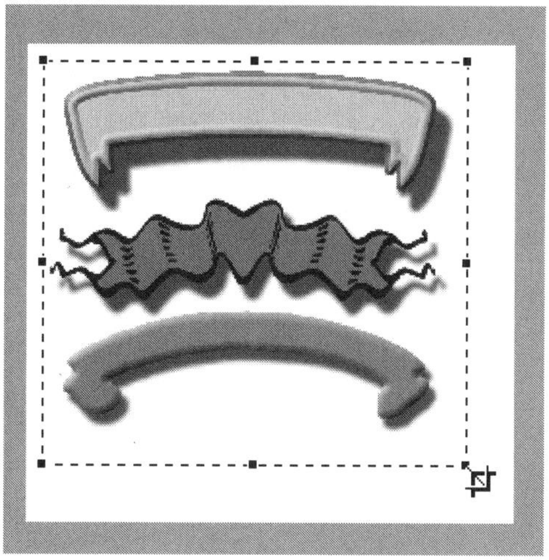

❿ *The* **Crop tool handles** *define the final canvas size after cropping.*

You can keep the size of the image constant while changing the area of the background. This adds space to, or deletes space from, the canvas outside the image area.

To change the canvas size numerically:

1. Choose **Modify > Document > Canvas Size** to open the Canvas Size dialog box ❽.
2. Enter new amounts in the New Size height and width fields.

TIP Use the current size as a reference.

3. Click the squares in the Anchor area to determine which area of the canvas will become larger or smaller.
4. Click OK.

To change the canvas size visually:

1. Choose the Crop tool from the toolbox ❾.
2. Drag with the Crop tool to create the handles ❿ that define the area you want to crop.
3. Double-click inside the crop area to apply the crop.

   or

   Double-click outside the crop area or choose a new tool to continue without applying the crop.

TIP The Crop handles can be extended outside the current canvas area to increase the size of the canvas.

When you reduce the size of your document, some objects that were visible on the canvas can be positioned outside the canvas in the inactive area. You have a choice as to whether or not Fireworks keeps those objects or deletes them.

To control objects off the canvas:

1. Choose File > Preference to open the Preferences dialog box **⓫**.

2. Choose Editing from the pop-up menu.

3. Select Delete Objects when Cropping.

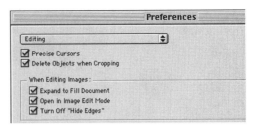

⓫ *Choose* **Delete Objects when Cropping** *from Editing Preferences to determine what happens to objects when the canvas is cropped.*

The canvas color is the color automatically applied behind all the images in a document. You can change the canvas color at any time while you work on a document.

To change the canvas color:

1. Choose **Modify** > **Document** > **Canvas Color** to open the Canvas Color dialog box **⓬**.

2. Click white, transparent, or custom.

TIP The transparent background is designated by a gray and white checkerboard **⓭**.

3. If you choose custom, click the Color Well to open the Swatches panel to choose a specific color.

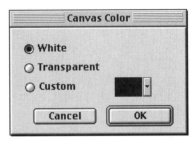

⓬ *The* **Canvas Color** *dialog box.*

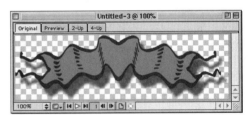

⓭ *The* **checkerboard grid** *indicates a transparent background.*

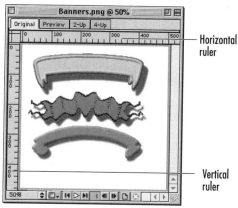

Horizontal ruler

Vertical ruler

⓮ *The* **rulers** *in the document window.*

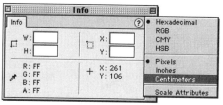

⓯ *Use the Info panel menu to* **change the unit** of measurement.

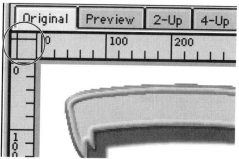

⓰ Drag the zero point cross hairs *(circled)* *onto the page to set the new zero point.*

Working with Rulers

In order to work precisely in your document, you need to work with the rulers.

To display the document rulers:

Choose **View** > **Rulers**. The rulers appear at the top and left sides of the document **⓮**.

TIP Two lines appear on the rulers to track your position as you move around the document.

Fireworks ships with pixels as the default unit of measurement for the rulers. You can change that unit at any time.

To change the unit of measurement:

1. Make sure the Info panel is open. If not, choose **Window** > **Info ⓯**.

2. Use the Info panel menu to choose a new unit of measurement. The choices are:
   - Pixels
   - Inches
   - Centimeters

Fireworks uses the upper left corner of a document as its *zero point*, or the point where the rulers start. You can change the zero point for a document. This can help you position items on the page.

To change the zero point:

1. Drag the zero point cross hairs onto the page **⓰**.

2. Double-click the zero point crosshairs in the corner of the document window to reset the zero point to the upper left corner.

Using Ruler Guides

The rulers also let you add guides that you can use to align objects.

To create guides:

1. Drag from the left ruler to create a vertical guide 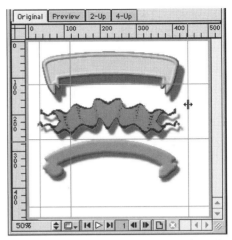. Release the mouse button to place the guide.

2. Drag from the top ruler to create a horizontal guide. Release the mouse button to place the guide.

3. Repeat to add as many horizontal or vertical guides as you need.

To position guides:

Drag an existing guide to move it to a new position.

or

Double-click the guide to open the Move Guide dialog box **⑱** and enter the exact position of the guide.

TIP Use **View** > **Guide Options** > **Snap To Guides** to have objects automatically snap, or align, to the guides.

⑰ Drag a guide *from the ruler onto the active area.*

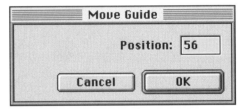

⑱ *The* **Move Guide** *dialog box.*

⑲ *The* **Guides** (Win) *dialog box.*

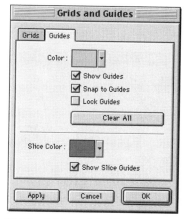

⑳ *The* **Grids and Guides** (Mac) *dialog box in the Guides mode.*

There are several ways you can edit or control the look of guides.

To edit guides:

1. Choose **View > Guide Options > Edit Guides** to open the Guides dialog box **⑲–⑳**.

2. Click the color box to open the color picker and choose a new color to make the guides look more or less obvious.

3. Click Show Guides to show or hide the guides.

4. Click Snap to Guides to turn this feature on or off.

5. Click Lock Guides to keep the guides from being moved.

TIP You can also lock the guides by choosing **View > Guide Options > Lock Guides**.

6. Click Clear All to delete all the guides from the document.

7. Click OK to apply the changes.

TIP (Mac) Click the Grid tab to switch from editing the guides to editing the grid *(see the steps on the next page)*.

Using Ruler Guides

Using the Document Grid

In addition to guides, Fireworks has a grid, which you can use to align objects.

To view the document grid:

Choose **View>Grid** to display the document grid ㉑. You can use the document grid to arrange your images into certain areas, or to make sure objects are aligned, or are the same size.

TIP You can use **View>Grid Options>Snap to Grid** to have objects automatically snap, or align, to the grid.

TIP When Snap to Grid is turned on, objects snap to the grid even if the grid is not visible.

You can also change the size of the grid. This makes it easy to create objects all the same size or shape.

To edit the document grid:

1. Choose **View>Grid Options>Edit Grid** to open the Grids and Guides dialog box ㉒–㉓.

2. Click the color box to open the color picker and choose a new color for the grid.

3. Use the horizontal control slider or type in the field to increase or decrease the horizontal spacing.

4. Use the vertical control slider or type in the field to increase or decrease the vertical spacing.

5. Click Snap to Grid to turn this feature on or off.

6. Click Show Grid to show or hide the document grid.

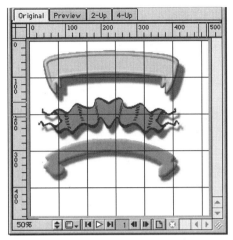

㉑ *The **document grid** shown over the art.*

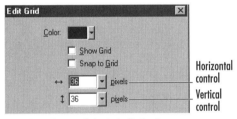

㉒ *The **Edit Grid** (Win) dialog box.*

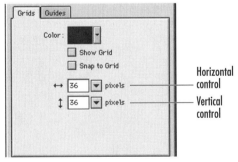

㉓ *The **Grids and Guides** (Mac) dialog box in the Grid mode.*

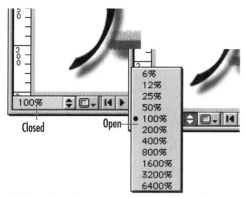

❷❹ *The* **Magnification control menu** *at the bottom of the document window.*

Magnification

You may need to zoom in or out to see specific areas of the big picture.

To use the magnification commands:

To zoom to a specific magnification, use the magnification control **❷❹**.

or

Choose **View** > **Magnification** and then choose a specific magnification.

or

Choose **View** > **Zoom In** or **View** > **Zoom Out** to jump to a specific magnification.

or

Choose **View** > **Fit Selection** to display the object selected.

or

Choose **View** > **Fit All** to display the entire document.

You can use the Zoom tool to jump to a specific magnification and position.

To use the Zoom tool:

1. Click the Zoom tool in the Toolbox **㉕**.

2. Click the Zoom tool on the area you want to zoom in on. Click as many times as you need to get as close as necessary to the area you want to see.

   or

   Drag the Zoom tool diagonally across the area you want to see. Release the mouse button to zoom in **㉖–㉗**.

   TIP Press Command/Ctrl and Spacebar to access the Zoom tool without leaving the tool that is currently selected.

   TIP Press the Option/Alt key while in the Zoom tool to zoom out from objects. The icon changes from a plus sign (+) to a minus sign (−).

㉕ *The* **Zoom tool** *in the toolbox.*

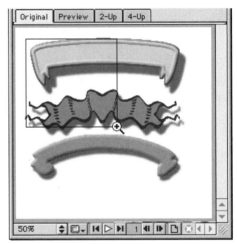

㉖ *Use the* **Zoom tool** *to zoom in on a specific area by dragging a marquee around that area.*

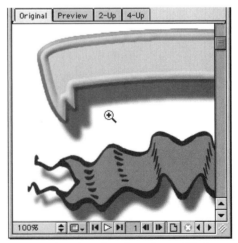

㉗ *After dragging, the* **selected area** *fills the window.*

Magnification

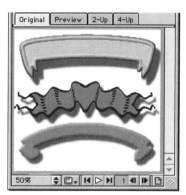

❷❽ *The* **Full Display** *mode shows all the fills, brushes, and effects for the objects.*

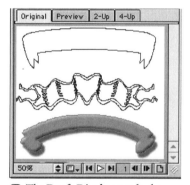

❷❾ *The* **Draft Display** *mode shows only the paths for the unselected objects. The selected object shows its fills, brushes, or effects.*

Display mode control

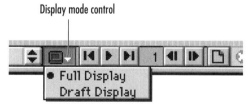

❸⓿ *The* **Display mode choices.**

Using the Display Options

Fireworks lets you work in two different display modes. The Full Display mode **❷❽** shows all the objects in the document with their fills, brushes, and effects.

The Draft Display mode **❷❾** shows only the paths for all the unselected objects. Only the selected object displays its fill, brush, or effect.

TIP Use the Draft Display mode to improve the screen re-draw speed.

To change the display options:

1. Press the Display mode control at the bottom of the document window **❸⓿**.

2. Choose between Full Display or Draft Display.

   or

   Choose **View** >**Full Display** to switch beetween the two display modes.

Using the Grabber Tool

If you have used a computer for any type of program, you should be familiar with the scroll bars of a window that let you see areas of the document that are outside the view of the window. Fireworks also has a Grabber tool that lets you move around the window without using the scroll bars.

31 *The* **Grabber tool** *in the toolbox.*

To use the Grabber tool:

1. Choose the Grabber tool in the toolbox **31**

2. Position the Grabber tool inside the document window and drag **32**. This reveals the areas of the image that were previously hidden.

TIP Hold the spacebar to access the Grabber tool without leaving the tool that is currently selected.

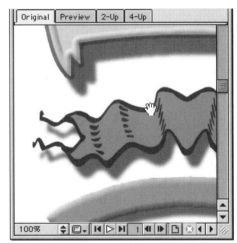

32 *The* **Grabber tool** *allows you to move an image within the document window.*

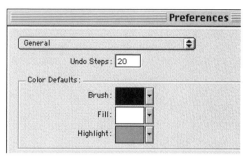

❸❸ *The* **Undo Steps field** *allows you to set how many actions can be reversed.*

Slider

❸❹ *The* **History panel** *shows a list of the undo steps.*

Controlling Actions

Like most other applications, Fireworks lets you undo or reverse actions and commands.

To undo actions:

1. Choose Undo from the Edit menu. This reverses the most recent action or command.

2. Choose Undo again to reverse the next most recent action.

To set the number of undo steps:

1. Choose **File** > **Preferences.**

2. Set the number of undo steps in the General preferences options **❸❸**.

TIP You must relaunch Fireworks for the change in the number of undo steps to take effect.

To jump to a previous action:

1. Choose **Window** > **History** to open the History panel. The panel shows a list of the most recent commands that can be reversed **❸❹**.

2. Drag the slide up to the point where you want to reverse the actions. You can continue to work from that point on.

TIP The History panel can also be used to make scripts that automate a series of commands. *(See Chapter 11, "Automation Features" for more information on working with the History panel to create scripts.)*

COLORS 3

When I worked in advertising, the low-budget print jobs were limited to just black and white. As I worked my way up to the big-budget clients, I got to work on four-color jobs.

Designers working on web graphics are luckier. Low-budget clients can afford color just like the big-budget companies. I think that's why so many designers enjoy creating web graphics.

Of course, there are some limitations as to the number and types of colors you can use. But, for the most part, you should not have to limit your graphics to black and white.

macromedia
FIREWORKS

Setting the Color Modes

Fireworks uses five different color modes to set color. You choose the different modes with the Color Mixer.

To use the Color Mixer:

1. If you do not see the Color Mixer, choose **Window** > **Color Mixer**.

   or

   Click the title bar of the Color Mixer panel to bring it in front of other onscreen elements.

2. Use the Mode menu to choose one of the five different color modes ❶.

One of the most common ways of defining colors for Web graphics is to use the RGB (red, green, blue) color system, also called *additive* color. *(See the color insert for a diagram of how additive colors can be mixed.)*

To define RGB colors:

1. Make sure the Color Mixer mode is set to RGB.

2. To choose the R (red) component, drag the slider or enter a value in the R field. Do the same for the G (green) component and the B (blue) component ❷.

   or

   Click anywhere along the RGB color ramp at the bottom of the Color Mixer to choose colors by eye, rather than by numeric values.

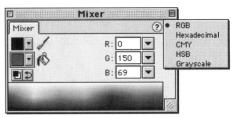

❶ *The* **five color mode choices** *of the Color Mixer.*

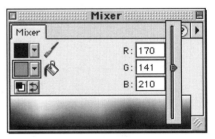

❷ **Drag the slider** *to set the value for one of the RGB color components. The RGB colors are set with numbers from 0 to 255.*

Understanding RGB Colors

Additive colors are formed from light. In the RGB additive color system, all three colors (red, green, and blue) combine to create white. Each of the RGB components is given a number between 0 and 255. So, for example, a yellow color could have the RGB values of R: 250, G: 243, and B: 117.

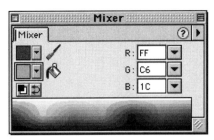

❸ **Hexadecimal colors** *use combinations of letters and numbers to define colors.*

Another way of defining colors is to use the *hexadecimal* color system. This is the same system used in HTML code.

To define hexadecimal colors:

1. Make sure the Color Mixer mode is set to Hexadecimal.

2. To choose the R (red) component, drag the slider or enter a value in the R (red) field. Do the same for the G (green) component and the B (blue) component ❸.

or

Click in the color ramp at the bottom of the Color Mixer to choose colors by eye, rather than by numeric values.

TIP The color ramp in the hexadecimal mode limits you to working with the 216 Web-safe colors *(see page 37)*.

TIP The hexadecimal system uses one or two combinations of the following numbers or letters: 0, 1, 2, 3, 4, 5, 6, 7, 8, 9, A, B, C, D, E, F. Other characters are ignored.

TIP You can also use the hexadecimal codes from your Fireworks graphics as part of the HTML code for your Web pages.

Understanding Hexadecimal Color

Text, links, and background colors of Web graphics are defined in HTML documents using a color system called *hexadecimal*. The hexadecimal system uses RGB color, but instead of numbers from 0 to 255, the hexadecimal system uses combinations of letters and numbers. So the yellow mentioned in the sidebar on the previous page would be defined in hexadecimal as R: FA, G: F3, B: 75.

There is no advantage to defining colors using hexadecimal values. However, you may find it easier to match the colors in HTML documents if you use hexadecimal values.

Setting the Color Modes

Fireworks also lets you define colors using CMY mode. This is a variation of the *subtractive* CMYK colors used in process-color printing *(See the color insert for a diagram of how subtractive colors can be mixed.)* The special CMY mode in Fireworks mixes cyan, magenta, and yellow to create colors.

To define CMY colors:

1. Make sure the Color Mixer mode is set to CMY.

2. To choose the C (cyan) component, drag the slider or enter a value in the C (cyan) field. Do the same for the M (magenta) component and the Y (yellow) component ❹.

   or

   Click anywhere along the CMY color ramp at the bottom of the Color Mixer to choose colors by eye, rather than by numeric values.

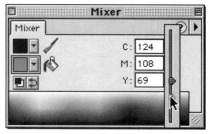

❹ **CMY colors** *use the numbers from 0 to 255 to set the amount of each color component.*

Setting the Color Modes

Understanding CMY Colors

The CMY colors in Fireworks are not the same as the CMYK colors used in printing. Theoretically (and in Fireworks), combining the three pure CMY colors produces black. In actual printing, combining the three CMY inks produces a muddy brown-black, so an extra black printing plate is added to create real black.

Fireworks provides the CMY mode as a convenience for those designers who (like this author) find it difficult to think in RGB. Our finger painting experiences make it easier for us to remember that magenta plus yellow make orange. We can't remember that you add green to red to make orange.

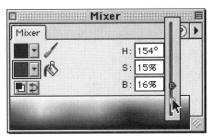

❺ **HSB colors** *use a combination of degrees around the color wheel for hue and percentages of saturation and brightness to define colors.*

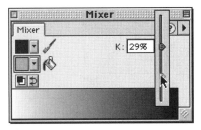

❻ **Grayscale colors** *use percentages of black to define colors.*

Understanding HSB Colors

The most classic form of defining colors is the HSB—hue, saturation, and brightness system. Hue uses the principle of arranging colors in a wheel. Changing the colors from 0° to 360° moves through the entire color spectrum. Saturation uses percentage values, where 100% is a totally saturated color. Lower saturation values create pastel versions of a color. Brightness uses percentage values, where 100% is a color with no darkness or black. The lower the brightness percentage, the more darkness or black is added to the color.

You can also define colors using the classic HSB or hue, saturation, and brightness system.

To define HSB colors:

1. Make sure the Color Mixer mode is set to HSB.

2. To choose the H (hue) component, drag the slider or enter a degree value in the H (hue) field ❺.

3. To choose the S (saturation) component, drag the slider or enter a percentage value in the S (saturation) field. Do the same for the B (brightness) component.

   or

   Click anywhere along the HSB color ramp at the bottom of the Color Mixer to choose colors by eye, rather than by numeric values.

While Fireworks graphics are exported in RGB or indexed colors, you may need to match colors used in grayscale images. So, the Color Mixer also lets you define colors using values of a single black (K) color plate.

To define Grayscale colors:

1. Make sure the Color Mixer mode is set to Grayscale.

2. To choose the K (black) component, drag the slider or enter a value in the K (black) field ❻.

   or

   Click anywhere along the grayscale color ramp at the bottom of the Color Mixer to choose colors by eye, rather than by numeric values.

Setting the Color Modes

Using the Swatches Panel

You would not want to have to go to the Color Mixer every time you need a certain color. The Swatches panel lets you store commonly used colors so they are always available.

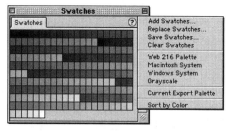

❼ *The* Swatches panel menu.

To use the Swatches panel:

1. If you do not see the Swatches panel, choose **Window > Swatches panel**.

   or

   If the Swatches panel is behind another panel, click the title bar of the Swatches panel to bring it in front of any other onscreen elements.

2. Use the Swatches panel menu to access the Swatches commands ❼.

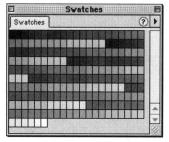

❽ *The* 216 Web-safe colors *in the Swatches panel. (See the color insert for the color version of this illustration.)*

One of the most important considerations in creating Web graphics is using *Web-safe colors.* You can access the 216 Web-safe colors via the Swatches panel.

To choose the Web 216 Palette swatches:

Open the Swatches panel menu and choose Web 216 Palette. The color swatches appear in the panel ❽.

What are Web-Safe Colors?

Web-safe colors are those that can be displayed predictably by different Web browsers as well as different computer systems. There are 216 Web-safe colors. If you limit your Fireworks graphics to only those 216 colors, you ensure that the colors of your document will not shift or change when they are displayed on different monitors using different browsers.

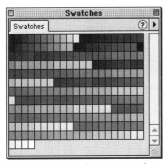

❾ *The* **Macintosh System colors** *in the Swatches panel. (See the color insert for the color version of this illustration.)*

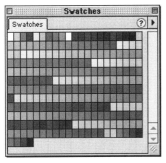

❿ *The* **Windows System colors** *in the Swatches panel. (See the color insert for the color version of this illustration.)*

⓫ *The* **Grayscale colors** *in the Swatches panel.*

You can also limit your colors to those found in the Macintosh operating system. To do so, you can choose the Macintosh System colors.

To choose the Macintosh System swatches:

Open the Swatches panel menu and choose Macintosh System. The 256 color swatches appear in the panel ❾.

Just as you can pick colors using the Macintosh System colors, you can also pick colors using the Windows System colors.

To choose the Windows System swatches:

Open the Swatches panel menu and choose Windows System. The 256 color swatches appear in the panel ❿.

You can also limit your colors to grayscale colors. This is done by choosing the Grayscale swatches.

To choose the Grayscale swatches:

Open the Swatches panel menu and choose Grayscale. The 256 grayscale color swatches appear in the panel ⓫.

Using the Swatches Panel

You can use the Swatches panel to store colors that you create in the Color Mixer. This makes it easy to maintain a consistent look in all your graphics.

To add colors to the Swatches panel:

1. Use the Color Mixer to define a color that you want to store.

2. Move the mouse over to the gray area at the end of the Swatches panel where there are no swatches. A paint bucket cursor appears ⓬.

3. Click the mouse button. The new color appears in its own color swatch.

You can also delete colors from the Swatches panel.

To delete colors from the Swatches panel:

1. Move the cursor over the swatch for the color you want to delete.

2. Hold the Command/Ctrl key. A scissors cursor appears ⓭.

3. Click to delete the color from the Swatches panel.

You can also delete all the colors from the Swatches panel at once.

To delete all the colors from the Swatches panel:

♦ Choose Clear Swatches from the Swatches panel menu.

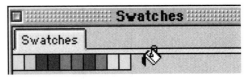

⓬ *The* **paint bucket cursor** *indicates you can store a color in the Swatches panel.*

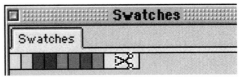

⓭ *The Command/Ctrl key displays the* **scissors cursor** *which allows you to delete a color from the Swatches panel.*

Before

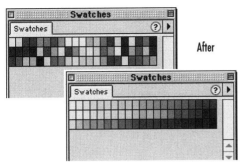

After

The Swatches panel before and after sorting the colors.

If you keep adding colors to the Swatches panel, you may want to arrange the swatches so that similar colors are grouped together.

To sort the swatches by color:

◆ Choose Sort by Color from the Swatches panel menu.

TIP The color swatches are sorted, first by hue and then from light to dark **14**.

Once you have created a custom Swatches panel with your own colors, you can save that Swatches panel to use at other times.

To save colors in the Swatches panel:

1. Choose Save Swatches from the Swatches panel menu.

2. Give the file a name and then save the file. The saved file can be loaded into the Swatches panel at any time.

To load colors to the Swatches panel:

1. Open the Swatches panel menu and choose Replace Swatches.

2. Navigate to find a saved Swatches panel file.

3. Choose Open. This replaces the current set of swatches with those from the saved file.

To add colors to the Swatches panel:

1. Open the Swatches panel menu and choose Add Swatches.

2. Navigate to find a saved Swatches panel file.

3. Choose Open. Unlike the Replace Swatches command, this adds the new swatches to those already in the Swatches panel.

Using the Swatches Panel

Using the Default Colors

Fireworks has a set of default colors for the brush and fill colors. These default colors can be accessed easily and changed to suit your needs.

To work with the default colors:

1. Click the default colors icon **⑮** in either the Toolbox or the Color Mixer to set the brush and fill colors to their default settings.

2. Click the swap colors icon **⑯** in either the Toolbox or the Color Mixer to reverse the brush and fill colors.

To change the default colors:

1. Choose File>Preferences to open the Preferences dialog box **⑰**.

2. Click the color box for the Brush or Fill Color Defaults.

3. Use the color picker to choose a new default color.

4. Click OK to apply the changes.

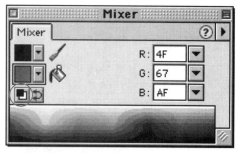

⑮ *Click the* **default colors icon** *(circled) in the Color Mixer to reset the brush and fill colors to their default setting.*

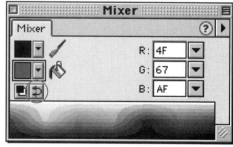

⑯ *Click the* **swap colors icon** *in the Color Mixer to reverse the brush and fill colors.*

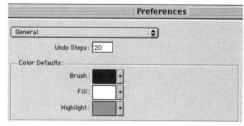

⑰ *The* **Preferences** *dialog box.*

Using the Default Colors

⓲ *The* **Eyedropper** *in the Toolbox.*

⓳ *The Eyedropper sampling for a* **Fill color.**

⓴ *The Eyedropper sampling for a* **Stroke** color.

㉑ *The* **Paint Bucket** *in the Toolbox.*

Sampling Colors

The Eyedropper tool lets you pick colors from objects or images.

To sample colors with the Eyedropper:

1. Choose the Eyedropper in the Toolbox ⓲.

2. Position the Eyedropper over the color you want to sample.

3. Click. The color appears as either the Fill or Stroke color.

TIP When the Fill color is chosen *(see page 98)*, the Eyedropper shows a black dot next to it ⓳.

TIP When the Stroke color is chosen in the Toolbox *(see page 114)*, the Eyedropper shows a curved line next to it ⓴.

The Paint Bucket lets you drop fills onto objects whether or not they are selected.

To fill objects with the Paint Bucket:

1. Choose the Paint Bucket in the Toolbox ㉑.

2. Click on an object. The object fills with the currently selected Fill color. *(For more information on working with fills, see Chapter 7, "Fills.")*

As you are working, you may want to know the exact composition of the color of an object or image. Fireworks lets you see the details of a color in the Info panel.

To use the Info panel:

1. Make sure the Info panel is open. If not, choose **Windows** > **Info**.

2. Pass the pointer over any object. The Info panel displays the values for the color the pointer is over **㉒**.

3. Click the triangle to open the Info panel menu **㉓**.

4. Use the Color Model list to change the way the Info panel displays the color values.

TIP Changing the way the Info panel displays colors does not actually change the colors. Colors in Fireworks are not set until they are exported as a finished file *(see Chapter 19, "Exporting")*.

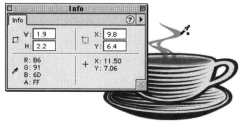

㉒ *The color readings of the* **Info** *panel.*

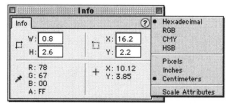

㉓ *The* **Info** *panel menu.*

PATH TOOLS | 4

Many of my students ask me which is better for them to know in order to learn Fireworks: a bitmapped editing program such as Photoshop or a vector illustration program such as Illustrator or FreeHand. Without a doubt the answer is a vector program.

While Fireworks does offer a bitmapped editing mode *(see Chapter 12, "Working with Pixels")*, the real power of the program comes from the fact that it creates images with vector paths. So, unlike pixels that are difficult to reshape, the paths in Fireworks remain "always editable, all the time."

If you are familiar with a vector program, you will quickly pick up the principles here. If you have never used a vector program, pay attention to this chapter because creating paths is the primary source of images in Fireworks.

Creating Basic Shapes

There are four tools that allow you to quickly make a variety of basic shapes: rectangles, ellipses, polygons, stars, and straight lines.

❶ *The* **Rectangle tool** *in the Toolbox.*

Although it is called the Rectangle tool, this tool lets you create rectangles, squares, and rounded-corner rectangles. With the Rectangle tool you can create buttons and banners for your Web graphics.

To create a rectangle:

1. Click the Rectangle tool in the Tool-box ❶. If the Rectangle tool is not visible, open the pop-up group to choose the Rectangle tool.

2. Move the pointer to the document area. The cursor changes to the plus (+) sign indicating that you can draw the rectangle.

3. Drag diagonally from one corner to the other of the rectangle you want to draw.

TIP Hold the Shift key as you drag to constrain the Rectangle tool into creating a square ❷.

TIP Hold the Option/Alt key as you drag to draw from the center point outward.

4. Release the mouse button to create the rectangle.

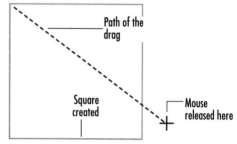

❷ **Holding the Shift key** *constrains the rectangle tool to create a square even if the path of the drag is not along the correct diagonal of the square.*

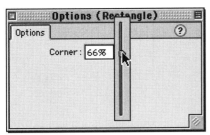

❸ *The* **Corner radius slider.**

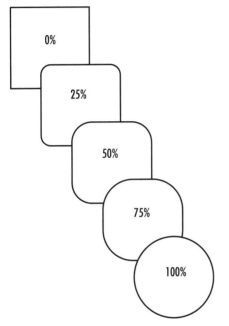

❹ *Rectangles drawn with different percentages for the corner radius.*

❺ *The* **Ellipse tool** *in the Toolbox.*

A rectangle with a rounded corner is a very popular look for buttons and other interactive Web elements.

To create a rounded-corner rectangle:

1. Double-click the Rectangle tool in the Toolbox. This opens the Tool Options for the Rectangle tool.

2. Drag the Corner slider to increase the size of the corner radius ❸.

TIP The size of the corner radius is a percentage of the length of the shorter side of the rectangle.

3. Drag as you would to create a regular rectangle. The corners of the rectangle are rounded by the percentage set for the corner radius ❹.

You can create ellipses or ovals using the Ellipse tool.

To create an ellipse:

1. Click the Ellipse tool in the Toolbox ❺. If the Ellipse tool is not visible, open the pop-up group to choose the Ellipse tool.

2. Move the pointer to the document area.

3. Drag a line that defines the diameter of the ellipse.

TIP Hold the Shift key as you drag to constrain the ellipse into a circle.

TIP Hold the Option/Alt key as you drag to draw from the center point outward.

4. Release the mouse button to complete the ellipse.

Creating Basic Shapes

You can use the Line tool to quickly create straight line segments.

To create a line:

1. Click the Line tool in the Toolbox **❻**.

2. Move the pointer to the document area. The cursor changes to the plus sign.

3. Drag to set the length and direction of the line.

TIP Hold the Shift key to constrain the angle of the line to 45° increments **❼**.

4. Release the mouse button to complete the line.

Polygons give your Web graphics a special look. The Polygon tool can create both polygons and stars.

To create a polygon:

1. Click the Polygon tool in the Toolbox **❽**. If the Polygon tool is not visible, open the pop-up group to choose the Polygon tool.

2. Double-click the Polygon tool to display the Polygon Options panel **❾**.

3. Choose Polygon from the pop-up list.

4. Use the slider or enter a number from 1 to 360 in the field to set the number of sides for the polygon.

5. Move the pointer to the document area and drag. The point where you start the drag is the center of the polygon.

TIP Hold the Shift key as you drag to constrain the orientation of the polygon to 45° increment angles.

6. Release the mouse button to create the polygon.

❻ *The **Line tool** in the Toolbox.*

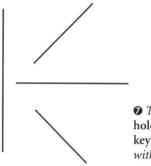

❼ *The results of* **holding the Shift key** *while drawing with the Line tool.*

❽ *The **Polygon tool** in the Toolbox.*

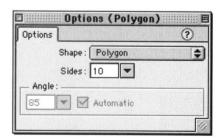

❾ *The **Polygon tool** options.*

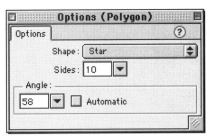

① *The Polygon tool set for the* **Star** *options.*

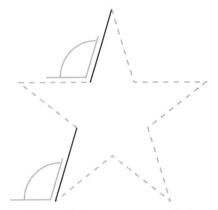

⑪ *The two black segments are parallel as a result of setting the star to* **Automatic.**

15° Acute angle   60° Obtuse angle

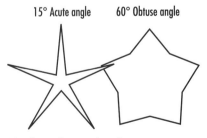

⑫ *Choose low angle values to create* **acute-angled stars** *with sharp points. Choose high angle values to create* **obtuse-angled stars** *with broad points.*

Fireworks also lets you create stars. When stars have many points they are sometimes called bursts. You can use bursts to call attention to special information.

To create a star:

1. Click the Polygon tool in the Toolbox. If the Polygon tool is not visible, open the pop-up group to choose the Polygon tool.

2. Double-click the Polygon tool to display the Polygon Options panel.

3. Choose Star from the pop-up list in the Polygon Options. This adds the Angle controls to the panel **①**.

4. Use the slider or enter a number from 1 to 360 in the field to set the number of sides for the star.

5. Check Automatic to create stars with parallel line segments **⑪**.

   or

   Use the slider to set the angle of the points. Low settings create acute angles. High settings create obtuse angles **⑫**.

Working with the Pen

One of the most important tools in any vector program is its Pen tool. The Pen tool allows you to precisely create a wide variety of shapes. The Fireworks Pen tool is similar to those found in Macromedia FreeHand and Adobe Illustrator. Before you learn to use the Pen, you should understand the elements of paths.

Anchor points define a path at points where the path changes. *Segments* are the paths that connect anchor points. *Conrol handles* extend out from anchor points; their length and direction control the shape of curves of the segments.

The best way to learn to use the Pen is to start by creating straight segments.

To create a straight path segment:

1. Click the Pen tool in the Toolbox **⑬**.

2. Move the pointer to the document area. The cursor changes to the plus (+) sign with a white square dot next to it. This indicates the start of the path **⑭**.

3. Click to create an anchor point which defines the beginning of the segment of the path.

4. Move the cursor to where you want the next anchor point of the path. The cursor changes to a plus sign without a dot next to it. This indicates that the next point is connected to the previous one.

5. Click. This connects the two anchor points with a straight line segment **⑮**.

6. Continue to create straight segments by repeating steps 4 and 5.

7. To finish the path, move the tool away from the path, hold down the Command/Ctrl key, and double-click.

⑬ *The* **Pen tool** *in the Toolbox.*

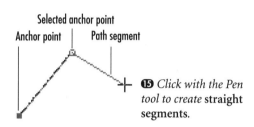

⑭ *The* **start icon** *for the Pen tool.*

Selected anchor point

Anchor point   Path segment

⑮ *Click with the Pen tool to create* **straight segments.**

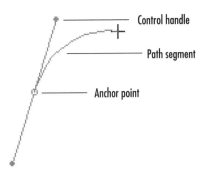

Control handle

Path segment

Anchor point

⑯ *Dragging with the Pen tool creates* **curved segments***.*

⑰ *A path with a series of curved segments.*

⑱ *Hold the Option/Alt key to pivot the handles and create a* **corner curve***.*

You can also create curved segments. Think of a curved segment as the shape that a roller coaster follows along a track.

To create a curved path segment:

1. Click the Pen tool in the Toolbox.

2. Move the pointer to the document area. The cursor changes to the plus sign with a white square dot next to it.

3. Press and drag to create an anchor point with control handles.

4. Release the mouse button. The length and direction of the handle controls the height and direction of the curve **⑯**.

5. Move the cursor to where you want the next anchor point of the path.

6. Press and drag to create the curved segment between the two anchor points.

7. Continue to create curved segments by repeating steps 3 and 4 **⑰**.

8. To finish the path, move the tool away from the path, hold down the Command/Ctrl key, and double-click.

Curves do not have to be smooth. A corner curve has an abrupt change in direction. The path of a bouncing ball is a corner curve.

To create a corner curve:

1. Press and drag to create an anchor point with control handles. Do not release the mouse button.

2. Hold the Option/Alt key and then drag to pivot the second handle **⑱**.

TIP The longer the handle, the steeper the curve.

3. Release the mouse button when the second handle is the correct length and direction.

Working with the Pen

Once you have created a curved segment with two handles, you can retract the second handle back into the anchor point. This allows you to make the next path segment a straight path.

To retract the handle into a point:

1. Drag to create an anchor point with two control handles.

2. Move the cursor back over the anchor point. A small arrow appears next to the plus sign.

3. Click. The handle retracts back into the anchor point ⓭.

4. Continue the path with either a straight segment or a curved segment.

TIP Click to make the next path segment straight. Drag to make the next path segment curved.

Once you click to create an anchor point with no control handles, you can extend a single handle out from that anchor point. This allows you to make the next path segment a curved path.

To extend a handle out from a point:

1. Click to create an anchor point with no control handles.

2. Move the pointer back over the anchor point you just created. A small arrow appears next to the plus sign.

3. Hold the Command+Option keys (Mac) or Ctrl+Alt keys (Win) as you drag out from the anchor point ⓴. A single control handle extends out from the anchor point.

4. Continue the path with a curved segment.

⓭ *Move the cursor back over a point and click to* **retract a handle** *along a curve.*

⓴ *Hold the Command+ Option keys (Mac) or Ctrl+Alt keys (Win) to* **extend a handle** *out from an anchor point.*

㉑ *An* **Open** *path.*

㉒ *The* **Closed path** *icon.*

There are two ways to finish a path in Fireworks. The first way is to leave the end points of the path open. An open path is like a piece of string.

To create an open path:

1. Move the pen away from the last point of the path.

2. Hold the Command/Ctrl key and double-click. This leaves the path open **㉑** and allows you to continue using the Pen tool.

   or

   Switch to another tool in the Toolbox. This leaves the path open.

The second way to finish a path is to join the last point of the path to the first. This creates a closed path. A closed path is like a rubber band.

To create a closed path:

1. Move the cursor to the first anchor point of the path. The cursor changes to a plus sign with a black square dot next to it **㉒**.

2. Click to close the path.

Using the Brush

Fireworks also has a Brush tool that lets you draw more freely, without worrying about how and where you place points.

23 *The* **Brush tool** *in the Toolbox.*

To draw with the Brush tool:

1. Click the Brush tool in the Toolbox **23**.

2. Move the pointer to the document area. The cursor changes to the brush icon.

3. Drag to create a path that follows the movements of the mouse.

4. Release the mouse button to end the path.

TIP To make a closed path with the Brush tool, move the mouse close to the starting point of the path. A small black dot appears **24**, indicating that the path will close when you release the mouse button.

24 The small black dot *next to the Brush tool indicates that the path will be closed.*

As you draw with the Brush tool, you can make straight lines in addition to the curved segments.

25 The plus sign *next to the Brush tool indicates that part of the path will be a straight line segment.*

To draw straight segments with the Brush tool:

1. Draw the curved portion of the path but do not release the mouse.

2. Hold the Shift key and then release the mouse button. The Brush cursor displays a small plus (+) sign indicating you are adding to the path **25**.

3. Still holding the Shift key, position the Brush cursor where you want the straight segment to end.

4. Press the mouse button and release the Shift key.

26 The plus sign *next to the Brush tool indicates that part of the path will be a straight line segment.*

TIP The straight line segment is not visible yet.

5. Drag with the mouse to draw the rest of the path. Release the mouse button to complete the path. The straight line segment appears **26**.

Using the Brush

㉗ *The* **Pencil tool** *in the Toolbox.*

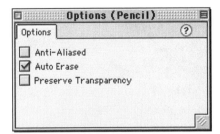

㉘ *The* **Pencil Tool options.**

Anti-Aliased off

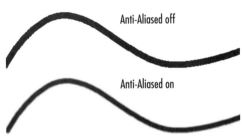

Anti-Aliased on

㉙ *The difference between drawing with the* **Anti-Aliased option** *on and off.*

Using the Pencil

The Pencil tool lets you draw without worrying about placing anchor points or creating handles. The Pencil tool can also be used in the image-editing mode to color individual pixels. *(For more information on working in the image-editing mode see Chapter 12, "Working with Pixels.")*

To draw with the Pencil:

1. Click the Pencil tool in the Toolbox **㉗**.
2. Move the pointer to the document area.
3. Drag to create a line that follows the movements of the mouse.
4. Release the mouse button to finish drawing the line.

TIP Release the mouse button where you started to close the path.

You can soften the look of Pencil lines by turning on the Anti-Aliased option. This adds lighter colors that blend to white to soften the edge of the line.

To add Anti-Aliased edges to pencil lines:

1. Double-click the Pencil tool in the Toolbox to display the Pencil Options **㉘**.
2. Click the Anti-Aliased option to soften the lines created by the pencil **㉙**.

TIP The anti-aliased option creates additional colors in artwork. This can add to the size of the final Web graphic.

Using the Pencil

The Auto Erase option lets you erase Pencil lines by drawing over them with the Fill color. *(For more information on Fill and Stroke colors, see Chapter 7, "Fills" and Chapter 8, "Strokes.")*

To use the Auto Erase:

1. Double-click the Pencil tool in the Toolbox. This opens the Options panel for the Pencil tool.

2. Click Auto Erase in the Options panel.

3. Place the Pencil over a path colored with the current Brush color.

4. Drag the Pencil. The path changes from the Brush to the Fill color **30**.

TIP When working in the path mode, the Auto Erase option of the Pencil does not actually change the colors of the previously drawn path. Rather, it creates a new path on top of the first one.

TIP The Auto Erase option works best when the path is not Anti-Aliased. This makes it easier to position the Pencil over a pixel colored exactly with the Brush color and not a shade created by the anti-aliasing.

TIP There is another option for the Pencil called Preserve Transparency. This option applies only to using the Pencil in the pixel-editing mode. *(For more information on using the pencil on pixel images, see Chapter 12, "Working with Pixels.")*

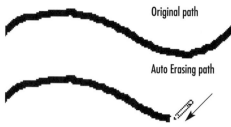

Original path

Auto Erasing path

30 *Dragging with the Pencil tool along a path with the **Auto Erase option** lets you erase the path by coloring it with the Fill color.*

③ *The* **Redraw Path tool** *in the Toolbox.*

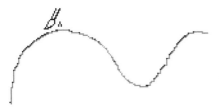

③ *The* **Redraw path icon.**

③ *A* **red line** *(circled) shows the original path as the Redraw Path tool creates the new path.*

Modifying Paths

Once you have created a path, you can modify its shape.

To modify a path:

1. Select a path.

TIP Paths are automatically selected after you finish drawing them. You can also select paths using any of the selection tools. *(See Chapter 5, "Selecting Paths.")*

2. Press the pop-up group in the Toolbox to choose the Redraw Path tool **③**.

3. Move the tool to the part of the path that you want to redraw. A small triangle sign appears next to the brush icon **③**. This indicates that the path will be redrawn.

4. Drag to create the new shape of the path. A red line appears that indicates the part of the path that is modified **③**.

5. Release the mouse to redraw the path.

TIP You can also modify the shape of a path by manipulating the anchor points and control handles of the path.

Modifying Paths

As you work with paths, you may find that you need to add points to a path. This makes it much easier to reshape an existing path. Adding and deleting points on a path requires selecting the path with the Subselection tool. *(See Chapter 5, "Selecting Paths" for more information on working with the Subselection tool.)*

To add points to a path:

1. Use the Subselection tool  to select the path with its points visible.

2. Choose the Pen tool and position the cursor on the segment where you want to add the point. A small caret (^) appears next to the cursor ③⑤.

3. Click. A new point appears.

To delete points from a path:

1. Select the path.

2. Use the Subselection tool to select the point or points.

3. Press the Delete/Backspace key on the keyboard. The point disappears from the path ③⑥.

③④ *The* **Subselection tool** *in the Toolbox.*

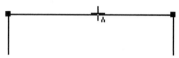

③⑤ *Click with the Pen tool to* **add a point** *to a path.*

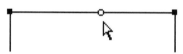

③⑥ *A* **selected** *point on a path can be* **deleted** *by pressing the delete/backspace key.*

Modifying Paths

SELECTING PATHS 5

When I was young, we didn't have personal computers. (Hey, that doesn't make me *that* old!) However, instead of computer graphics, we had other types of arts and graphics. (Yes, there were arts and graphics before computers.) One of my favorites was nail-and-string art.

You started with a plywood rectangle and spent the entire morning hammering thin nails into the wood in a grid pattern. (If the nail-and-string art was created as part of a school class, the room became very noisy during this period.) After lunch, you took colored string and used the nails to create shapes (a much quieter activity).

That's why I enjoy working with the vector paths in Fireworks. The anchor points are like the nails and the paths are the string. However, unlike the nails of my old art projects, Fireworks anchor point are much more flexible.

Selecting Entire Objects

The main selection aid is the Pointer tool. The Pointer tool selects objects as complete paths, not individual points.

To use the Pointer tool:

1. Click the Pointer tool in the Toolbox **❶**.

TIP Hold the Command/Ctrl key to temporarily access the Pointer tool. Release the key to return to the original tool.

2. Position the Pointer arrow over an object and click. A highlight color appears along the path indicating that the object is selected **❷**.

TIP If the object has no fill color, you must click the path or stroke color to select the object.

TIP If you are working in the Draft Display mode *(see page 35)*, you must click the path directly to select the object.

3. Hold the Shift key and click to select any additional objects.

4. Hold the Shift key and click to deselect any objects.

❶ *The **Pointer tool** in the Toolbox.*

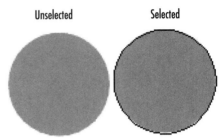

Unselected Selected

❷ *A highlight color appears on the path of a selected object.*

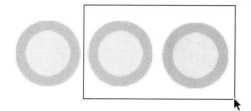

❸ *Drag with the Pointer tool to select objects within the* **rectangular marquee.**

You can also select many objects at once by dragging a marquee with the Pointer tool.

To select objects with a marquee:

1. Place the Pointer tool outside the area of the objects you want to select.

2. Drag diagonally with the Pointer tool to create a rectangle that encloses your selection.

3. Release the mouse button. All objects inside the rectangle are selected ❸.

Once you have a selection of objects, you can add objects to, or subtract from the selection.

To add or subtract objects from a selection:

◆ Hold the Shift key and click to select any additional objects.

or

◆ Hold the Shift key and click to deselect any objects.

TIP Sometimes it is easier to marquee-select a group of objects and then use the Shift key to deselect the one or two you do not want as part of the selection.

In addition to the selection tools, the commands in the Select menu allow you to select and deselect objects.

To use the Select menu commands:

◆ Choose **Select** >**Select All** to select all the objects in a file.

or

◆ Choose **Select** >**Deselect** to deselect any selected objects. These commands can also be used when working in the Image Editing mode *(see Chapter 12, "Working with Pixels").*

TIP You can also deselect any objects in a file by clicking the empty space in a document with the Pointer tool.

Selecting Entire Objects

Selecting Points

Instead of selecting the entire object, you can also select individual points and manipulate them to change the shape of the path. The Subselection tool is used to select individual anchor points.

❹ *The* **Subselection tool** *in the Toolbox.*

To use the Subselection tool:

1. Click the Subselection tool in the Toolbox ❹.

2. Click the object to select the object. The anchor points will be displayed but not selected.

TIP Anchor points filled with the highlight color are unselected ❺.

3. Click a specific point or marquee-drag to select multiple points. The anchor points of the object are selected.

4. Hold the Shift key and click to select additional points.

TIP Selected anchor points are white ❺.

5. Use the Subselection tool to move the selected points ❻.

TIP If you switch from the Pointer tool to the Subselection tool while an object is already selected, you see the unselected anchor points for that object.

Object selected but points unselected

Object and points selected

❺ *The* **Subselection tool** *allows you to see the individual anchor points of a selected object. Click to select the specific points.*

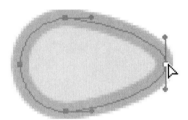

❻ **Drag with the Subselection tool** *to change the position of anchor points.*

The **Select Behind tool** *in the Toolbox.*

The Select Behind tool was used to select the star behind the other two objects. The first click selected the square. The second click selected the circle. The third click selected the star.

Selecting Behind Objects

Because transparency is so important in creating Fireworks graphics, you may find that your artwork consists of many objects stacked on top of each other. This could make it difficult to select an object behind the rest. The Select Behind tool makes it easy to select through other objects to one at the back.

To use the Select Behind tool:

1. Press the pop-up group for the Pointer tool to choose the Select Behind tool ➐.

2. Click with the Select Behind tool over the objects you want to select. The first click selects the object on top of the others.

3. Click as many times as necessary to select the object you want ➑.

TIP Hold the Shift key as you click to add each object to the selection.

Controlling Selections

If you are working with many overlapping objects, it may be difficult to determine which object you are about to select. The Mouse Highlight feature allows you to know which object is about to be selected with the next click.

To set the Mouse Highlight:

1. Double-click the Pointer, Subselection, or Select Behind tool to open the Options panel.
2. Select Mouse Highlight in the panel ❾.
3. Move the selection tool over an object. A red line appears around the object indicating that the object can be selected with the next mouse click.

The Preview Drag option controls what the object looks like as you move it.

To set the Preview Drag:

1. Double-click the Pointer, Subselection, or Select Behind tool to open the Options panel.
2. Select Preview Drag in the panel.
3. Move an object. With Preview Drag turned on you see the fill, stroke, and effects of an object as you move it. With Preview Drag turned off, you see only the path shape of the object ❿.

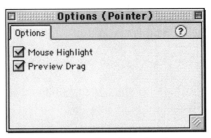

❾ *The* **Pointer tool options** *for the selection tools.*

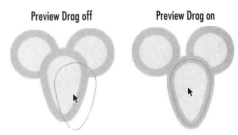

❿ *The* **Preview Drag** *controls what you see when an object is moved.*

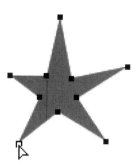

⓫ *The* **Hide Edges** *command hides the highlight along a path but keeps the anchor points and control handles visible when you use the Subselection tool.*

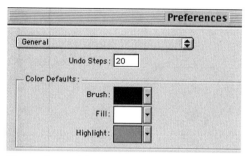

⓬ *Use the* **Highlight Color Well** *in the Preferences dialog box to change the color of the path highlight.*

If you find the highlight effect interferes with your work, you can hide the highlight while keeping the object selected.

To control the highlight of selected objects:

♦ Choose **View** > **Hide Edges**. This hides the highlight along the path of an object.

or

♦ To reveal the highlight, choose **View** > **Hide Edges** when there is a checkmark in front of the command.

TIP Anchor points and control handles are still visible when the Hide Edges command is applied ⓫.

You may not be able to see the path highlight color if it is too similar to the color of the brush stroke around an object. You can use the Preferences to change the path highlight color.

To change the highlight color:

1. Choose **File** > **Preferences** to open the Preferences dialog box ⓬.

2. Click the Highlight Color Well. The Color Picker dialog box appears.

3. Choose the color for the highlight and then click OK.

TIP The highlight color is an application preference. Changing it changes the highlight color for all Fireworks documents.

Controlling Selections

Working with Groups

If you have an button that consists of several objects and text, you may find it easier to select all together as a single unit, or group.

⑬ *A Grouped object displays four points when selected.*

To group selected objects:

1. Select two or more objects.

2. Choose **Modify > Group**. Small anchor points appear around the objects indicating that they are a group **⑬**.

TIP Fireworks lets you group a single object. This lets you select the object without highlighting its path.

3. You can add objects to the group by selecting the group and additional objects and then choosing the Group command again.

To ungroup objects:

1. Select the grouped objects.

2. Choose **Modify > Ungroup** to release the objects from the group.

TIP (Win) You can also use the Group/Ungroup icons on the Modify toolbar.

Grouped objects are considered a single object. However, you do not have to ungroup to select a specific object within the group.

To select objects within groups:

1. Choose either the Pointer, Subselection, or Select Behind tool.

2. Hold the Option/Alt key and click the individual object of the group.

TIP Hold the Shift and Option/Alt keys to add other items to the selection.

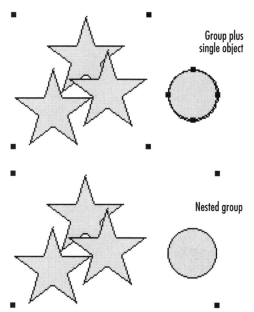

Group plus
single object

Nested group

⑭ *A* **nested group** *is a group that contains a subgroup.*

Groups can be nested within other groups so that one group contains subgroups.

To create a nested group:

1. Select two or more groups or one group and some other objects.

2. Choose **Modify** > **Group**. The original selections are now subgroups of the nested group **⑭**.

3. Continue to select additional objects and choose the Group command to create more nested groups.

The Subselect and Superselect commands make it easy to work with nested groups. The Subselect command lets you select a group and then easily select the individual members of the group.

To use the Subselect command:

1. Select a nested group.

2. Choose **Edit** > **Subselect**. This lets you see and work with the original objects of the nested group.

The Superselect command lets you select an individual object in a group and then easily select the entire group.

To use the Superselect command:

1. Select a single item in a nested group.

2. Choose **Edit** > **Superselect**. This selects the group that contained the selection.

TIP You can reapply both the Subselect and Superselect commands to further select groups within nested groups.

Working with Groups

WORKING WITH OBJECTS 6

When I was a kid, I had an art toy called Colorforms®. In case you don't know what Colorforms is, my set consisted of black pages onto which I could stick shiny cutout vinyl shapes. The vinyl pieces stuck to the black pages without any glue or tape, which I found quite remarkable.

Forty plus years later, as I play with Fireworks, I see how similar it is to Colorforms. However, unlike the plastic Colorforms objects, objects on my Fireworks pages can be stretched, distorted and otherwise transformed into unlimited variations.

Hundreds of pieces came in my Colorforms set, but I can duplicate Fireworks objects over and over—there is no limit to how many objects I have on the page.

Moving Objects

Once you have selected an object, you can move it by dragging the mouse.

To move an object by eye:

1. Select the object.

2. Using any of the selection tools, drag the object to the new position.

TIP Drag anywhere on the object except on a point to avoid reshaping the object.

You can also move an object by changing its coordinates in the Info panel.

To move an object numerically:

1. Select the object.

2. Choose **Window** > **Info**. The Info panel appears ❶.

3. Change the number in the **X** field to set the position of the left edge.

4. Change the number in the **Y** field to set the position of the top edge.

TIP Use the **W** and **H** fields to change the width and height of an object.

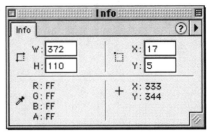

❶ *The* **Info panel** *lets you change the position of an object using the X and Y coordinates.*

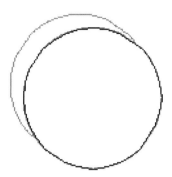

❷ *The* **Duplicate** *command copies the selected object.*

❸ **Holding the Option/Alt keys** *as you move an object creates a copy of that object while leaving the original in place.*

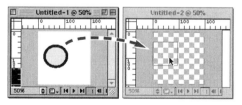

❹ *You can* **drag and drop** *an object from one document to another. (The dashed line indicates direction of the drag and drop.)*

Duplicating Objects

To copy and paste an object:
1. Select the object.
2. Choose **Edit** > **Copy**.
3. Choose **Edit** > **Paste** to paste the object into the same position as the original.

To clone an object:
1. Select the object.
2. Choose **Edit** > **Clone**. A duplicate of the object appears in the same position as the original.

To duplicate an object:
1. Select the object.
2. Choose **Edit** > **Duplicate**. A duplicate of the object appears slightly offset from the original **❷**.

To copy an object as you move it:
1. Choose any of the selection tools.
2. Hold the Option/Alt key as you move the object. A small plus sign (+) appears next to the arrow as you move the object **❸**.
3. Release the mouse button. A copy of the object appears.

You can also drag and drop objects from one document to another.

To drag and drop an object:
1. Position two document windows so that both are visible.
2. Use any of the selection tools to drag an object from one document to the other.
3. Release the mouse button. A copy of the object appears **❹**.

TIP Clone, Duplicate, Drag and Drop, and Option/Alt-Drag leave the contents of the Clipboard unchanged.

Duplicating Objects

Transforming Objects

Transformations change the size, shape, or orientation of an object. Fireworks provides many different ways to transform objects.

Scaling changes an object's size.

❺ *The* **Scale tool** *in the Toolbox.*

To scale an object:

1. Choose the Scale tool in the Toolbox ❺.

   or

   Choose **Modify > Transform > Scale.** The transformation handles appear around the object.

2. Place the cursor directly over any of the handles. A small double-headed arrow appears ❻.

3. Drag toward the object to reduce it or away to enlarge it.

   TIP Drag one of the corner handles to scale both the horizontal and vertical dimensions of the object.

   TIP Drag the edge handles to change just the horizontal or vertical dimensions.

4. Double-click within the bounding box of the transformation handles to apply the transformation.

   or

   Click the Transform button in the Transform Options panel ❼.

   TIP To exit the transformation mode without applying the transformation, switch to any other tool in the Toolbox or press the Esc key on the keyboard.

   TIP *For a description of the Scale Attributes and Auto-crop Images controls, see page 83.*

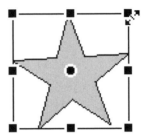

❻ *Drag a corner handle with the* **Scale tool** *to change the horizontal and vertical dimensions of the object proportionally.*

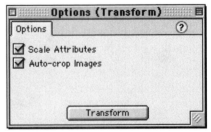

❼ *The* **Transform** *Options panel.*

❽ *The* **Skew tool** *in the Toolbox.*

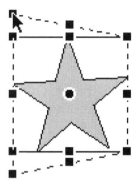

❾ *Drag a corner handle with the* **Skew tool** *to change the dimension of that side of the object.*

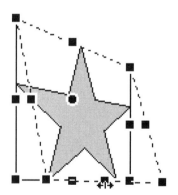

❿ *Drag a side handle with the* **Skew tool** *to change the angles along that side of the object.*

The *skewing* transformation moves two sides of the bounding box together or two control handles in opposite directions. Skewing creates three-dimensional effects for objects or for text *(see page 147).*

To skew an object:

1. Choose the Skew tool in the Toolbox **❽**.

   or

   Choose **Modify** > **Transform** > **Skew**. The transformation handles appear around the object.

2. Place the cursor directly over any of the handles.

3. Drag one of the corner handles in or out to move that handle and the one opposite it. This changes the dimension of that side of the object **❾**.

4. Drag one of the side handles to change the angle of that side of the object **❿**.

5. Double-click within the box created by the transformation handles to apply the transformation.

   or

   Click the Transform button in the Transform Options panel.

TIP To leave the transformation mode without applying the transformation, switch to any other tool in the Toolbox or press the Esc key on the keyboard.

Transforming Objects

The *distortion* transformation allows you to distort the shape of an object by changing the shape of the box that defines the object. Unlike skew, the distortion transformation allows you to manipulate each corner handle individually.

⑪ *The* **Distort tool** *in the Toolbox.*

To distort an object:

1. Choose the Distort tool in the Toolbox ⑪.

   or

   Choose **Modify > Transform > Distort.** The transformation handles appear around the object.

2. Place the cursor directly over any of the handles.

3. Drag one of the side handles to change the shape of the object ⑫.

4. Double-click within the box created by the transformation handles to apply the transformation.

   or

   Click the Transform button in the Transform Options panel.

TIP To exit the transformation mode without applying the transformation, switch to any other tool in the Toolbox or press the Esc key on the keyboard.

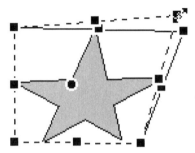

⑫ *Drag a handle with the* **Distort tool** *to change the shape of an object.*

Transforming Objects

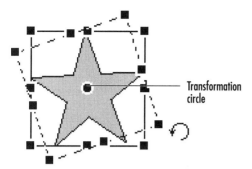

— Transformation circle

⓭ *Drag with the* **Rotation cursor** *to change the orientation of an object.*

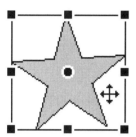

⓮ *The* **four-headed arrow** *appears while moving an object in the transformation mode.*

An additional transformation, *rotation*, is available when you use any of the three transformation tools.

To rotate an object:

1. Choose any of the Transformation tools.

2. Position the cursor outside of the handles. A rounded arrow appears.

3. Drag either clockwise or counter-clockwise to rotate the object **⓭**.

TIP Move the small transformation circle to change the point around which the object rotates.

4. Double-click within the box created by the transformation handles to apply the transformation.

   or

   Click the Transform button in the Transform Options panel.

TIP To leave the transformation mode without applying the transformation, switch to any other tool in the Toolbox or press the Esc key on the keyboard.

You can also move an object while in the transformation mode.

To move an object in the transformation mode:

1. Choose any of the Transformation tools.

2. Position the cursor inside the box created by the transformation handles. A four-headed arrow appears **⓮**.

3. Drag to move the object.

4. Continue working with the transformation tools or apply the transformation by double-clicking within the box created by the transformation handles.

Transforming Objects

Fireworks also gives you a set of transformation menu commands that make it easy to rotate or flip objects 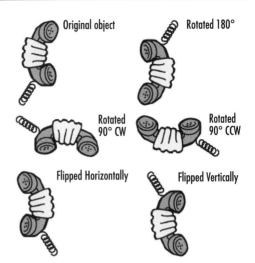.

To use the Transform menu commands:

1. Select an object.

2. Choose one of the commands from the **Modify** > **Transform** menu to rotate or flip the object. For example, to rotate an object so that it is upside down, choose **Modify** > **Transform** > **Rotate 180°**.

TIP (Win) You can also use the rotate buttons on the Modify toolbar to easily apply rotations.

The Numeric Transform dialog box makes it easy to scale, resize, or rotate an object using numeric values, rather than by judging by eye.

To use the Numeric Transform dialog box:

1. Select an object.

2. Rotate or flip the object by choosing a command from the **Modify** > **Transform** > **Numeric Transform**. The Numeric Transform dialog box appears.

3. Use the pop-up list to choose Scale, Resize, or Rotate.

4. In the Scale mode 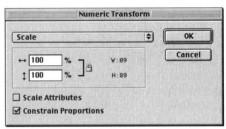, enter the percentage of change in the width or height fields.

   or

   In the Resize mode 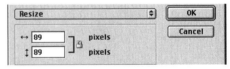, enter the pixel amount in the width or height fields.

   or

   In the Rotate mode 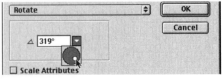, use the wheel or enter the angle in the field.

5. Click OK to apply the transformation.

TIP Both Scale and Resize change the size of the object. Scale does so using percentages. Resize does so by changing the pixel dimensions.

15 *The effect of* **Transform** *menu commands on the original object (upper left).*

16 *The* **Numeric Transform** *dialog box set to the* **Scale controls.**

17 *The* **Resize controls** *of the Numeric Transform dialog box.*

18 *The* **Rotate controls** *of the Numeric Transform dialog box.*

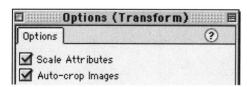

⓳ *The* **Transform** *Options panel.*

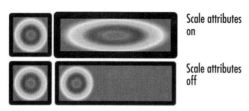

Scale attributes on

Scale attributes off

⓴ *The difference between scaling with the* **Scale Attributes** *option on and off. The size of the stroke and the gradient change when the option is turned on. The stroke and gradient do not change when the option is turned off.*

Auto-crop Images on

Auto-crop Images off

㉑ *The difference between rotating with the* **Auto-crop Images** *option on and off. The bounding box around the rotated image shrinks when the option is on. The bounding box expands when the option is off.*

Controlling Transformations

Two options control how the Transformation tools work.

Scale Attributes controls how the scale tool affects the attributes of an object.

To set the Scale Attributes option:

1. Double-click any of the Transformation tools in the Toolbox. The Transform Options panel appears **⓳**.

2. Choose Scale Attributes to extend any scaling to the size of the stroke, pattern fill, gradient fill, or effect applied to the object **⓴**.

   or

   Deselect Scale Attributes to restrict scaling only to the size of the object, not the stroke, pattern fill, gradient fill, or effect applied to the object.

Auto-crop Images controls whether or not the bounding box of a pixel-based image shrinks to fit a transformed image. *(For information on pixel-based images, see Chapter 12, "Working with Pixels.")*

To set the Auto-crop Images option:

1. Double-click any of the Transformation tools in the Toolbox. The Transform Options panel appears.

2. Choose Auto-crop Images to automatically shrink the bounding box of an image to fit the new area of any transformed image **㉑**.

   or

   Deselect Auto-crop Images to leave control of the size of the bounding box to Fireworks.

Controlling Transformations

Reshaping Objects

Once you have created an object, you may find it difficult to work with the control handles to reshape the path. Fireworks gives you several ways to easily change the object's shape.

⓶ *The* **Freeform tool** *in the Toolbox.*

The Freeform tool allows you to change the shape of an object without worrying about adding or modifying points.

To set the Freeform tool options:

1. Double-click the Freeform tool in the Toolbox ⓶ to open the Freeform Options panel ⓷.

2. Use the slider or click in the Size field to set the size of the tool. This controls how large an area is pushed by the tool.

3. If you have a pressure-sensitive pen and tablet, click Pressure to allow your pressure on the tablet to affect the size of the effect.

   TIP If you do not have a pressure-sensitive tablet, press the left arrow, left bracket ([), or 1 key as you drag to decrease the size of the Freeform tool effect.

   TIP If you do not have a pressure-sensitive tablet, press the right arrow, right bracket (]), or 2 key as you drag to increase the size of the Freeform tool effect.

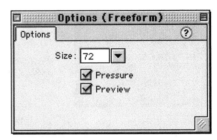

⓷ *The* **Freeform tool** *options.*

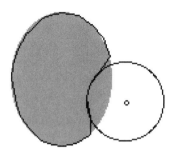

㉔ *The* **Push Freeform tool** *cursor.*

㉕ *The* **Push Freeform tool**
allows you to push on the edges
of an object to reshape it.

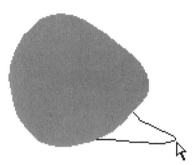

㉖ *The* **Pull Freeform tool** *cursor.*

㉗ *The* **Pull Freeform tool** *allows you*
to pull out segments from an object.

There are two modes to the Freeform tool:
the Push mode and the Pull mode. In the
Push mode the Freeform tool acts like a
rolling pin to modify the shape of the path.

To use the Freeform tool in the Push mode:

1. Set the Freeform tool options, as
   described on the previous page.

2. Move the cursor near, but not on, the
   edge of a selected object. The cursor
   displays the Push Freeform tool icon, an
   arrow with a circle next to it **㉔**.

3. Drag around the edge of the object.
   The shape of the object changes
   accordingly **㉕**.

TIP As you drag, the Push Freeform tool
icon changes to a circle that indicates
the size of the effect of the tool.

TIP The Push Freeform tool can work from
either the inside or the outside of an
object.

TIP Check Preview in the Freeform Options
panel to turn off the highlight color
on the object as you use one of the
Freeform tools.

In the Pull mode the Freeform tool acts like
a magnet that pulls out new segments from
the path.

To use the Freeform tool in the Pull mode:

1. Set the Freeform tool options, as
   described on the previous page.

2. Move the cursor to the edge of a
   selected object. The cursor displays the
   Pull Freeform tool arrow icon **㉖**.

3. Drag in or out from the edge of the
   object. The shape of the object changes
   accordingly **㉗**.

Reshaping Objects

The Reshape Area tool also lets you distort paths without manually adding or modifying anchor points or handles.

To set the Reshape Area tool options:

1. Choose the Reshape Area tool in the Toolbox **28**.

2. Double-click the Reshape Area tool in the Toolbox to open the Reshape Area Options panel **29**.

3. Use the slider or click in the Size field to set the size of the Reshape Area tool. The greater the amount, the larger the area that the tool distorts **30**.

4. Use the slider or type in the Strength field to set how long the tool will work during a drag—the higher the setting, the longer the tool distorts the path **31**.

5. If you have a pressure-sensitive tablet, check the Size or Strength boxes to set how the pressure on the tablet affects the tool.

TIP If you do not have a pressure-sensitive tablet, press the 1, left bracket ([), or left arrow key as you drag to decrease the size of the Reshape Area tool effect.

TIP If you do not have a pressure-sensitive tablet, press the 2, right bracket (]), or right arrow key as you drag to increase the size of the Reshape Area tool effect.

28 *The* **Reshape Area tool** *in the Toolbox.*

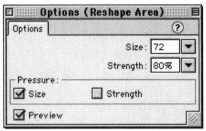

29 *The options for the* **Reshape Area tool.**

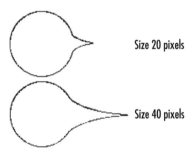

Size 20 pixels

Size 40 pixels

30 *The effect of changing the* size *of the* **Reshape Area tool.**

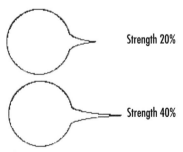

Strength 20%

Strength 40%

31 *The effect of changing the* **strength** *of the* **Reshape Area tool.**

32 *The* **Reshape Area tool** *allows you to distort the path of objects.*

33 *The* **Eraser tool** *in the Toolbox.*

34 *Cutting an object with the Eraser tool.*

The Reshape Area tool modifies paths as if they were taffy. The size of the tool controls the amount that is pulled. The strength of the tool controls the length of the pull.

To use the Reshape Area tool:

1. Choose the Reshape Area tool.

2. Position the tool either inside or outside the path.

3. Drag to reshape the path **32**.

You can also reshape paths by cutting them with the Eraser tool.

To use the Eraser tool:

1. Choose the Eraser tool in the Toolbox **33**.

2. Drag the Eraser tool across a path. This cuts the path **34**.

TIP Segments created by the Eraser tool can be moved away from the other objects with any of the selection tools.

TIP The Eraser tool also erases pixels in the Image Editing mode *(see page 178)*.

TIP The Eraser tool cursor resembles an X-acto knife when used to cut paths. It resembles a rubber eraser when erasing pixels.

Reshaping Objects

Combining Objects

One of the secrets to working with vector objects is to use commands that combine simple path shapes into more complex shapes. Some vector programs call these commands Path Operations. In Fireworks they are the Combine commands. Each of the Combine commands creates a new object from two or more overlapping objects.

The Union command allows you to create one path that is a combination of two or more objects.

To unite overlapping objects:

1. Select two or more overlapping objects.

2. Choose **Modify** > **Combine** > **Union.** The outside path of the new object follows the original outside path of the overlapping objects ⑤.

The Intersect command creates one path from the intersection of two or more paths.

To form the intersection of overlapping objects:

1. Select two or more overlapping objects.

2. Choose **Modify** > **Combine** > **Intersect.** The path of the new object follows the shape of the area where the two paths overlapped ㊱.

Original objects   Objects after Union command

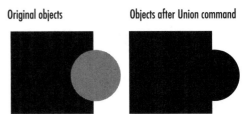

㉟ The Union command *forms one object from the combination of two or more overlapping objects.*

Original objects   Objects after Intersect command

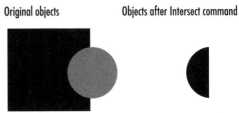

㊱ The Intersect command *creates an object from the area where two or more objects overlapped.*

Combining Objects

Original objects   Objects after Punch command

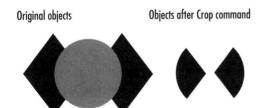

37 **The Punch command** *uses one object to punch a hole in the objects below it.*

Original objects   Objects after Crop command

38 **The Crop command** *trims away all the area outside the top object.*

The Punch command allows one object to act like a cookie cutter to punch a hole in the objects below it.

To create a hole where objects overlap:

1. Select two or more overlapping objects.

2. Choose **Modify** > **Combine** > **Punch**. The top object punches holes in all the objects below it **37**.

The Crop command is the reverse of the Punch command. Instead of punching a hole in the objects below, cropping discards the parts that are outside the top object.

To crop overlapping objects:

1. Select three or more overlapping objects.

2. Choose **Modify** > **Combine** > **Crop**. This trims away parts of the paths that were outside the original top object **38**.

TIP The object created by the Combine commands take their appearance from the bottommost object.

Combining Objects

Using the Alter Path Commands

You can also change the shape of paths using the Alter Path commands.

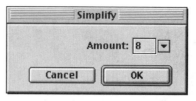

39 *The* **Simplify** *dialog box.*

For instance, you can simplify the number of points on a path.

To simplify the shape of a path:

1. Select a path.

2. Choose **Modify** > **Alter Path** > **Simplify**. The Simplify dialog box appears **39**.

3. Enter an amount of simplification in the dialog box and click OK. Fireworks removes as many points as possible to simplify the path **40**.

TIP The higher the number, the greater the distortion that may occur.

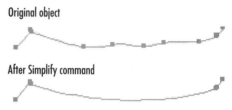

Original object

After Simplify command

40 *The* **Simplify** *command reduces the number of points on a path.*

You can also expand the stroke of an open path into a closed path. This lets you apply a fill such as pattern or a gradient. *(For more information on open and closed paths, see page 59. For more information on using patterns and gradient blends as fills, see Chapter 7, "Fills.")*

To expand a path:

1. Select a path.

2. Choose **Modify** > **Alter Path** > **Expand Stroke**. The Expand Stroke dialog box appears **41**.

3. Enter the desired width or thickness of the path (in pixels).

4. Set shape of the corners.

5. Enter an amount for the Miter Limit to control the length of the points of any corners.

6. Set the shape of the ends of the path.

7. Click OK. The path is converted into a filled shape **42**.

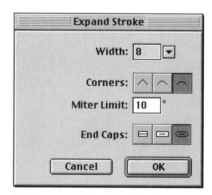

41 *The* **Expand Stroke** *dialog box.*

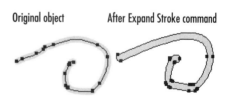

Original object   After Expand Stroke command

42 *The* **Expand Stroke** *command converts an open path into a filled shape.*

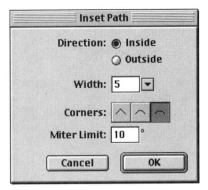

43 *The* Inset Path *dialog box.*

44 *The* Inset Path command *changes the shape of the object so that it lies inside or outside the original.*

Fireworks also lets you increase or decrease the size of a path using the Inset Path command. While it might seem like this is the same as the Scale command *(see pages 79 or 82)*, it is actually different and allows you to create a smaller or larger path that exactly follows the contours of the original.

To inset a path:

1. Select a path you want to inset.

2. Choose **Modify** > **Alter Path** > **Inset Path.** The Inset Path dialog box appears **43**.

3. Choose the direction of the inset. Inside moves the contours of the path inside the original. Outside moves the contours of the path outside the original **44**.

4. Enter the width or amount that the path should be changed.

5. Set shape of the corners.

6. Enter an amount for the Miter Limit to control the spikes of any corners.

7. Click OK. The path is converted into a filled shape.

TIP Use the Clone command before applying the Inset Path. This keeps the original image and moves the object created by the Inset Path command inside or outside the original.

Using the Alter Path Commands

Aligning Objects

You can use the Align menu commands to align the objects or distribute them along the horizontal or vertical axis ⓯–⓰.

To use the Align menu commands:

1. Select two or more objects to align.

   or

   Select three or more objects to distribute.

2. Align or distribute the objects by choosing a command from the **Modify** > **Align** menu, for example, **Modify** > **Align** > **Left**.

TIP Fireworks uses the leftmost object as the point to align to on the left. It uses the rightmost object to align to the right.

TIP Fireworks uses the topmost object to align to the top. It uses the bottommost object to align to the bottom.

The Modify toolbar (Win) gives you buttons to apply many object commands. All the Align commands are available in a pop-up list on the Modify toolbar.

To use the Align pop-up list (Win):

1. Select two or more objects to align.

   or

   Select three or more objects to distribute.

2. Press the Align button on the Modify toolbar ⓭ and choose an alignment or distribute command.

④ *The results of using the **Align** commands for the vertical axis.*

④ *The results of using the **Align** commands for the horizontal axis.*

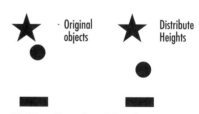

④ *The effect of applying the **Distribute Heights** command.*

④ *The effect of applying the **Distribute Widths** command.*

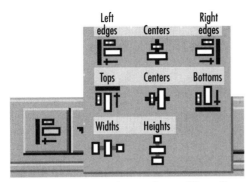

49 *The* **Align pop-up list** *on the Modify toolbar (Win).*

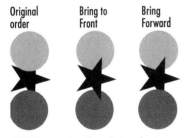

50 *The results of applying the* **Arrange** *menu commands to the star.*

Just as in other vector programs, the order in which overlapping objects appear depends on the order in which they were created. Objects that were created first are at the back of the file. Objects that were created later are in front. You can also change the order of the objects using the Arrange menu commands **50**. Objects can be moved to the front or back of a layer.

To send objects to the front or back of a layer:

1. Select the object.
2. Choose **Modify** > **Arrange** > **Bring to Front** to move the object in front of all the other objects on that layer.

   or

   Choose **Modify** > **Arrange** > **Send to Back** to move the object behind all the other objects on that layer.

   TIP (Win) You can also use the Front/Back icons on the Modify toolbar to easily move objects within a layer.

Objects can also be moved forward or backward one place at a time in their layer.

To move objects forward or backward in a layer:

1. Select the object.
2. Choose **Modify** > **Arrange** > **Bring Forward** to move the object in front of the next object in the layer.

   or

   Choose **Modify** > **Arrange** > **Send Backward** to move the object behind the next object in the layer.

3. Repeat as necessary to put the object where you want it.

   TIP (Win) You can also use the Forward/Backward icons on the Modify toolbar to easily move objects in front or behind each other.

Aligning Objects

Working with Layers

As you add more objects to your documents, you may want to take advantage of the Fireworks Layers panel. This panel lets you show and hide objects on each of the layers, lock the layers from changes, and change the order in which objects appear.

To work with the Layers panel:

1. Open the Layers panel by choosing **Window>Layers 🚱**. The two default layers, Layer 1 and Web Layer, appear in the panel.

   TIP The Web layer holds objects used to add Web addresses to images and to slice them for exporting. *(For more information on working with Web addresses and HTML information in Fireworks, see Chapter 16, "Hotspots and Links" and Chapter 17, "Slices.")*

2. To make all the objects on a layer invisible, click the Show/Hide icon for that layer.

   TIP To make all the layers invisible, hold the Option/Alt key as you click the view icon for any layer.

3. To prevent any objects on a layer from being selected, click the space in the lock area. A padlock icon appears indicating the layer is locked.

   TIP Click the layer's padlock icon to unlock the layer.

4. Click the name of a layer to make that layer the active layer. New objects are automatically on that layer.

5. Drag the name of a layer up or down to a new position in the panel to move the that layer to a new position.

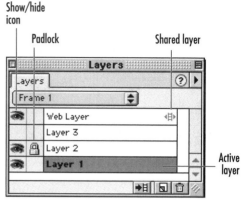

Show/hide icon

Padlock

Shared layer

Active layer

🚱 *The* Layers panel.

New   Delete
Layer   Layer

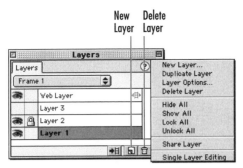

⑤ *The* **Layers** *panel menu.*

⑤ *The* **Layers Options** *dialog box.*

The Layers panel menu controls additional features of the Layers panel.

To use the Layers panel menu:

1. Press the triangle at the top of the Layers panel to view the panel menu ⑤.

2. Choose New Layer or click the icon to add a new layer.

3. Choose Duplicate Layer to duplicate the layer currently selected along with its contents.

4. Choose Layer Options to change the name of the currently selected layer.

5. Choose Delete Layer or click the icon to delete a layer.

6. Choose Hide All or Show All to change the display status of all the layers in the document.

7. Choose Lock All or Unlock All to change the protection applied to all the layers in the document.

8. Choose Share Layer to display the objects on a layer on all the frames of a document. *(For more information on working with frames, see Chapter 15, "Animations.")*

To change the name of a layer:

1. Choose Layer Options from the Layer panel menu.

   or

   Double-click the name of the layer. This opens the Layer Options dialog box ⑤.

2. Type the new name for the Layer.

3. Click OK to apply the name change.

Working with Layers

The Single Layer Editing mode makes it easy to work only with the objects on one layer.

To use Single Layer Editing:

◆ Choose Single Layer Editing from the Layers panel menu. The currently selected layer becomes the only layer you can work on. Objects on other layers cannot be selected.

You can also move objects from one layer to another.

To move an object between layers:

1. Select the object. A small square appears next to the name of the layer that the object is on.

2. Drag the small square to the layer where you want the object **54**.

TIP Objects can also be copied and pasted from one layer to another.

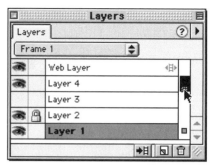

54 Drag the small object square *to move an object from one layer to another.*

Working with Layers

The objects in Fireworks are like the Colorforms shapes I played with as a child. However, the original plastic Colorforms shapes came only in solid colors. So a blue shape had to stay blue. You couldn't change the color. (Later on Colorforms came in all sorts of images and designs.)

Fireworks objects can be filled with colors, textures, patterns, gradients, and even other Fireworks objects. Even better, once an object has one type of fill, you can still go back later and change it. Also, Fireworks objects don't have to be hard edged objects. They can have a slight softening or fade applied to their edges.

Note: In case you are wondering, I found that Colorforms are still popular—even in this age of computer and video games. I can't think of a better toy for any child. In fact, a box of Colorforms is great preparation for any budding artist. I found them at the Web site www.areyougame.com.

macromedia
FIREWORKS

Creating Basic Fills

Fills are the colors, patterns, and gradients that are applied inside paths.

To apply a solid color fill:

1. Choose **Window** > **Fill** to open the Fill panel.
2. Choose Solid from the Fill category pop-up list. This displays the options for solid fills **❶**.
3. Click the Fill color button to open the Color Well Swatches panel to pick a color.

   or

   Use the Color Mixer to select a color. *(For more information on working with the Color Mixer, see Chapter 3, "Colors.")*

You can also set an object to have no fill. This makes the inside of the object completely transparent.

To set a Fill to None:

Choose None from the Fill category pop-up list. The object will become transparent **❷**.

TIP You can also apply the None fill by clicking the None button in the Color Well Swatches panel *(see page 11)*.

TIP Click the edge to select an object with a None fill, or use a selection marquee.

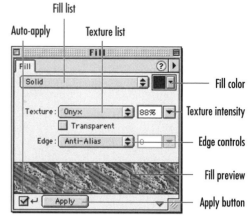

❶ *The* Fill *panel.*

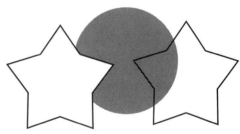

❷ *The difference between a white fill and a fill of* **None** *becomes obvious when the objects appear over another image.*

Dither preview   Actual Color control

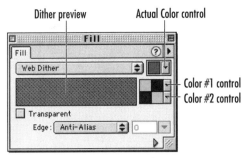

Color #1 control
Color #2 control

❸ *The* Web Dither Fill *controls.*

Creating a Web Dither Fill

In additon to a solid color fill, Fireworks offers a Web Dither Fill. This allows you to choose two colors that are combined together in a pattern (also called a *dither*) to simulate a third color. This gives you more control over the number of colors in your document. *(For a color print-out of a Web Dither Fill, see the color insert pages.)*

To apply the Web Dither Fill setting:

1. Choose Web Dither from the Fill category pop-up list. This displays the options for Web Dither fills ❸.

2. Use the Color #1 control to set the first of the two dithered colors.

3. Use the Color #2 control to set the second of the two dithered colors. The Dither preview shows how the combination of the two colors will look.

TIP Use the Actual Color control to convert the dithered color into a solid color.

Creating a Web Dither Fill

Creating Gradient Fills

In addition to solid colors, Fireworks lets you fill objects with gradients, which gradually blend one color into another.

To apply a gradient fill:

1. Select an object.

2. Choose one of the types of gradient fills from the Fill category pop-up list **❹**.

   TIP Each of the gradients controls how the colors of the gradients are manipulated. *(For a print-out of the default settings of the gradients, see Appendix A.)*

3. If necessary, change the colors by choosing from the gradient colors list **❺**.

To edit the colors a gradient fill:

1. With a gradient selected, choose Edit gradient from the Fill panel menu **❻**. This opens the Edit Gradient dialog box **❼**.

2. Click one of the square gradient controls along the gradient ramp. Drag the control to change the position of the color.

3. Click in the empty area below the gradient ramp to add a new gradient control.

   TIP To delete a gradient control, drag it off of the area below the ramp.

4. Double-click a gradient control to open the Color Mixer. Choose the color you want and then click OK to apply the color to the gradient.

5. Use the preset pop-up list to change the colors in the gradient.

6. Click OK to apply the changes to the gradient.

   TIP For a color print-out of the default gradient colors, see the color insert.

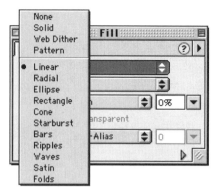

❹ *The gradient category list.*

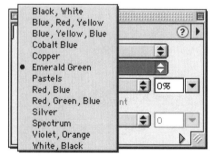

❺ *The gradient colors list.*

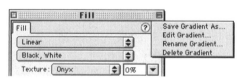

❻ *The Fill panel menu.*

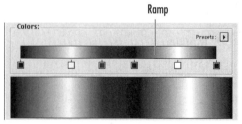

❼ *The Edit Gradient dialog box. Click in the area below the gradient ramp to add a new gradient control.*

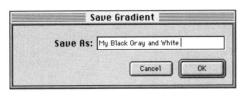

❽ *The* **Save Gradient** *dialog box.*

If you want to use your gradient in other Fireworks documents, you need to save your own gradient preset.

To save a gradient:

1. Choose Save Gradient As from the Fill panel menu. This opens the Save Gradient dialog box **❽**.

2. Give the gradient a name and click OK.

TIP If you give the gradient a new name, you add a new preset to the list.

TIP Gradient colors are saved in the document where they were created. To have a gradient available for all documents, use a style. *(For more information on working with styles, see Chapter 11, "Automation Features.")*

TIP (Mac) When you change the colors of a gradient, a plus sign appears next to its name. This indicates that the gradient has not been saved as a gradient preset.

You can also delete gradients from the Fill panel menu.

To delete a gradient fill:

1. Select the gradient preset you want to delete.

2. Choose Delete Gradient from the Fill panel menu. A dialog box appears asking you to confirm the deletion of the gradient.

3. Click OK. The gradient is deleted from the list.

In addition to controlling the colors in a gradient, you can also change the appearance of a gradient by changing its direction, length, and center.

To change the appearance of a gradient:

1. Select an object filled with a gradient.

2. Click the Paint Bucket tool in the Toolbox **❾**. The vector controls appear in the object **❿**.

3. Move the circle control to change the start point of the gradient **⓫**.

4. Drag the square control to change the end point of the gradient **⓬**.

TIP Some gradients provide two control handles to control two axes of the gradient.

5. Drag the line of the control to change the rotation of the gradient **⓭**.

TIP Double-click with the Paint Bucket tool to reset the vector controls to the default setting.

❾ *The* **Paint Bucket** *in the Toolbox.*

❿ *The* **vector controls** *over a gradient.*

⓫ *The* **circle control** *defines the start point of a gradient.*

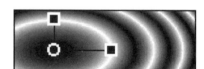

⓬ *A* **square control** *defines the end point of the gradient. A short gradient repeats to fill the object.*

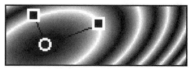

⓭ *The* **angle of the controls** *defines the rotation of the gradient.*

Creating Gradient Fills

Pattern preview

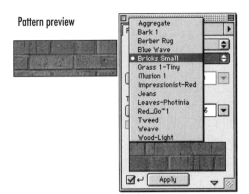

⓮ *The* **Patterns** *pop-up list.*

⓯ *An* **individual pattern** *inside an object.*

Working with Patterns

In addition to gradients, Fireworks has a set of patterns that you can apply to objects as a fill.

To apply a pattern fill:

1. Choose Pattern from the Fill category pop-up list. The pattern list appears.

2. Choose one of the preset pattern fills from the pattern list **⓮**. *(For a complete print-out of all the default patterns, see Appendix A.)*

TIP A small preview appears next to each name as you move through the list.

TIP The vector controls can also be used to modify the appearance of patterns as well as gradients *(see previous page).*

In addition to the patterns that ship with Fireworks you can add your own artwork to use as patterns. There are three ways to add patterns: individually, to the pattern folder, or as a second pattern folder.

To add individual patterns:

1. Choose Other from the pattern list.

2. Navigate and select the file you want to use as a pattern.

3. The name of the file appears at the end of the pattern list and can be applied to any object **⓯**.

TIP Individual patterns are contained in that document only.

TIP You can transfer an individual pattern from one document to another by copying an object that contains the pattern to another file.

TIP Use the same technique to add individual textures to files. *(See page 105 for information about working with textures.)*

Working with Patterns

Fireworks ships with fourteen patterns that appear in the Fill panel. You can add to the patterns that ship with Fireworks or create your own pattern folder.

To add to the pattern folder:

1. Scan or create artwork that can be tiled as a pattern.

2. Give the file a name and save it as any file format Fireworks can read. *(See the sidebar on this page for a list of those file formats.)*

3. Put the file in the Patterns folder (Fireworks: Settings: Patterns). The name of the file appears as the name of the pattern in the pop-up list.

TIP Use the same technique to add files to the Textures folder (Fireworks: Settings: Textures). *(See the next page for information on working with textures.)*

To add a second pattern folder:

1. Place the files that you want to be patterns in a folder (directory).

2. Choose **File** > **Preferences.**

3. Choose Folders from the pop-up menu ⑯.

4. Choose Patterns and then use the Browse button to navigate to the folder that holds the files.

TIP The patterns will not be available until the next time you launch Fireworks.

TIP Use the same technique with the Textures control to add a second folder for textures. *(See the next page for information on working with textures.)*

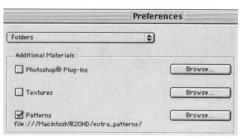

⑯ *Use the* **Folders Preferences** *to specify a second folder to hold patterns.*

Adding Patterns and Textures

Fireworks supports any file format that it exports as a file format for patterns and textures. So if you use Fireworks to create your patterns or textures, you can save the file as a PNG or any of the other formats Fireworks exports to.

If you use another program, such as Adobe Photoshop, you can save the file as a PNG, TIFF, or other bit-mapped formats.

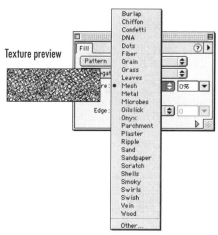

Texture preview

⓱ *The* Texture *pop-up list.*

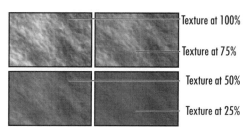

Texture at 100%

Texture at 75%

Texture at 50%

Texture at 25%

⓲ *Different settings of the Parchment texture on a solid fill.*

Transparency off

Transparency on

⓳ *The effect of the* Transparent *settings for a texture.*

Using Textures

Textures change the intensity of fills. You can apply textures to any of the fills—solids, patterns, or gradients. Once a texture is applied to a fill, you can then change the intensity of the texture.

To apply a texture to a fill:

1. Choose one of the textures from the Texture pop-up list ⓱. *(For a complete print-out of all the default textures, see Appendix A.)*

TIP There is always a texture applied to every fill. However, with an intensity of 0% the effect of the texture is not visible.

2. Use the slider or enter a number in the Intensity field to see the effects of the texture on the fill ⓲.

3. Check Transparent to allow background objects to appear in the light-colored areas of the texture ⓳.

Using Textures

Applying Transparency

Not only can you change the fill of objects, you can also control the object's transparency or opacity. Transparency—or lack of opacity—allows you to see through an object to the one underneath.

To change an object's transparency:

1. Choose **Window**>**Object** to open the Object panel 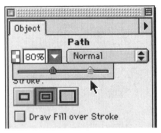.

2. Select the object you want to change.

3. Drag the Opacity slider or type a new percentage in the Opacity field **㉑**.

TIP The Opacity controls in Fireworks are similar to the layer opacity controls in Adobe Photoshop. However, in Fireworks, each object on a layer can have its own opacity setting. In Photoshop all the objects on a layer share the same opacity setting.

You can also have one object punch a transparent hole in another.

To create a hole in an object:

1. Select two or more objects.

2. Choose **Modify**>**Join**. The areas where the objects overlap are transparent **㉒**.

TIP Text characters that have two or more parts, such as the letters *D*, *B*, *o*, or *g* are automatically joined when you convert the text to paths (see page 150).

To fill the hole in an object:

1. Select the joined objects.

2. Choose **Modify**>**Split**.

TIP (Win) You can also use the Join and Split icons on the Modify toolbar to easily change objects.

⓴ *The **Opacity** slider of the Object panel.*

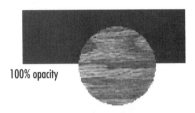
100% opacity

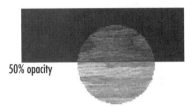
50% opacity

㉑ *The effects of changing the **opacity** of an object.*

㉒ *Applying the **Join** command creates a hole where two objects overlap.*

Before

After

23 *A Mask Group set to* **Mask to Path.** *Only the parts of the photo that fit within the top object are visible.*

Before

After

24 *A Mask Group set to* **Mask to Image.** *The lightness and darkness of the top object change the visibility of the object below.*

Working with Masks

Masking is the technique that uses the shape of one object as a contour to crop—or clip—other objects. Only those parts of the objects in the mask are visible. Fireworks has two types of masks: path shape and image.

To use a path as a mask:

1. Position the objects to be masked below the object that is to act as the mask.

2. Select all the objects and choose **Modify > Mask Group > Mask to Path.** This lets you see the bottom objects within the mask **23**.

   TIP You can also use the **Edit > Paste Inside** command to create a Path mask.

To use an image as a mask:

1. Position the objects to be masked below the object that is to act as the mask.

2. Select all the objects and choose **Modify > Mask Group > Mask to Image.** The bottom objects can be seen through the dark areas of the mask **24**.

   TIP Fireworks' Mask To Image command uses the same principles as Photoshop's layer masks. This uses the *alpha channel* values of the image.

Working with Masks

To change the mask setting:

1. Use the Selection tool to select the entire Mask Group.

2. Choose **Modify** > **Mask Group** and then choose the other type of mask.

   or

   In the Object panel, change the setting for the type of Mask **㉕**.

   TIP You can also use the Object panel to change a group into a Mask Group.

㉕ *Selecting a Mask Group displays the* **Mask Group controls** *in the Object panel.*

To release a mask:

1. Use the Selection tool to select the entire Mask Group.

2. Choose **Modify** > **Ungroup** to release the mask.

   or

   In the Object panel, change the setting from Mask Group to Group.

To select objects within a Mask Group:

1. Use the Subselection tool to select the objects you want to modify.

2. Make any changes to the object.

   or

   Choose **Edit** > **Clear** delete the object.

㉖ *The* **Mask handle** *lets you move the contents inside a mask.*

Once you have created a mask, you may want to move the objects inside the mask. This technique works with both types of masks.

To move objects within a Mask Group:

1. Select the mask with the Pointer tool. A small mask handle appears **㉖**.

2. Drag the mask handle. This moves the items within the mask.

Working with Masks

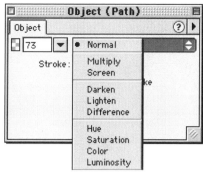

❷❼ *The* **Blending mode** *pop-up list.*

Using the Blending Modes

The Object panel lets you change how the colors of one object interact with objects below. This is similar to the layer blending modes in Adobe Photoshop.

To change the object blending mode:

1. Select the top object you want to change.

2. Use the blending mode pop-up list to choose the blending mode for the object **❷❼**.

For a color print-out of the blending modes shown in figures **❷❽**–**❹⓿**, *see the color insert.*

The Normal Blending Mode

Choose **Normal** **❷❽** to have the top object not interact with the objects below it.

❷❽ *The results of the* **Normal** *blending mode.*

The Multiply Blending Mode

Choose **Multiply** to add the colors of the top object to the objects below **❷❾**. This is similar to the results of overprinting one object over another.

❷❾ *The results of the* **Multiply** *blending mode.*

The Screen Blending Mode

Choose **Screen** to subtract the colors of the top object from the objects below **❸⓿**. This is similar to the results of bleaching out one image from the other.

❸⓿ *The results of the* **Screen** *blending mode.*

The Darken Blending Mode

Choose **Darken** to have the colors of the top object visible only where they are darker than the objects below **❸❶**.

❸❶ *The results of the* **Darken** *blending mode.*

The Lighten Blending Mode

Choose **Lighten** to have the colors of the top object visible only where they are lighter than the objects below **❸❷**.

❸❷ *The results of the* **Lighten** *blending mode.*

Using the Blending Modes

The Difference Blending Mode

Choose **Difference** to have the colors of the top object create a difference between them and the objects below. The greater the difference, the lighter the color ❸❸.

❸❸ *The results of the* **Difference** *blending mode.*

The Hue Blending Mode

Choose **Hue** to have the hue of the top object applied to the objects below ❸❹.

❸❹ *The results of the* **Hue** *blending mode.*

The Saturation Blending Mode

Choose **Saturation** to have the saturation of the top object applied to the objects below ❸❺.

❸❺ *The results of the* **Saturation** *blending mode.*

The Color Blending Mode

Choose **Color** to have the hue and saturation of the top object applied to the objects below ❸❻.

❸❻ *The results of the* **Color** *blending mode.*

The Luminosity Blending Mode

Choose **Luminosity** to have the lightness information of the top object applied to the objects below ❸❼.

❸❼ *The results of the* **Luminosity** *blending mode.*

The Invert Blending Mode

Choose **Invert** to have the shape of the top object reverse the colors of the objects below—for instance, black becomes white and green becomes red. The object's color has no effect on the Invert blend ❸❽.

❸❽ *The results of the* **Invert** *blending mode.*

The Tint Blending Mode

Choose **Tint** to have the color of the top object tint the objects below ❸❾.

❸❾ *The results of the* **Tint** *blending mode.*

The Erase Blending Mode

Choose **Erase** to have the shape of the top object act like a mask on the objects below. Only objects outside the top object will be visible. The color of the top object has no effect on the results of the Erase blend ❹⓪.

❹⓪ *The results of the* **Erase** *blending mode.*

Using the Blending Modes

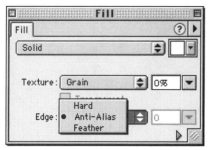

④ The **Fill Edge list** *controls the appearance of the edges of filled objects.*

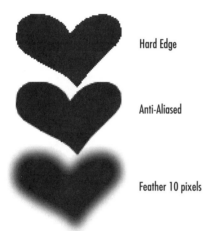

Hard Edge

Anti-Aliased

Feather 10 pixels

④ *The three different* **edge** *choices.*

Modifying Fill Edges

Once you have filled an object, you can control how the edges of the object are filled.

To change the edges of a fill:

1. Select and fill an object.

2. Use the Fill edge list **④** to change the edge treatment of the fill **④**.

   • Choose Hard Edge to leave the edge of the object as single-colored pixels.
   • Choose Anti-Alias to soften the edge of the object.
   • Choose Feather and then use the slider to blur the edge of the object.

   TIP The feather amount is in pixels and is applied equally to both sides of the edge of the path.

STROKES 8

In addition to fills, Fireworks also lets you change the appearance of objects by applying a stroke to the edge of the path. In an ordinary vector program, strokes are limited to just colors or dashes. In Fireworks, however, strokes are much more versatile than the ones found in ordinary vector programs.

Fireworks lets you set strokes to resemble all sorts of natural media such as paint brushes, crayons, chalk, pencils, oils—even toothpaste and confetti! You can also apply textures to strokes for even more varied appearances.

Finally, you can set strokes in Fireworks so that they work with pressure-sensitive tablets. Or you can simulate the look of a tablet, even if you work with a mouse.

Setting Stroke Attributes

A stroke in Fireworks can be a simple colored line resembling a pencil stroke, or it can be a multicolored paint splatter. You control the look of strokes with the Stroke panel.

To view the Stroke panel:

Choose **Window**>**Stroke** to open the Stroke panel **❶**.

The best way to understand strokes is to start with a basic stroke and then work your way up to the more sophisticated effects.

To apply a basic stroke:

1. Select the Brush tool in the Toolbox **❷**.

   TIP Although strokes can be applied to closed paths, such as rectangles, it is easier to understand strokes by creating open paths with the Pen, Pencil, or Brush tools.

2. Open the Stroke panel and select Basic from the stroke category pop-up list.

3. Drag the Brush tool in the document area. A brush stroke appears along the path you just created.

4. Use the Stroke Color Well to choose a Stroke color.

   TIP You can also use the Color Well in the Color Mixer or the Toolbox to set the stroke color. *(For more information on working with the Color Mixer, see Chapter 3, "Colors.")*

   TIP When you create a path with the Brush or Pencil tools, the fill automatically changes to None. This gives the look of a simple brush stroke, rather than a vector object.

Category list

Stroke list Softness Softness
             preview   control

Stroke panel menu

Stroke color

Stroke size

Stroke preview

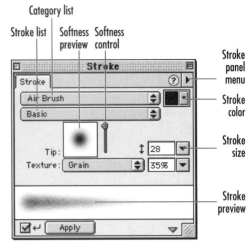

❶ *The* Stroke *panel.*

❷ *The* **Brush tool** *in the Toolbox.*

Differences Between Paths and Strokes

Paths are the objects that you create in Fireworks. A stroke is applied to the edge of paths.

So you might have a path that doesn't contain a stroke, but you'll never have a stroke that isn't applied to a path.

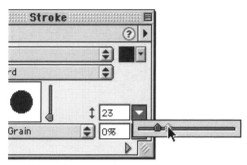

❸ *The* Stroke size *slider.*

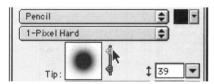

❹ *The* Stroke softness *slider.*

❺ *Two different textures applied to the stroke and fill of an object.*

The easiest way to understand the nature of strokes is by experimenting with the attributes of a selected path.

To change the stroke attributes:

1. Start with the basic stroke created in the previous exercise.

2. In the Stroke panel, drag the size slider or enter an amount in the field to change the size of the stroke ❸.

3. Drag the softness slider to blur the edge of the stroke ❹.

TIP You may need to increase the size of the stroke to see the difference in the edge softness.

4. Choose one of the preset strokes from the stroke name pop-up list to change the shape of the stroke.

TIP Each of the 11 stroke categories has its own preset strokes making a total of 48 different strokes to choose from. *(For a print-out of all the default stroke categories, see Appendix A.)*

Just as with fills, you can apply a texture to a stroke.

To apply a texture to a stroke:

1. Select a Stroke.

2. Open the Stroke panel and choose one of the textures from the Texture pop-up list. *(For a complete print-out of all the default textures, see Appendix A.)*

TIP The list of texture for strokes is the same as the list of textures used for fills. However, a Stroke can have a different texture than the fill for the object ❺.

3. Use the slider or enter a number in the Intensity field to see the effects of the texture on the fill.

TIP As with patterns, you can create your own textures to use within Fireworks *(see page 103).*

Setting Stroke Attributes

Saving Stroke Settings

Any changes you make to the Stroke panel, such as the size, edge softness, or texture, are modifications of the original stroke preset. You can save those changes as your own stroke preset.

To save Stroke panel settings:

1. Make whatever changes you want to the Stroke panel settings.

TIP (Mac) A plus appears next to the stroke name indicating that the stroke has been modified.

2. Choose Save Stroke As from the Stroke panel menu ❻. The Save Stroke dialog box appears.

3. Type the name of the new stroke and click OK. The new stroke appears as one of the stroke presets.

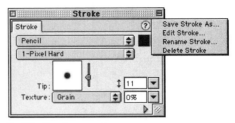

❻ *The* **Stroke** panel *menu.*

❼ *The* **Pencil tool** *in the Toolbox.*

Using the Pencil

The Pencil tool creates paths like the Brush tool. However, the size and shape of the Pencil tool creates the thin lines of a pencil.

To use the Pencil tool:

1. Click the Pencil tool in the Toolbox ❼.

2. Drag a path on the page. The Stroke panel settings automatically change to the Pencil tool settings.

3. Choose one of the preset settings for the Pencil tool ❽.

4. Drag to create a Pencil path.

TIP When you select the Brush or the Pencil tools, any fill that was set in the Fill panel resets automatically to None.

TIP Paths created by the Pencil tool can be changed by applying any of the stroke categories.

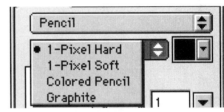

❽ *The* **Pencil tool** *presets.*

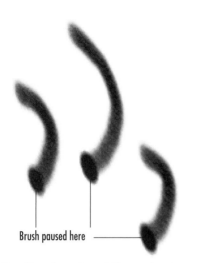

Brush paused here

❾ *The effect of pausing while creating three brush strokes.*

Creating Pressure Effects

Pressure means more than just meeting tight deadlines. If you work with a pressure-sensitive tablet, you can see how Fireworks strokes respond to changes in how you press with the stylus. Even if you draw with a mouse, you can still make a more natural stroke based on how you drag with the mouse.

To create a natural brush stroke:

1. Select the Brush tool.

2. Choose a brush such as Airbrush set to Basic or Calligraphy set to Quill.

TIP These strokes respond very well to variations in mouse movements.

3. Drag along a path pausing without releasing the mouse button. The width of the stroke increases where you pause in the drag **❾**.

You can also alter the look of the stroke after it has been applied to a path by using the Path Scrubber tool. This tool allows you to increase or decrease the pressure on a path. The Path Scrubber has two modes: Path Scrubber Plus and Path Scrubber Minus.

TIP If you have a pressure-sensitive tablet, you can use the Path Scrubber to further refine the look of the path. If you do not have a pressure-sensitive pen and tablet, you can use the Path Scrubber to simulate those effects.

To use the Path Scrubber tool:

1. Select a path with a stroke.
2. Choose the Path Scrubber Plus tool in the Toolbox ❿. (If you do not see the Path Scrubber Plus tool, press the pop-up group to select the tool.)
3. Drag along the path. The width of the stroke increases as you drag ⓫.
4. Choose the Path Scrubber Minus tool in the Toolbox ⓬.
5. Drag across to intersect the path. The width of the stroke decreases as you drag ⓭.

TIP Hold the Option/Alt key to switch between the Path Scrubber Plus and Minus modes.

❿ *The* **Path Scrubber Plus tool** *in the Toolbox.*

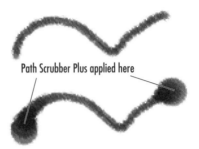

Path Scrubber Plus applied here

⓫ *The effects of the Path Scrubber Plus tool on a brush stroke.*

⓬ *The* **Path Scrubber Minus tool** *in the Toolbox.*

Path Scrubber Minus applied here

⓭ *The effects of the Path Scrubber Minus tool.*

Creating Pressure Effects

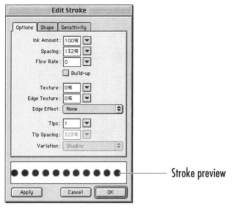

⓮ *The* Stroke Options *dialog box.*

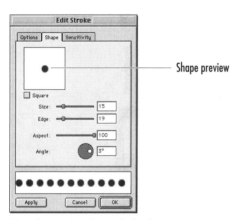

⓯ *The* Stroke Shape *dialog box.*

⓰ *The* Stroke Sensitivity *dialog box.*

Editing Strokes

In addition to the settings in the Stroke panel, other controls can affect the appearance of strokes. You do not have to open these settings to use Fireworks. However, as you become more comfortable with the program, you may want to experiment with these controls. For instance, these controls let you create strokes that are dashed or dotted lines.

To create your own strokes:

1. Choose Edit Stroke from the Stroke panel menu. The Edit Stroke dialog box appears.

2. Click the tab for Options to control the appearance of the stroke ⓮.

3. Click the tab for Shape to control the size, edge softness, shape, roundness, and angle of the stroke ⓯.

TIP You can override the settings for size by changing the size and edge in the main Stroke panel.

4. Click the tab for Sensitivity to control how the stroke reacts to changes in the mouse or stylus movements ⓰.

Modifying Stroke Positions

Unlike other vector programs, Fireworks gives you a choice as to where a stroke is displayed on a path.

To change the position of a stroke on a path:

1. Select the path.

2. Choose **Window**>**Object** to open the Object panel ⓱.

3. Click the Centered, Inside, or Outside buttons to change the position of the stroke along the path ⓲.

When a path has both a stroke and a fill, you have a choice as to how the fill interacts with the stroke.

To change how the fill meets a stroke:

1. Select the path.

2. Choose **Window**>**Object** to open the Object panel.

3. Check Draw Fill Over Stroke to have the fill of the object extend over the path ⓳.

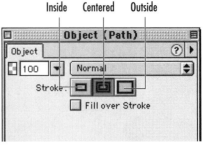

⓱ *The Stroke Position controls in the* **Object** panel.

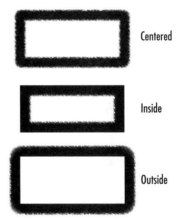

⓲ *The three choices for the* **position of a brush on a path.**

⓳ *The effects of changing the* **Draw Fill Over Brush** *setting.*

EFFECTS 9

You could think of fills and strokes as the basic utilitarian features to styling objects. Effects, however, are the razzle-dazzle features that alter the look of objects. Unlike fills and strokes that are limited to just the inside or the outside of objects, Fireworks effects can change the look of either the inside or the outside of objects.

For instance, you can add a bevel effect to the inside or the outside of an object. A shadow effect added to the outside of an object makes the object appear to be floating above its background. However, a shadow effect added inside an object will make it look like it is punching a hole in the background.

Applying Effects

Effects are applied using the Effect panel.

To open the Effect panel:

Choose **Window**>**Effect** to open the Effect panel ❶.

or

Click the Effect panel tab to change from the Fill or Brush panel.

When you first open the Effect panel, it will be empty. You need to add effects to the panel list.

To add to the Effect panel list:

1. Select an object.

2. Use the Effect pop-up list ❷ to add effects to the panel.

3. Choose Use Defaults to add the default effects to the panel ❸. *(See page 137 for information on how to change the default settings for the Effect panel.)*

   or

   Choose a specific effect from one of the effects categories.

Effect panel list

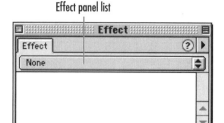

❶ *The* Effect panel *without an effects chosen.*

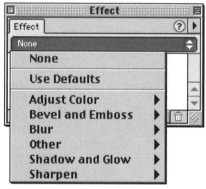

❷ *The* Effect pop-up list *lets you add to the Effect panel.*

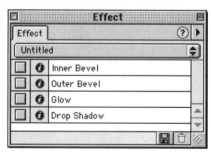

❸ *The* Effect Defaults.

Applying Effects

❹ *Different looks that can be created using the* Inner and Outer Bevels.

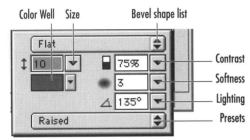

Color Well   Size   Bevel shape list

— Contrast

— Softness

— Lighting

— Presets

❺ *The* Outer Bevel *controls.*

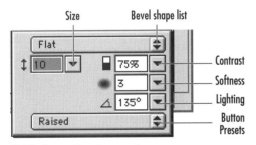

Size   Bevel shape list

— Contrast

— Softness

— Lighting

— Button Presets

❻ *The* Inner Bevel *controls.*

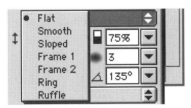

❼ *The bevel* shape choices.

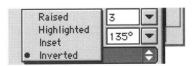

❽ *The bevel effects* button presets.

Applying Bevel Effects

The bevel effects simulate the look of 3D objects such as chiseled letters or carved forms **❹**. Fireworks lets you apply bevels to either the inside or outside of objects.

To apply an outer or inner bevel:

1. Select an object.

2. Choose Outer Bevel from the Effect list. The Outer Bevel controls appear **❺**.

   or

   Choose Inner Bevel from the Effect list. The Inner Bevel controls appear **❻**.

3. Choose one of the bevel shapes from the Bevel shape list **❼**. *(For a display of the bevel shapes, see Appendix A.)*

4. Use the Size control to change the size of the bevel.

5. If you have chosen Outer Bevel, use the Color Well to change the color of the bevel.

   TIP The color of an inner bevel comes from the color of the original object.

6. Use the Contrast control to change the intensity of the light creating the bevel highlights and shadows.

7. Use the Softness control to change the hardness of the edges of the bevel.

   TIP If the bevel around curved objects appears bumpy, increase the softness to smooth the bevel.

8. Use the Lighting control to change the angle of the light on the beveled edge.

9. Use the Button presets **❽** to apply special effects to the bevels. *(See the next page for a discussion on how to use the button presets.)*

Applying Bevel Effects

The Button menu for the bevel effects is used to easily apply variations to the bevels. The four states are Raised, Highlighted, Inset, and Inverted.

Using the bevel button choices menu:

The four states change bevels as follows 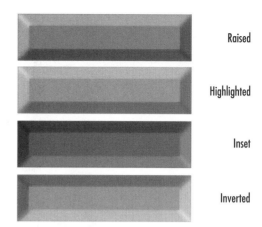:

- **Raised** leaves the object as originally styled.

- **Highlighted** lightens the object as if a 25% white tint were applied over it.

- **Inset** reverses the lighting of the bevel to invert the 3D effect.

- **Inverted** reverses the lighting and lightens the object with a tint.

TIP The four states of the Button menu are provided as a convenience for quickly changing the appearance of buttons. They do not actually create the code for buttons. *(For more information on creating rollover buttons, see Chapter 18, "Behaviors.")*

Raised

Highlighted

Inset

Inverted

❷ *The effects of applying the* Bevel Preset choices.

⑩ *Different looks that can be created using the* Inner Shadow *and* Drop Shadow *effects.*

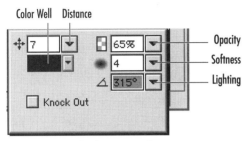

Color Well Distance

Opacity
Softness
Lighting

Knock Out

⑪ *The* Drop Shadow *controls.*

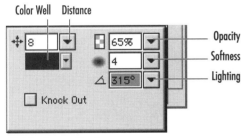

Color Well Distance

Opacity
Softness
Lighting

Knock Out

⑫ *The* Inner Shadow *controls.*

Applying Shadow Effects

The shadow effects simulate the look of objects casting a shadow on a wall or cutting out a hole in a background **⑩**.

To apply a Drop Shadow or Inner Shadow effect:

1. Choose Drop Shadow from the Effect list. The Drop Shadow controls appear **⑪**.

   or

   Choose Inner Shadow from the Effect list. The Inner Shadow controls appear **⑫**.

2. Use the Opacity control to change the transparency of the shadow. The lower the number, the more transparent the object.

3. Use the Softness control to change the softness or feather applied to the edge of the shadow.

4. Use the Lighting control to change the angle of the light casting the shadow.

5. Use the Distance control to change how far the shadow falls from the object.

6. Use the Color Well to choose a color for the shadow.

7. Select Knock Out to have only the shadow appear, not the object casting the shadow.

Applying Shadow Effects

Applying Emboss Effects

The emboss effect pushes the shape of one object into or out from the background or other objects .

⓭ *Different looks that can be created using the* Inset Emboss and Raised Emboss effects.

To apply a Raised Emboss or Inset Emboss effect:

1. Choose Raised Emboss from the Effect list. The Raised Emboss controls appear **⓮**.

   or

   Choose Inset Emboss from the Effect list. The Inset Emboss controls appear **⓯**.

2. Use the Width control to change the width or size of the embossed edge.

3. Use the Contrast control to change the intensity of the light creating the embossing highlights and shadows.

4. Use the Softness control to change the sharpness of the edges of the embossing.

5. Use the Lighting control to change the angle of the light on the embossing.

   TIP Embossing always takes its appearance from the object it is over, the canvas color of the document, or any placed image.

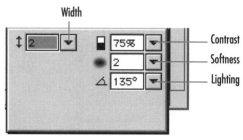

⓮ *The* **Raised Emboss** *controls.*

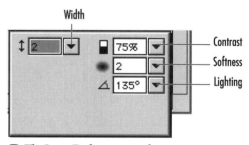

⓯ *The* **Inset Emboss** *controls.*

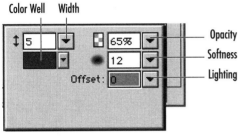

⓰ *Different looks that can be created using the* **Glow effect.**

Color Well   Width

Opacity
Softness
Lighting

⓱ *The* **Glow controls.**

Applying Glow Effects

The glow effect lets you add a color all around the edges of an object **⓰**.

To apply a Glow effect:

1. Choose Glow from the Effect category pop-up list. The Glow effect choices appear **⓱**.

2. Use the Opacity control to change the transparency of the glow. The lower the number, the greater the transparency.

3. Use the Softness control to change the softness, or feather, applied to the glow.

4. Use the Width control to change the size of the glow.

5. Use the Offset control to add a space between the object and the glow.

6. Use the Color Well to choose a color for the glow.

Applying Glow Effects

Applying Blur Effects

The blur effects soften the details in objects. This can be used to make one object appear to be behind others. The effects are most obvious when applied to pixel-based images, but they also affect patterns, textures, and gradients applied to objects.

TIP The blur effects work by changing some of the blacks and whites in an image to shades of gray. This means that some of the detail of an image is lost.

To apply the Blur or Blur More effects:

◆ Choose Blur or Blur More from the Effect category pop-up list. The name of the effect appears in the Effect panel.

TIP The Blur **18** and Blur More **19** effects apply a finite amount of blur and do not have a dialog box that controls the amount of the blur.

You can also apply a Gaussian Blur, which lets you control the amount of the blur.

To apply the Gaussian Blur effect:

1. Choose Gaussian Blur from the Effect category pop-up list. The Gaussian Blur dialog box appears **20**.

2. Use the slider to increase or decrease the amount of the blur.

3. Check Preview to see the effects of the blur on the selected object.

4. Click OK. The name of the effect appears in the Effect panel as the effect is applied **21**.

Original   Blur effect

18 *The results of applying the* **Blur effect** *to an image.*

Original   Blur More effect

19 *The results of applying the* **Blur More effect** *to an image.*

20 *The* **Gaussian Blur** *dialog box.*

Original   Gaussian Blur

21 *The result of applying the* **Gaussian Blur effect** *to an image.*

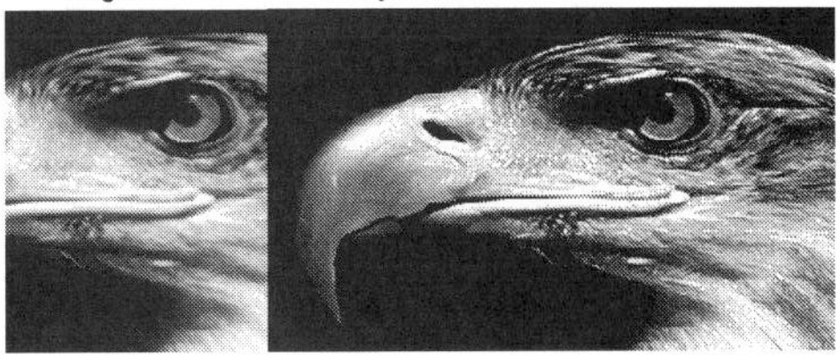

Original | Sharpen effect

22 *The effect of applying the* **Sharpen effect** *to an image.*

Original | Sharpen More effect

23 *The effect of applying the* **Sharpen More** **effect** *to an image. Notice the added contrast created around the eye and below the mouth.*

Applying Sharpening Effects

Just as you can blur images, so can you sharpen them. This is especially useful when working with scanned images that tend to look a little soft, or out of focus.

TIP The sharpen effects work by changing some gray pixels in the image to black or white. Although it may seem that more detail is revealed, strictly speaking some of the detail is lost.

To apply the Sharpen or Sharpen More effects:

◆ Choose Sharpen or Sharpen More from the Effect category pop-up list. The name of the effect appears in the Effect panel.

TIP The Sharpen **22** and Sharpen More **23** effects apply a finite amount of sharpening and do not have a dialog box controlling the amount of the blur.

The other type of sharpening effect goes under the unlikely name Unsharp Mask. This comes from a traditional photographic technique.

To apply the Unsharp Mask effect:

1. Choose Unsharp Mask from the Effect category pop-up list. The Unsharp Mask dialog box appears ㉔.

2. Drag the Sharpen Amount slider to change the amount of contrast that is applied—the greater the amount, the greater the sharpening.

3. Drag the Threshold slider to set how different the pixels must be before they are sharpened.

TIP A Threshold of 0 means that all the pixels in the image are sharpened.

TIP A high threshold means that only those pixels that are very different in brightness are sharpened. For instance, in illustration ㉕, a high threshold means that only the sharp line in the beak would be sharpened. A low threshold means that the gray feathers in the lower right corner would also be sharpened.

5. Drag the Pixel Radius slider or type in the field to set the number of pixels around the edge that have the sharpening effect applied.

6. Check Preview to see the effects of the blur on the selected object.

7. Click OK. The name of the effect appears in the Effect panel as the effect is applied.

TIP High Unsharp Mask settings with a high sharpen and low threshold settings can cause an unwanted halo or glow around objects ㉖.

㉔ *The* **Unsharp Mask** *dialog box.*

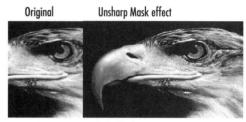

㉕ *The effect of applying the* **Unsharp Mask effect** *to an image.*

㉖ *The Unsharp Mask effect at a* **high sharpen and low threshold** *can create an unnatural glow around details in an image.*

Original Find Edges and Invert effects

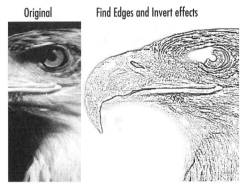

㉗ *The results of applying the* **Find Edges effect** *and then the* **Invert effect** *to an image.*

Applying the Find Edges Effect

The Find Edges effect changes the colors of the pixels so that a line appears where there was an edge.

To apply the Find Edges effect:

◆ Choose Find Edges from the Effect pop-up list. The image is converted and the name of the effect appears in the Effect panel.

TIP Use the Invert effect *(see page 132)* after the Find Edges effect to convert the image to black on white **㉗**.

㉘ *To* **create an Alpha mask,** *draw a rectangle over an image and then apply a gradient.*

㉙ *The* **Convert to Alpha** effect *applies a transparency to the gray areas of the gradient.*

㉚ *The* **Mask Group** *fades the original image according to the values in the gradient.*

Using the Convert to Alpha Effect

The Convert to Alpha effect converts an object into its grayscale values.

TIP The Mask Group command set to Image *(see page 107)* gives you the same display as the Convert to Alpha Effect.

To mask using the Convert to Alpha effect:

1. Find an object or image to mask.

2. Add an image that covers the image you want to mask and position it over the original object or image **㉘**.

TIP Alpha areas that are black allow the images underneath to be seen. Alpha areas that are white make the images underneath transparent.

3. With the rectangle selected, choose Convert to Alpha from the Effect pop-up list. This converts the object to a grayscale image **㉙**.

4. Select both the image and the mask and choose **Modify > Mask Group** to see the image through the Alpha mask **㉚**.

TIP The Alpha masks in Fireworks are similar to the Alpha channels in Adobe Photoshop.

Applying the Adjust Color Effects

Fireworks also has a set of effects that alter the appearance of colors in objects and images. These effects are similar to those found in image editing programs such as Adobe Photoshop.

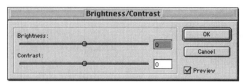

③① *The* **Brightness/Contrast** *dialog box.*

To apply the Brightness/Contrast effect:

1. Choose Brightness/Contrast from the Adjust menu of the Effect category pop-up list. The Brightness/Contrast dialog box appears **③①**.

2. Use the Brightness slider to increase or decrease the lightness of the image.

3. Use the Contrast slider to increase or decrease the contrast of the image.

4. Check Preview to see how the controls affect the image.

5. Click OK. The name of the effect appears in the Effect panel.

To apply the Curves effect:

1. Choose Curves from the Adjust menu of the Effect category pop-up list. The Curves dialog box appears **③②**.

2. Drag a point on the graph to change the straight line to a curve. Move the curve up to lighten the area. Move the curve down to darken the area.

3. Use the Eyedroppers to choose the image's black, neutral, and white points.

4. Check Preview to see how the controls affect the image.

The Invert effect reverses selected images into negatives.

To apply the Invert effect:

◆ Choose Invert from the Adjust menu of the Effect category pop-up list. The colors of the image are reversed **③③** and the name of the effect is added to the Effect panel.

Modification point   Eyedroppers

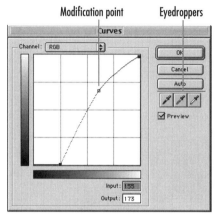

③① *The* **Curves** *dialog box.*

Original   Invert effect

③② *The result of applying the* **Invert effect** *to an image.*

Black point   Midpoint   White point Eyedroppers

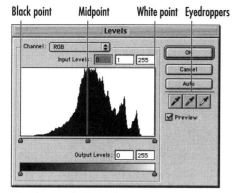

❸❹ *The* Levels *dialog box.*

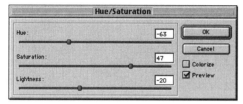

❸❺ *The* **Brightness/Contrast** *dialog box.*

To apply the Levels effect:

1. Choose Levels from the Adjust menu of the Effect category pop-up list. The Levels dialog box appears **❸❹**.

2. Drag the Black point, Midpoint, or White point sliders to adjust the tonal range of the image.

    or

    Use the Eyedroppers to select the black, white, and neutral points on the image.

3. Drag sliders for the output ramp to change the appearance of the image.

To apply the Auto Levels effect:

◆ Choose Auto Levels from the Adjust menu of the Effect category pop-up list. This applies a preset adjustment to the levels of the object.

To apply the Hue/Saturation effect:

1. Choose Hue/Saturation from the Adjust menu of the Effect category pop-up list. The Hue/Saturation dialog box appears **❸❺**.

2. Use the Hue slider to change the range of colors in the image.

3. Use the Saturation slider to increase or decrease the saturation of the colors in the image.

4. Use the Lightness slider to increase or decrease the lightness of the image.

5. Click Colorize to convert the image to monotone.

6. Click Preview to see the effects of the controls on the image.

7. Click OK. This converts the image and adds the name of the effect to the Effect panel.

Applying the Adjust Color Effects

Using the Eye Candy Filters

Fireworks 3 also ships with a gift for you—two free filters from Alien Skin Software's Eye Candy collection. These filters are automatically installed as part of the regular Fireworks application.

The Eye Candy Cutout effect is a more sophisticated version of the Fireworks inner shadow effect *(see page 125).*

To apply the Eye Candy Cutout effect:

1. Choose Cutout from the Eye Candy 3.1 LE menu of the Effect category pop-up list. The Cutout dialog box appears **36**.

2. Use the Cutout controls **37** to change the effect as follows:
   - Direction changes the angle of the shadow in the cutout.
   - Distance controls how large a shadow is created.
   - Blur softens the edge of the shadow.
   - Opacity changes the transparency of the shadow.
   - Shadow color changes the color of the shadow.
   - Solid color changes the background color to transparent.
   - Fill color changes the color of the background.

3. Click the Apply button **38** to add the effect to the object.

   or

   Click the Cancel button to leave the dialog box without applying the effect.

Original image   Preview image

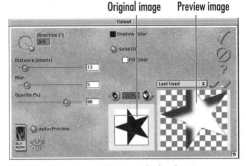

36 *The* Eye Candy Cutout *dialog box.*

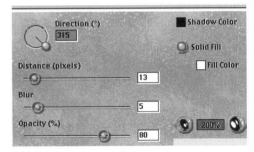

37 *The* **Cutout controls.**

Apply

Cancel

38 *The* **Apply and Cancel controls** *for the Eye Candy effects.*

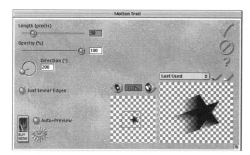

39 *The* Eye Candy Motion Trail *dialog box.*

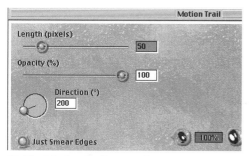

40 *The* Motion Trail controls.

The Eye Candy Motion Trail effect simulates the look of an object moving so fast it creates a blurred image behind it.

To apply the Eye Candy Motion Trail effect:

1. Choose Motion Trail from the Eye Candy 3.1 LE menu of the Effect category pop-up list. The Eye Candy Motion Train dialog box appears **39**.

2. Use the Motion Trail controls **40** to change the effect as follows:
   - Length changes the how long the trail extends from the object.
   - Opacity changes the transparency of the trail.
   - Direction controls the angle that the trail extends from.
   - Just Smear Edges extens the trail only from the outside edge of the object.

3. Click the Apply button to add the effect to the object.

   or

   Click the Cancel button to leave the dialog box without applying the effect.

Using the Eye Candy Filters

Working with the Effect Panel

The Effect panel controls the look of objects that have effects applied to them.

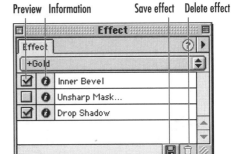

Preview Information Save effect Delete effect

⓬ *The* **Effect panel** *with multiple effects.*

To modify an effect:

1. Click the information icon in the Effect panel **⓬**. This opens the effect controls.

   TIP If the effect is set by a dialog box, such as the Gaussian Blur, the information icon opens the dialog box.

2. Make whatever changes you want.

3. Click the name of the effect in the panel to apply the new control settings.

To change the display of an effect:

◆ Click the Preview icon in the Effect panel **⓬**. This turns the effect on and off.

   TIP Use the All On or All Off commands in the Effect panel menu to temporarily turn on and off all the effects.

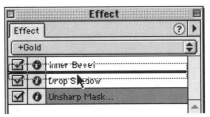

⓬ Drag an effect to a new position *in the Effect panel to change how the effect is applied.*

To delete an effect:

◆ Drag the name of the effect onto the Delete Effect icon.

   or

◆ Use the Delete Effect command in the Effect panel menu to delete the selected effect.

To apply multiple effects:

◆ Add as many effects as you want from the Effect pop-up list.

   TIP Each effect is applied in the same order that it appears in the Effects panel.

   TIP Drag the effects up or down the list to change the order that the effect is applied to the image **⓬**.

   TIP Different orders create different looks **⓭**.

⓭ *The difference between positioning the Drop Shadow effect above the Inner Bevel (left) or positioning the Drop Shadow below the Inner Bevel (right).*

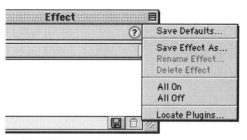

⓬ *The* Effect panel menu.

⓭ Saved effects *appear in the pop-up list in the Effect panel.*

Once you create an effect or a series of effects in the Effect panel, you can easily save them so they are available for other objects or documents.

To save an effect:

1. Apply the effects you want to an object.

2. Choose Save Effect As from the Effect panel menu **⓬**. The Save Effect dialog box appears.

3. Type the name of the new effect and click OK. The new effect appears as one of the effect presets **⓭**.

TIP Use the Rename Effect command in the Effect panel menu to change the name of an effect.

You can also change the setting for the default effects used as the Use Defaults command *(see page 122)*.

To set the default effects:

1. Apply a certain set of effects to an object.

2. Choose Save Defaults from the Effect panel menu. An alert box appears, asking you to confirm that you want to save these settings as the new defaults.

3. Click OK. The next time you choose Use Defaults, the new effects will appear.

Fireworks also supports many third party plug-ins such as those in Adobe Photoshop and Kai's Power Tools. These appear in the effects panel 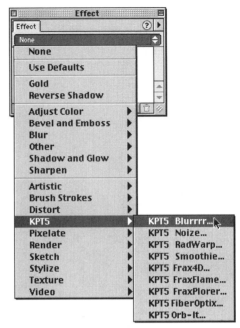. This allows you to apply those filters and adjust them later.

To add third party plug-ins using the Effect panel:

1. Choose Locate Plug-ins from the Effect panel menu.

2. Use the dialog box to navigate to the folder that contains the plug-ins.

3. Select the folder. An alert box informs you that the next time you launch Fireworks, the plug-ins will be available in the Effect panel.

TIP This technique also adds plug-ins to the Xtras menu *(see page 180).*

To add third party plug-ins using Preferences:

1. Choose File > Preferences to open the Preferences dialog box 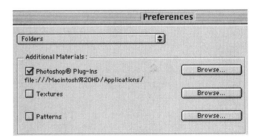.

2. Use the dialog box to navigate to the folder that contains your Photoshop plug-ins.

3. Select the folder.

4. Quit and re-launch Fireworks to see the plug-ins in the Effect panel.

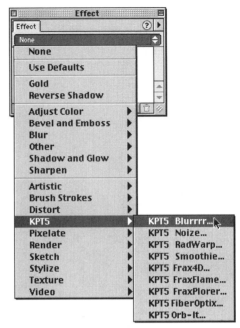

46 Plug-ins *from Adobe and other companies appear in the Effect panel list.*

47 *Use the* **Preferences dialog box** *to locate the folder that contains the additional plug-ins.*

TEXT 10

Whoever said a picture is worth a thousand words underestimated by several hundred kilobytes. Pictures and graphics create much bigger Web files than ordinary HTML text. This means that pages with graphics take much longer to appear on the viewers' computer screens.

All text created in Fireworks is eventually exported onto Web pages as graphics. So why would someone want to convert fast-downloading text into slow-downloading graphics?

It might be to create labels, create a banner design, or just make sure the text looks the same no matter what fonts or system the viewer has. Whatever the reason, Fireworks has many features for working with text.

macromedia
FIREWORKS

Typing Text

You access text in Fireworks by using the Text tool. You should find working with text similar to the methods you have used in any graphics or page-layout program.

❶ *The* **Text tool** *in the Toolbox.*

To use the Text tool:

1. Choose the Text tool in the Toolbox **❶**.

2. Click inside the document area or drag to create the area where you want the text to stay inside. This opens the Text Editor **❷**.

TIP If you click with the Text tool, the text box starts at that spot and extends to the edge of the document area.

To use the Text Editor:

1. Type the text inside the Preview area.

2. Use any of the ordinary text techniques to select text, make corrections, or insert new text within the Preview area.

3. Click Show Font and Show Size & Color to see the text as it will appear in the document.

TIP Turn off the Font and Size & Color options if you find it difficult to read the text within the Text Editor.

4. Click Apply to see the formatting changes without leaving the Text Editor.

5. Click OK to close the Text Editor.

To reopen the Text Editor:

Choose **Text** > **Editor**.

or

Double-click the text block.

❷ *The* **Text Editor.**

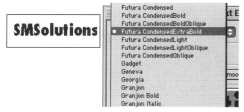

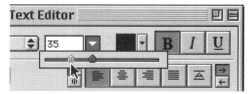

❸ *The side area of the* **font list** *in the Text Editor displays a representation of the selected text in the typeface in the font list.*

❹ *The* **point size** *control in the Text Editor.*

❺ *The* **styling** *controls in the Text Editor include the buttons for applying bold, italic, and underline style to text.*

Setting the Text Attributes

Once you have opened the Text Editor, you can control the various text attributes.

To set the font:

1. Use the font pop-up list ❸ to choose the typeface.
2. Type text inside the Preview area.
3. Use the font pop-up list to change to a different typeface.

TIP A small area appears next to the font list that displays a representation of the selected typeface. The representation is either the selected text or the name of the typeface.

To set the point size:

◆ Use the point size slider or type in the field ❹ to change the point size.

Fireworks also lets you add bold or italic styling to text.

To add electronic styling:

1. Select the text.
2. Click the bold or italic buttons to change text ❺.

TIP Electronic styling is discarded when text is converted into paths *(see page 150)*.

You can apply different text attributes within the Text Editor.

To apply different text attributes:

1. As you are typing the text, make whatever changes you want. The next text you type will reflect those changes.

   or

   Select the text you want to change.
2. Apply the changes to that text.

Kerning is adjusting the space between two letters. Fireworks lets you kern text within the Text Editor.

To kern the text:

1. Click between the two letters you want to kern.

2. Use the Kern slider or type in the field ❻ to kern the text closer together or further apart. Negative values decrease the space; positive values increase the space ❼.

TIP Click Auto-Kern in the Text Editor to have Fireworks use the built-in kerning pairs from the typeface.

TIP The Preview does not show the effects of kerning. To see those effects, position the Text Editor outside the document area and then use the Apply button to see how the text changes as you enter the kerning amounts.

Range kerning is kerning applied to a selection of text. (Range kerning is sometimes called *tracking* in other programs.)

To set the range kerning:

1. Drag across a selection of the text.

2. Use the Range Kerning slider or type in the field to change the range kerning for the text ❽. Negative values decrease the space; positive values increase the space ❾.

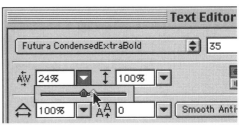

❻ *The* **kerning** *controls in the Text Editor.*

People Inc.
People Inc.

❼ *The result of kerning to close up the space between the letters* **Pe, pl,** *and* **le.**

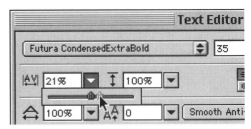

❽ *The* **range kerning** *controls in the Text Editor.*

People Inc.
People Inc.

❾ *The results of applying range kerning to increase the spaces between the characters.*

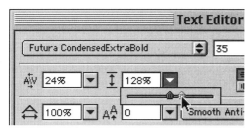

⑩ *The* **leading** *controls in the Text Editor.*

⑪ *The* **baseline shift** *controls in the Text Editor.*

People Inc.
People Inc.

⑫ *The results of applying a positive baseline shift to the characters* **nc.** *(The baseline is indicated by the dashed line.)*

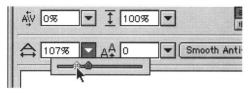

⑬ *The* **horizontal scale** *controls in the Text Editor.*

People Inc.
People Inc.

⑭ *The results of applying horizontal scale to the letter* **P.**

Leading, or *line spacing,* is the space between multiple lines of text. (Leading is pronounced *ledding* after the metal pieces of lead that were inserted in early typesetting equipment.) If your text is only on a single line, you do not have to worry about setting leading.

To set the leading:

Use the Leading slider or type in the field to change the leading for the text **⑩**.

TIP Fireworks measures leading as a percentage of the point size. 100% means the leading is the same as the point size.

TIP Leading is applied to an entire paragraph, not individual characters.

Baseline shift is the technique of raising or lowering text from its *baseline,* or the line that the text sits on.

To add a baseline shift:

1. Select the text.
2. Use the baseline slider or type in the field **⑪** to raise or lower the text in points from the baseline.

TIP Positive numbers raise the text. Negative numbers lower the text **⑫**.

Text can also be distorted using a technique called horizontal scaling. This changes the width of the text without changing the height.

To change the horizontal scale:

1. Select the text.
2. Use the horizontal scale slider or type in the field **⑬** to increase or decrease the horizontal scaling. Amounts lower than 100% make the text width smaller. Amounts higher than 100% make the text wider **⑭**. *(See the sidebar on the following page for a discussion on using the horizontal scale controls.)*

Text can also be set with a wide variety of alignment options. The text can be set either horizontally or vertically. Horizontal text reads from left to right.

To set the horizontal alignment:

1. Select the text.

2. Click one of the five horizontal alignment settings: left, right, centered, justified, or stretched alignment **⑮**.

TIP Justified alignment increases the range kerning so the line fills the width of the text block **⑯**.

TIP Stretched alignment distorts the shape of the text as it increases the horizontal scale, so the line fills the width of the text block **⑰**. This could cause typographic purists to cringe *(see the sidebar on this page)*.

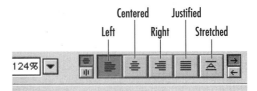

⑮ *The* **alignment** *controls in the Text Editor.*

People Inc.

People Inc.

⑯ *The results of the* **justified alignment.**

People Inc.

People Inc.

⑰ *The results of the* **stretch alignment.**

Should You Use Horizontal Scale?

Typography purists (such as this author) disdain the look of electronically scaled type. They say it causes ugly distortions to the look of the original typeface.

They also say that if you need to fit text into a specific area you should use the proper condensed or expanded typeface. However, even the purists cannot always tell if small amounts have been applied.

Setting the Text Attributes

Swatches Palettes

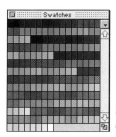

216 Web-safe colors *discussed on page 44.*

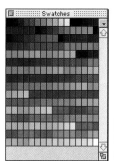

Macintosh System Colors *discussed on page 45.*

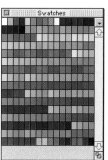

Windows System Colors *discussed on page 45.*

Gamma Correction

Use the View menu to see the effects of the Windows or Macintosh gamma on artwork (see page 191).

Artwork as seen in the **Windows Gamma.**

Artwork as seen in the **Macintosh Gamma.**

Choosing GIF Optimization

The type of artwork that should be exported as a **GIF image.** *This image uses 27 colors in the GIF Adaptive palette.*

Choosing JPEG Optimization

The type of artwork that should be exported as a **JPEG image.** *This exports the image with millions of colors available.*

Applying Web-safe colors

As you shift and reduce the number of colors you may want to add dithering.

The original art contains a variety of non–Web-safe colors.

*Using **24 Web-safe colors** shifts the colors but reduces the file to 3.29K.*

*Dithering the **24 colors** helps improve the look but increases the size to 3.91K.*

*At **12 colors** the file size drops to 2.66K. While some details are lost, the image is still usable.*

*At **6 colors** the file size drops to 1.93K. However, the image is hardly usable.*

Handling GIF Blends

GIF images with blends need special techniques to avoid banding. *(For more information on optimzing GIF images, see pages 192–193.)*

Using the Web-safe palette creates banding in the blend.

Adding dithering reduces the banding but may not be desirable.

Using the Adaptive palette reduces the banding almost completely.

Adding a small amount of dithering to the Adaptive palette reduces the banding even further.

Color Table

The settings of the Color Table change the look of a GIF image. (*For more information on the Color Table, see pages 194–196.*)

The original color table for this image consists of mostly red and gray colors.

When a new color table is loaded, the colors of the image change to match the new combination of blue colors.

JPEG Comparisons

As you decrease the quality of a JPEG image, the file size decreases. Notice how the quality of the image degrades only slightly while the file size is reduced greatly. Notice also the effects of smoothing. (*For more information on JPEG optimization, see pages 197–198.*)

JPEG at 100% Quality *(16.58K).*

JPEG at 80% Quality *(5.00K).*

JPEG at 40% Quality *(2.80K).*

JPEG at 40% Quality, Smoothing of 4 *(2.52K).*

Color Insert

GIF Loss

The Loss control in the GIF Optimize panel decreases the file size while keeping the number of colors constant *(see page 193)*. However, it can cause distortions in the image.

The original GIF image with no Loss applied has a file size of 9.89K.

The original GIF image with 100% Loss applied has a file size of 4.63K.

Web Palette or Adpative Palette

The differences between an Adaptive palette or a Web palette *(see pages 192)*.

*An **Adaptive palette** maintains as many of the original colors as possible. Notice the subtle shade for the face and hands.*

*A **Web 216 palette** with **dithering on** creates a pattern of dots in the shirt, face, and hands to simulate non-Web colors. This is unacceptable for flat color art.*

*The **Web 216 palette** with **dithering off** shifts the colors in the shirt, face, and hands to the closest Web-safe color.*

Effects of 8-bit monitors

Because 8-bit monitors can not display more than 256 colors, there are some changes that occur when images are displayed.

The original image as displayed with **millions of colors.**

With **256 colors** *the image looks similar with only a little banding in the brown.*

When viewed on an **8-bit monitor** *the image becomes very dithered.*

When the palette is converted to **Web-safe** *there is a color shift and a reduction in the dithering.*

Web Dither Fill

The Web Dither Fill allows you to use two colors in a checkerboard pattern to create the illusion of a third color (see page 99).

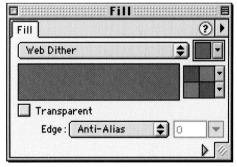

The Fill panel set to Web Dither shows the mixture of the two colors.

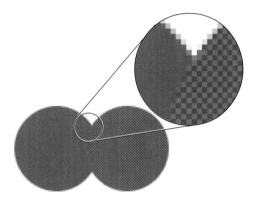

The **Web Dither** *fill in the right circle approximates the purple in the left circle. The blowup shows the color is actually a pattern.*

The Default Gradient Colors

For more information on working with gradients, see pages 100–102.

*The **Black, White** gradient.*

*The **Pastels** gradient.*

*The **Blue, Red, Yellow** gradient.*

*The **Red, Blue** gradient.*

*The **Blue, Yellow, Blue** gradient.*

*The **Red, Green, Blue** gradient.*

*The **Cobalt Blue** gradient.*

*The **Silver** gradient.*

*The **Copper** gradient.*

*The **Spectrum** gradient.*

*The **Emerald Green** gradient.*

*The **Violet, Orange** gradient.*

The Blending Modes

For a detailed explanation of these modes, see pages 109–110.

*The **Normal** blending mode.*

*The **Multiply** blending mode.*

*The **Screen** blending mode.*

*The **Darken** blending mode.*

*The **Lighten** blending mode.*

*The **Difference** blending mode.*

*The **Hue** blending mode.*

*The **Saturation** blending mode.*

*The **Invert** blending mode.*

*The **Tint** blending mode.*

*The **Color** blending mode.*

*The **Luminosity** blending mode.*

*The **Erase** blending mode.*

Color Insert

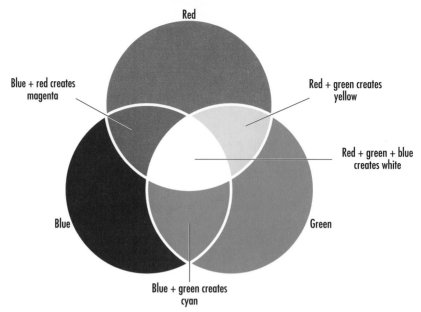

An example of additive colors, sometimes called RGB. *(For more information see page 40.)*

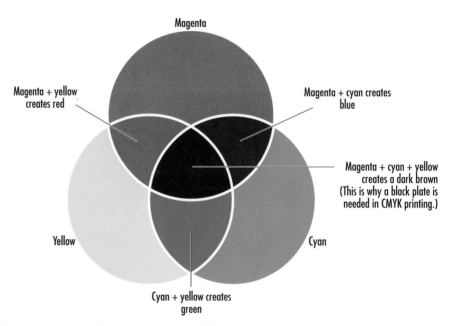

An example of subtractive colors, sometimes called process color. *(For more information see page 42.)*

Horizontal   Vertical

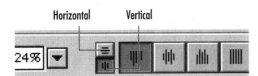

⓲ *The* **vertical alignment** *controls.*

Normal   Reversed

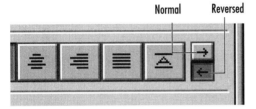

⓳ *The* **text flow** *controls.*

S M S C
C S M S

⓴ **Text reversed** *to read from right to left.*

㉑ The Anti-Aliased settings *pop-up menu.*

No Anti-Alias
Crisp Anti-Alias
Strong Anti-Alias
Smooth Anti-Alias

㉒ *The effects of the anti-alias settings on text.*

Text can also be set so it reads from top to bottom. This is very useful for creating vertical buttons.

To set the vertical alignment:

1. Select the text.

2. Click the vertical alignment button **⓲** to access the five vertical alignment settings: top, bottom, centered, justified, or stretched alignment.

TIP Vertical alignment does not show in the Text Editor. Use the Apply button to see the actual vertical alignment.

Another special effect you can create with text is to have the text read from right to left. This can also be useful when working with certain foreign typefaces.

To reverse the text flow:

Click the Reversed button **⓳**. All the text in that text block changes so that the letters flow from right to left **⓴**.

Text that is displayed as part of Web pages may need to be softened around the edges so it appears less jagged. This is called anti-aliasing.

To set the Anti-Aliasing amount:

1. Select the text.

2. Choose the Anti-Alias setting from the pop-up menu **㉑**.

TIP Anti-aliasing does not show in the Text Editor. Use the Apply button to see the effect **㉒**.

Working with Text Blocks

Once text is in a text block, you do not have to open the Text Editor to make certain formatting changes.

To modify text inside a text block:

1. Drag any of the text block handles to rewrap the text within the block ❷❸.

2. With the text block selected, choose any of the following commands:
    *   **Text > Font** lets you change the typeface.
    *   **Text > Size** lets you change the point size.
    *   **Text > Style** lets you apply one of the electronic styles.
    *   **Text > Alignment** lets you apply one of the horizontal or vertical alignment settings.

TIP Changes applied from the Text menu are applied to all the text in the text block. You cannot apply the changes to just some of the text.

TIP You can also select multiple text blocks and apply changes to them all at once.

❷❸ **Drag the text block handles** *to change the way the text wraps within the block.*

㉔ *The results of applying a distortion to the text within a text block.*

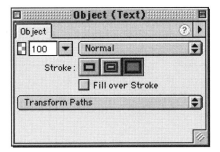

㉕ *The* **Object Properties** *panel when a text block is selected.*

You can use the transformation tools on text with some spectacular results.

To transform text in a text block:

1. Select the text block.

2. Use any of the the Transform tools *(see pages 78–83)* to distort the text within the block **㉔**.

TIP The transformation tools change the size of the text by distorting the text, not by changing the point size.

TIP Choose **Modify** >**Transform**>**Remove Transformations** to restore the text to its original formatting.

When you distort text, you have a choice as to how the text is distorted. This is controlled by the object properties for text.

To set the object properties for a text block:

1. Select the text block.

2. Choose **Window**>**Object** to open the Object Properties panel **㉕**.

3. Choose Transform Paths or Transform Pixels.

TIP Transform Paths results in distortions that preserve crisp text. Transform Pixels results in distortions in which the text may be blurred.

Working with Text Blocks

Working with Text on a Path

One of the most popular effects in graphics is to attach text so it flows along a path.

To attach text to a path:

1. Select the text block.

2. Select the path.

3. Choose Text > **Attach to Path**. The text automatically aligns to the path **26**.

TIP Text attached to a path can still be edited using the Text Editor *(see page 140)*.

Once you have text on a path you can change the alignment, or the position where the text appears on the path.

To change the alignment of text on a path:

1. Select the path that has the text attached to it.

2. Choose Text > **Align** and then choose one of the alignment settings from the submenu. This changes where the text is positioned **27** on the path.

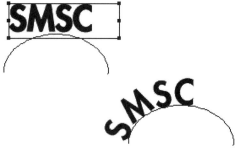

26 *The results of* **attaching text to a path.**

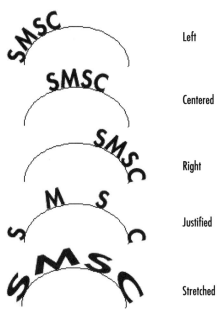

Left

Centered

Right

Justified

Stretched

27 *The results of* **applying the different alignment settings** *to text on a path.*

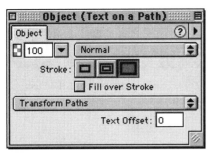

㉘ *The Object Properties dialog box for* **text attached to a path.**

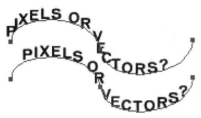

㉙ *The effects of adding a 20 pixel* **text offset** *to shift the text along a path.*

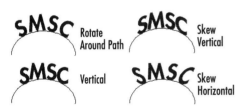

㉚ *The results of applying the* **different orientation** *settings to text on a path.*

㉛ *The results of applying the* **Reverse Direction** *command settings to text on a path.*

You can also control where the text is positioned along the path. This is called the text offset.

To change the text offset along a path:

1. Select the text that has been attached to the path.
2. Choose **Window** > **Object** to show the Object panel **㉘**.
3. Change the amount in the Text Offset field and then click Apply or OK. The text moves along the path **㉙**.

You can also change how the individual characters of the text are positioned in relation to the angle of the path. This is called the *orientation* of the text.

To change the orientation of the text:

Choose **Text** > **Orientation** and then choose one of the orientation settings to change how the text is positioned on the path **㉚**.

- **Rotate Around Path** has the text keep a perpendicular orientation as it moves around the path.

- **Vertical** makes each character stand up straight no matter how the path curves.

- **Skew Vertical** maintains a vertical rotation but distorts the characters' shapes as the text follows the path.

- **Skew Horizontal** exaggerates the text's horizontal tilt up to a 90° rotation and distorts the characters' shapes as the text follows the path.

You can also flip the text to the other side of the path.

To reverse the direction of text on a path:

Choose **Text** > **Reverse Direction** to flip the text so that it flows on the other side of the path **㉛**.

Working with Text on a Path

149

Adding Special Text Effects

You can apply any of the path attributes—fills, strokes, or effects—to text **32**.

To apply path attributes to text:

1. Select a text block or text on a path.

2. Use any of the Fill settings to change the inside of the text.

3. Use any of the Stroke settings to add a stroke around the edge of the text.

4. Use any of the Effect settings to add effects to the text.

The text in a text block or attached to a path is called editable text. This means that you can work with the text—change the font or the letters—at any time. There are some effects that require that the text be converted into paths.

To convert text to paths:

1. Select the text block or text on a path.

2. Choose **Text > Convert to Paths**. This converts the text into grouped paths.

3. Use any of the path selection tools to manipulate the paths **33**.

TIP Once you convert text to paths, you can no longer edit it in the Text Editor; you can then edit it only as path objects.

32 *The results of* **applying various fill, brush, and effect settings** *to text.*

People Inc.

People Inc.

33 *The results of* **converting text to paths** *and then manipulating the converted paths.*

AUTOMATION FEATURES

One of the challenges of creating Web graphics is that a typical Web site has hundreds of different images for graphics, buttons, and navigational elements. Once you've created those items you may find it necessary to repeatedly change the look of many different elements.

Would you want to open each file for the different elements and make the changes manually? Maybe if you were being paid by the hour, but not if you're trying to get the job done quickly.

Fortunately Fireworks provides you with many ways to automate creating objects and making changes. While all these features use different aspects of the program, they all have the benefit of helping you work faster and more efficiently.

Paste Attributes

If you have created an object with a certain set of intricate fill settings—for instance a special gradient, feathering, and texture—it might be cumbersome to reapply all those settings to another object created later. Rather, you can copy the settings from one object to another **❶**.

To paste attributes from one object to another:

1. Select the object with the attributes you want to copy.

2. Choose **Edit > Copy**.

3. Select the object with the attributes you want to change.

4. Choose **Edit > Paste Attributes**. The second object takes on all the settings of the first.

TIP Changes made using the vector controls *(see page 102)* are not saved when copying and pasting attributes.

Item copied

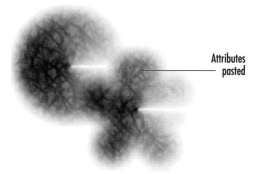

Attributes pasted

❶ *The results of applying the* **Paste Attributes** *command.*

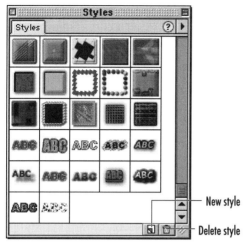

❷ *The* **Styles panel** *stores visual previews of the styles. These styles all come preset with Fireworks.*

❸ *The* **Edit Style dialog box** *lets you name the style and select which properties are included as part of the style.*

Using Styles

Styles are simply a way to store all the information about the fill, stroke, effect, or text settings. You can then easily apply the style to other objects without applying all the settings one by one.

The Styles panel comes with an assortment of object and text styles that you can use. There are still more styles located on the Fireworks CD. However, most likely you will want to define your own styles.

To define an object style:

1. Open the Styles panel by choosing **Window > Styles** ❷.

2. Select an object and use the Fill, Stroke, and Effect panels to give the object any look you want.

3. With the object selected, click the New Style button at the bottom of the Styles panel. The Edit Style dialog box appears ❸.

4. Name the style.

5. Check the boxes for the properties you want the style to control.
   - Fill Type controls a pattern, gradient, or Web dither.
   - Fill Color controls the color of a fill.
   - Effect controls the effect.
   - Stroke Type controls the size and type of stroke.
   - Stroke Color controls the color of a stroke.

6. Click OK to store the style in the Styles panel.

TIP The preview in the Styles panel is always a square, regardless of the shape that was used to define the style.

Using Styles

In addition to styles for objects, you can also define styles that apply text properties.

To define a text style:

1. Select a text block and use the Text Editor as well as the Fill, Stroke, and Effect panels to format the text.

2. With the formatted text block selected, click the New Style icon at the bottom of the Styles panel. The Edit Style dialog box appears ❹.

3. Use the Name field to name the style.

4. In addition to the object properties described on the previous page, check the boxes for which text properties you want the style to control.
   - Check Text Font to control the font.
   - Check Text Size to control the point size ❺.
   - Check Text Style to control styling such as Bold or Italic.

5. Click OK to store the style in the Styles panel.

TIP The preview in the Styles panel is always *ABC*, regardless of the text that was used to define the style.

Once you have defined a style, it is easy to apply that style to objects.

To apply a style to objects:

1. Select the object or objects to which you want to apply the style.

2. Click the preview of the style ❻. The object changes according to the definition of the style.

TIP Unlike the styles in FreeHand or other programs, styles can't be used to update objects. Changing the definition of the style doesn't change the objects that have had the style applied to them.

❹ *The Edit Style dialog box lets you name the style and set which properties are included as part of the style.*

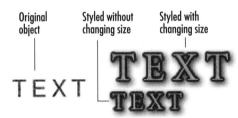

❺ *The difference between applying a style that does not change the text size and one that does change the size.*

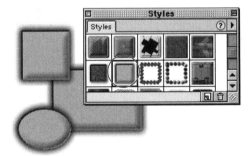

❻ *Click the style preview (circled) to apply a style to a selected object.*

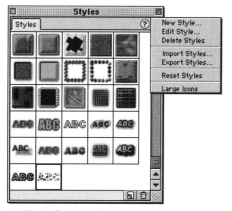

❼ *The* Styles panel menu.

Once you define a style, it continues to appear in the Styles panel where you can access it for other documents. You can also save styles and export them to share with other people working on the same project.

To export styles:

1. In the Styles panel, select the style you want to export.

2. Select additional styles by holding the Command/Ctrl key and clicking the styles.

TIP To select adjoining styles, select the style at one end of the group, hold down the Shift key, and click the style at the other end of the group. All styles between the first and last style are selected.

3. Choose Export Styles from the Styles panel menu ❼. A dialog box appears.

4. Use the dialog box to name the document that contains the styles and click Save.

To import styles:

1. Choose Import Styles from the Styles panel menu ❼.

2. Navigate to find the document that contains the styles you want to import.

3. Choose Open. The styles appear in the Styles panel.

TIP Exporting and then importing styles lets you clear the Styles panel so that it contains only the styles applicable to the project you are working on.

Using Styles

Once you have defined a style, you can edit which properties of the style are applied to objects.

To edit styles:

1. Choose Edit from the Styles menu. This opens the Edit Style dialog box.

2. Make whatever changes you want and click OK.

TIP You must create a new style and then apply it to objects to change the fill, stroke, effect, or text settings.

You can change the way styles are displayed in the Styles panel.

To change the Styles panel views:

1. Choose Large Icons from the Styles panel menu. This increases the size of the preview in the Styles panel.

2. If Large Icons is already chosen, choose it again to change the previews to the Small Icons ❽.

If you have many styles in the panel, you can delete the ones you do not need.

To delete styles:

1. Select the styles you want to delete.

2. Click the Delete Style button at the bottom of the Styles panel.

   or

   Open the Styles panel menu and choose Delete Styles.

If you have added and deleted styles, you can reset the Styles panel to the original styles that shipped with Fireworks.

To reset the styles to the defaults:

1. Choose Reset Styles from the Styles panel menu.

2. Click OK when the dialog box asks for confirmation.

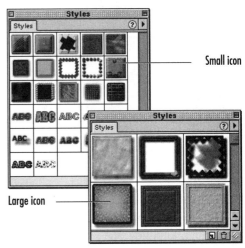
Small icon

Large icon

❽ *The difference between the* Small icons *and the* Large Icons *in the Styles panel.*

❾ *The* **Find and Replace** *panel.*

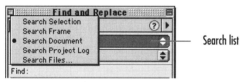

Search list

❿ *The* **Search choices** *for Find and Replace.*

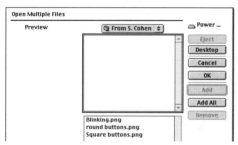

⓫ *The* **Open Multiple Files** *dialog box where you can add a list of files to change using the Find and Replace panel.*

Working with Find and Replace

The Find and Replace panel lets you change the formatting of multiple objects. For instance, you can find all instances of a certain font or color, and then change them to something else.

To use the Find and Replace panel:

1. Choose **Window**>**Find and Replace** to open the Find and Replace panel **❾**.
2. Use the Search list as described below to specify the locations where the Find and Replace commands should search.
3. Choose which type of attributes, as described on pages 158–160.
4. Use the Find, Replace, and Replace All buttons as described on page XXX to control which elements should be replaced.

To set the Find and Replace search location:

1. Choose **Window**>**Find and Replace** to open the Find and Replace panel **❾**.
2. Open the Search In pop-up menu **❿** and choose a place for the Find and Replace to occur as follows:
   - Search Selection searches among the currently selected items.
   - Search Frame searches in the current frame of the document. *(For more information on working with Frames, see Chapter 15, "Animations.")*
   - Search Document searches throughout the current document.
   - Search Project Log searches within all the files listed in the Project Log. *(For information on adding files to the Project Log, see page 161.)*
   - Search Files searches within a specific list of files.
3. If you choose Files, use the dialog box that appears **⓫** to navigate to add files from different locations.

To set the search attributes:

◆ Choose one of the five attributes from the Find list ⓰.

- Find Text searches for specific words and changes them to others.
- Find Font searches and changes text attributes such as font, style, and point size.
- Find Color searches and changes colors of Fireworks objects.
- Find URL searches and changes the URLs within a document. *(For more information on working with URL links, see Chapter 16, "Hotspots and Links.")*
- Find Non-Web 216 Colors searches and changes colors so that they are part of the Web 216 palette.

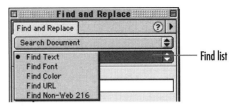

⓰ *The* **Find list** *in the Find and Replace panel allows you to specify the type of search.*

To find and replace text attributes:

1. Choose Find Text from the attribute list. The text attributes appear ⓱.

2. In the Find field, type the text you want to locate.

3. In the Change to field, type the replacement text.

4. Check Whole Word to make sure the text only appears as a whole word and not part of another word.

5. Check Match Case to make sure the upper- and lowercase letters match the text exactly as typed.

6. Check Regular Expressions to use special control characters in your search and replace text strings.

TIP For instance entering the regular expression tag *s$* searches for the letter *s* that appears only at the end of a word or line. *(See Appendix C for a list of some Regular Expression controls.)*

⓱ *The* **text attributes** *in the Find and Replace panel.*

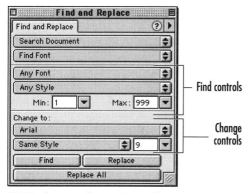

⓮ *The* **font attributes** *in the Find and Replace panel let you change the font, style, and point size of text.*

⓯ *The* **color attributes** *in the Find and Replace panel allow you to search for one color and replace it with another.*

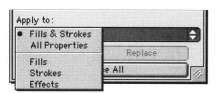

⓰ *The* **Apply to** *list for the attributes changes.*

To find and replace Font attributes:

1. Choose Find Font from the Attribute list. The font attributes appear **⓮**.

2. Choose the typeface to search for from the Font list in the Find controls.

3. Set the replacement typeface from the Font list in the Change controls.

4. Set the type style to locate from the Style list in the Find controls.

TIP Use Any Font or Any Style to include all fonts or all styles in the search.

5. Set the replacement type style from the Style list in the Change controls.

TIP Use Same Style to not change the typestyle in the search.

6. Set a range of point sizes to be changed by entering minimum and maximum amounts in the Min and Max fields in the Find controls.

TIP To set a single point size to change, delete any amount in the Min field and enter an amount in the Max field.

7. Set the point size to be changed by entering the amount in the Size list in the Change controls.

To set the Color attributes:

1. Choose Find Color from the Attribute list. The color attributes appear **⓯**.

2. Use the Find color well to select the color to change.

3. Use the Change color well to set the replacement color.

4. Use the Apply to list **⓰** to set which properties should change.
   - Fills & Strokes changes the fills and strokes but not effects.
   - All Properties changes the fills, strokes, and effects.
   - Fills, Strokes, or Effects changes just one of those attributes.

Working with Find and Replace

To find and replace URL attributes:

1. Choose Find URL from the attribute list. The URL attributes appear .

2. In the Find field, type the URL to search for.

3. Type the replacement URL in the Change to field.

TIP Set the Whole Word, Match Case, and Regular Expressions as described on page 158.

To search for Non-Web 216 Colors:

1. Choose Find Non-Web 216 from the attribute pop-up list. The Non-Web 216 attributes appear .

2. Use the Apply to list to set which properties should change *(see the description on the previous page)*.

To use the Find, Replace, and Replace All buttons:

1. Click Find  to select the first object that meets the search criteria.

2. Click Replace  to change that one instance.

   or

   Click Replace All  to change all the elements that meet the search criteria.

TIP If you choose Replace All, a dialog box appears telling you when the search is complete and how many changes were made 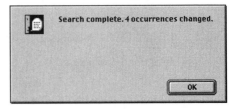.

⑰ *The* **URL attributes** *in the Find and Replace panel.*

⑱ *The* **Non-Web 216 attributes** *in the Find and Replace panel.*

⑲ *The* **Find, Replace,** *and* **Replace All** *buttons in the Find and Replace panel.*

⑳ *The* **Search complete** *dialog box tells you the results of the Find and Replace command.*

Frame Date

The Project Log panel.

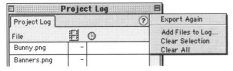

The Project Log menu.

The Open Multiple Files dialog box allows you to add multiple files to the Project Log.

Using the Project Log

It may become difficult to remember all the files associated with a specific Web site or project. The Project Log gives you an easy way to organize these files into groups. You can use the Project Log as part of a Find and Replace routine *(see pages 157–160).*

To add or delete Project Log files:

1. Choose **Window**>**Project Log** to open the Project Log panel ㉑.

2. Choose Add Files to Log from the Project Log menu ㉒. The Open Multiple Files dialog box appears ㉓.

3. Use the Open Multiple Files dialog box to select the files to be added to the Project Log.

4. Select an item or items in the Project Log and then choose Clear Selection to delete the selected files from the Project Log.

   or

   Choose Clear All to delete all the files from the Project Log.

   TIP The Project Log frame and date columns show which frames have been altered and the most recent modification date using Find and Replace.

The files in the Project Log can also be exported using the current export settings.

To export files from the Project Log:

1. Set the Export defaults as desired. *(See Chapter 15, "Exporting," for setting the Export defaults.)*

2. Select the files in the Project Log that you want to export.

3. Choose Export Again from the Project Log menu. This lets you save each of the exported files.

Using the Project Log

Scripting Commands

Scripting Commands

Fireworks also lets you replay a series of actions recorded in the History panel (*see page 37*).

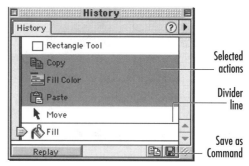

㉔ *The* **History** panel *allows you to replay actions and turn them into scripts.*

To replay a set of actions:

1. If the History panel is not visible, choose **Window** > **History** to open the History panel **㉔**.

2. Use the Shift key to select the range of actions you want to replay.

TIP Fireworks displays a divider line between actions that cannot be replayed together. For instance, you cannot use the mouse to choose a new selected object and play that action with others.

3. Click the Replay button.

   or

   Choose Replay Selected Steps from the History panel menu **㉕**.

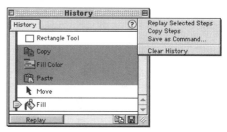

㉕ *The* **History** panel menu.

To store actions as a script:

1. Select a range of actions in the History panel.

2. Use the Shift key to select the range of actions you want to replay.

3. Click the Save as Command button.

   or

   Choose Save as Command from the History panel menu **㉕**.

4. Use the Save Command dialog box **㉖** to name the command. The command automatically appears under the Commands menu in the menu bar.

TIP Commands are stored as .jsf files in the folder located at Fireworks 3: Settings: Commands.

㉖ *The* **Save Command** *dialog box allows you to name a command created by the History panel.*

To play back commands:

◆ Choose the command listed under the Commands menu.

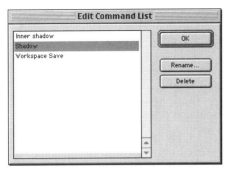

27 *The* **Edit Command List** *dialog box allows you to rename or delete commands that appear in the Commands menu.*

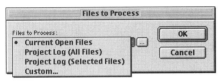

28 *The* **Files to Process** *dialog box allows you to select which files should have the script applied to them.*

Commands in Dreamweaver

Macromedia Dreamweaver 3 also uses .jsf commands. This makes it possible to have a command in Dreamweaver that also controls Fireworks. For more details on coordinating the commands between the applicaitons, read *The Dreamweaver 3 Bible* by Joseph Lowery.

Fireworks lets you save the layout of onscreen panels as a command. This makes it easy to rearrange your panels.

To save a panel layout:

1. Arrange the panels and toolbars in the configuration you want to save.
2. Choose **Commands> Panel Layout.**
3. Name the layout and click OK. The panel layout appears under the Panel Layouts Sets submenu in the Commands menu.

To use the Panel Layout command:

◆ Select the panel arrangement from the **Commands >Panel Layout Sets** submenu.

To edit the commands:

1. Choose **Commands >Edit Command List.** The dialog box appears **27**.
2. Select the command you want to edit.
3. Click Rename to rename a command.
4. Click Delete to delete commands you no longer want on the list.

TIP The Delete command cannot be undone.

You can also apply scripts to many files at the same time. This is the Batch a Command feature.

To Batch a Command:

1. Choose **Commands >Batch a Command.**
2. Navigate to find a stored .jsf file and click OK.
3. Use the Files to Process dialog box **28** to select which files to apply the script to.
4. Click OK. The files are automatically opened and the script is applied and the files are saved and closed.

Batch Processing Changes

Batch processing allows you to combine the Find and Replace feature together with the exporting features into one command that can be applied to many files at once.

TIP Batch processing is not the same as the Batch a Command described on the previous page. Batch processing only combines Find and Replace with exporting. Batch a Command can apply any script such as those created by the History panel.

The first part of batch processing is to determine what files will be processed.

To set the files for batch processing:

1. Choose **File**>**Batch Process**. The Batch Processing dialog box appears ㉙.

2. Use the Files to Process pop-up list ㉚ to choose which files should be included in the batch processing.

   • Current Open Files includes all files currently open.
   • Project Log (All Files) includes all the files listed in the Project Log. *(See page 161 for information on working with the Project Log.)*
   • Project Log (Selected Files) includes only the selected files in the Project Log.
   • Custom opens the Open Multiple Files dialog box *(see page 161)* which allows you to pick a specific set of files to batch process.

3. Set the replacement and export options, as described on the next page.

4. Set the backup and script options, as described on page 166.

5. Click OK to batch process the files.

㉙ *The* Batch Processing *dialog box.*

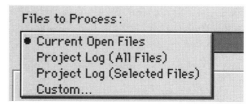

㉚ *The* Files to Process *options for Batch Processing.*

Batch Processing Changes

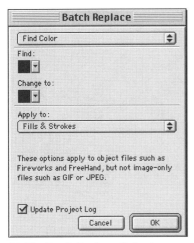

❸❶ The **Batch Replace** *dialog box.*

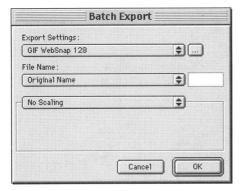

❸❷ The **Batch Export** *dialog box.*

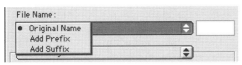

❸❸ The **File Name options** *lets you choose how the new files should be named.*

❸❹ The **Scaling options** *control the size of new files. Each option in the list opens fields that allow you to enter the amounts to scale.*

Once you have set the files for batch processing, you need to set the actions to perform on all the files.

To set Batch Replace options:

1. Check the box for Find and Replace under the Actions label in the Batch Processing dialog box. This opens the Batch Replace dialog box **❸❶**.

TIP If the box is already checked, click the Find and Replace ellipsis (…) to open the dialog box.

2. Set the options for the Find and Replace settings covered on pages 157–160.

3. Check Update Project Log change the status of the files in the Project Log.

4. Click OK.

TIP The Batch Processing options only apply to vector objects, not bitmapped images.

To set Batch Export options:

1. Check the box for Export under the Actions label in the Batch Processing dialog box. This opens the Batch Export dialog box **❸❷**. *(For more information on exporting files, see Chapter 19, "Exporting.")*

TIP If the box is already checked, click the Export ellipsis (…) to open the dialog box.

2. Set the Export Settings to use the setting from the file, a custom setting or a specific export preset.

3. Use the File Name pop-up list **❸❸** to keep the original name of the file or to add a suffix or prefix.

4. Use the Scaling pop-up list **❸❹** to control the dimensions of the exported file.

5. Click OK.

The batch processing options also let you keep backups of the original versions of the file after they are modified.

To set batch Backup Original Files options:

1. Open the Batch Processing dialog box and change any necessary processing and export settings.

2. Click the Backup Original Files ellipsis (…) in the Batch Processing dialog box to open the Save Backups dialog box **35**.

2. Choose Overwrite Existing Backups to keep only the previous version of the file and not any versions created before.

3. Choose Incremental Backups to keep all previous versions of the file, renaming any older versions if necessary.

Fireworks lets you save batch processing settings as a script that can be applied later or to other files.

To save the batch process settings as a script:

1. Open the Batch Processing dialog box and change any necessary processing and export settings.

2. Click the Script button in the Batch Processing dialog box **36**. This opens a dialog box where you can save the script as a .jsf file.

TIP Fireworks scripts are written in the JavaScript language and can be edited using a word processing program **37**.

To run a script:

1. Choose File > Script.

2. Choose a previously saved script from the dialog box.

3. Click OK.

35 *The* **Save Backups** *dialog box.*

36 *The* **Script button** *in the Batch Processing dialog box.*

```
theDoc.save();
if (theDoc.filePathForSave == null) {
    // this should never happen.
    alert(Errors.EInternalError);
    break;
}
}

if (batch.exportOptions != null) {

    var curExportFormatOptions;
    if (batch.useFormatOptionsFromEachFile) {
        curExportFormatOptions =
```

37 *A portion of a* **Fireworks JavaScript** *as displayed in a word processing program.*

Batch Processing Changes

WORKING WITH PIXELS 12

It is the vector objects in Fireworks that make it so easy to use. But what if you want to use images such as photographs or scanned art that cannot be created by vector objects?

Fortunately there is an alter ego to the vector side of Fireworks—a complete set of features for creating, importing, and working with pixel-based artwork.

Technically the correct term for these graphics is pixel-based images. However, it is easier to call them *image objects* to differentiate them from the vector objects covered previously.

Please note that the title of this chapter, *Working with Pixels*, has nothing to do with my cat, Pixel, even though she would like to think I wrote an entire chapter all about her.

Switching to Image Editing

If you want to work with photographs, scans, or other pixel images, you must switch to the image-editing mode.

To switch to the image-editing features:

◆ Choose File>Open and choose a scanned or pixel-based image.

TIP The thick striped line around the image indicates that the image-editing tools are available ❶.

or

◆ With either the Pointer or Subselection tools chosen, double-click a pixel-based image.

or

◆ Use the Marquee, Lasso, or Magic Wand tools to make a selection in the image. *(See pages 171–175 for working with the selection tools.)*

To switch back to vector drawing:

◆ Choose **Modify**>**Exit Image Edit**. This brings you back to the normal vector-drawing mode.

or

◆ Click the Exit image-edit button ❶.

To create an image from scratch:

1. Choose **Insert**>**Empty Image**. The striped line appears around the edge of the image, indicating you are working in the Image Edit Mode.

2. Use any of the image-editing tools to paint or modify the area inside the empty image ❷.

3. Choose **Modify**> **Exit Image Edit**. The area of the empty image shrinks to the size of the area that was painted or modified.

Striped line   Exit image-edit button

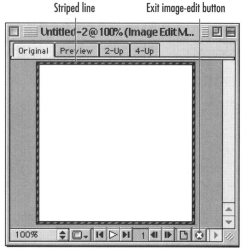

❶ *The* **striped line** *indicates the artwork can be edited using the image-editing tools.*

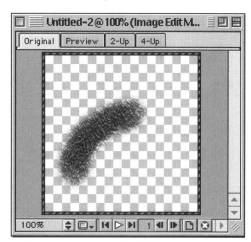

❷ *An* **empty image** *allows you to use any of the image-editing tools to paint inside the area.*

❸ *The* **corner symbol** *for imported artwork.*

❹ *Dragging the corner symbol places the imported artwork at a specific size. (The arrow indicates the direction of the drag.)*

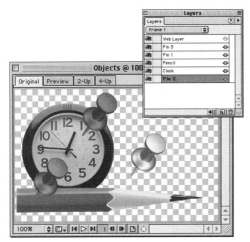

❺ Layers from Photoshop *are imported with the objects on their own Fireworks layers.*

Importing Pixels

You can import or place pixel-based images into Fireworks files. These can be files created by programs such as Adobe Photoshop or Metacreations Painter.

To import pixel-based images:

1. With a file open, choose **File >Import** and then find the file you want to import.

2. Click OK. A small corner symbol **❸** indicates the file is ready for placing on the currently selected Fireworks layer.

3. Drag the corner symbol to draw a rectangle that scales the image to fit **❹**.

   or

   Click to simply place the image at its original size.

You can also open pixel-based images in Fireworks.

To open pixel-based images:

1. Choose **File >Open**.

2. Find the Photoshop file and click OK.

3. The file opens as a Fireworks document.

TIP If the Photoshop file contains layers, each of the layers appears as its own pixel-based image **❺**.

Importing Pixels

Manipulating Pixels

If you have image objects in your Fireworks files, you may want to crop those images so they take up less space in the file.

To crop image objects:

1. Select a pixel-based image.
2. Choose **Edit > Crop Selected Image**. A set of handles appears around the image **❻**.
3. Drag the handles so that they surround the area you want to keep.
4. When you have defined the area you want, double-click inside the handles. The excess image is deleted.

❻ *The* **crop handles** *let you discard portions of imported images.*

You can also combine imported images, turn vector objects into image objects, or add vector objects to image objects.

To combine or convert objects:

1. Select the objects you want to combine or convert **❼**.

TIP Select a single vector object to convert it to a pixel-based image object.

2. Choose **Modify > Merge Images**. Vector objects are converted to pixels and imported images are combined into one image object **❽**.

TIP If you convert vector objects into image objects, you lose the ability to edit the paths that defined the vector objects.

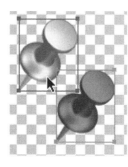

❼ *Two imported images can be moved or manipulated as separate images.*

❽ *The* **Merge Images** *command combines the two imported images into one image object.*

Manipulating Pixels

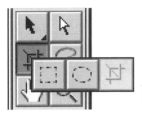

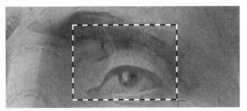

❾ *The* **Marquee tools** *in the Toolbox.*

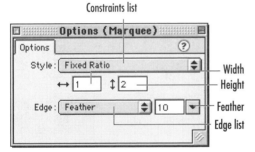

❿ *The* **marching ants** *of the marquee surround the selected area.*

Constraints list

❶❶ *The* **Marquee Options** *panel.*

Selecting Pixels

Unlike vector objects, pixels are selected as areas of the image. The basic selection tools are the two Marquee tools and the two Lasso tools.

To use the Marquee tools:

1. Press the Marquee tool in the Toolbox and choose either the rectangular or elliptical shape ❾.

2. Move the cursor over the image area and drag diagonally to create a selection. A series of moving dashes (sometimes called *marching ants*) indicates the selected area ❿.

TIP Press the mouse and then hold the Option/Alt key to draw the selection from the center outward.

TIP Press the mouse and the hold the Shift key to constrain the selection to a square or circle.

3. Position the cursor inside the selection and drag to move that portion of the image to a new area.

The marquee tool *constraints* allow you to change the tool so that the area selected is a certain size or proportion.

To change the Marquee tool constraints:

1. Double-click either of the marquee tools in the Toolbox to open the Marquee Tool Options panel ❶❶.

2. Use the Constraints list to choose Normal, Fixed Ratio, or Fixed Size.

3. In the Fixed Ratio mode, enter the ratio for the width and the height of the selection. This constrains the marquee to those proportions.

4. In the Fixed Size mode, enter the pixel amounts for the width and height of the selection. This constrains the marquee area to that size.

Selecting Pixels

You can also change the appearance of the edges of a marquee selection.

To change the Marquee tool edges:

1. In the Marquee Options panel, press the edge list to choose Hard Edge, Anti-Alias, or Feather .

   - Choose Hard Edge to give the selection a jagged edge ⑬.
   - Choose Anti-Alias to give the selection a smoother edge ⑬.
   - Choose Feather to blur the edges of the selection ⑬.

2. If you choose the Feather, set the amount of the blur with the feather control slider or type the amount of the feather (in pixels) in the field.

⑫ *The* Edge list *choices.*

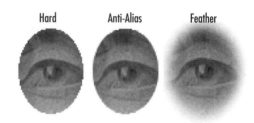

⑬ *The effects of* changing the edge choices *of a selection.*

You might want to select shapes besides rectangles and ellipses. To do so, you can use either of the Lasso tools.

To use the Lasso tools:

1. Press the Lasso tool in the Toolbox and choose either the regular or the polygon lasso ⑭.

2. In the regular lasso mode, drag around the area you want to select. The marching ants indicate the selected area ⑮.

3. In the polygon lasso mode, click the cursor around the area you want to select. Each click creates a point of the polygon ⑮.

4. Use the edge list in the Options panel to choose among Hard Edge, Anti-Alias, or Feather.

TIP The regular lasso is useful for following the curved contours of images. The polygon lasso is best for creating selections with straight sides.

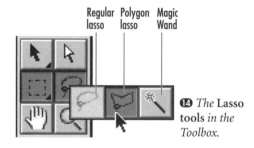

⑭ *The* Lasso tools *in the Toolbox.*

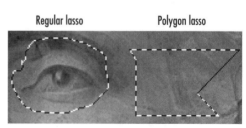

⑮ *A comparison of the Regular lasso and the Polygon lasso.*

⑯ *The* **Magic Wand** *in the Toolbox.*

Edge list

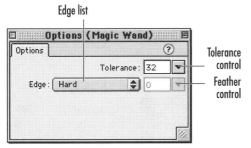

Tolerance control

Feather control

⑰ *The* **Magic Wand Tool Options.**

⑱ *The* **area selected with the Magic Wand.**

You can also select areas by their color. For instance, you might want to select the background behind an image and then delete it or change its color. To do this, you use the Magic Wand.

To use the Magic Wand:

1. Press the Lasso tool to choose the Magic Wand in the Toolbox **⑯**.

2. In the Magic Wand Tool Options panel **⑰**, use the Tolerance control to set how many colors the Magic Wand selects.

3. Use the Edge list in the Tool Options panel to choose among Hard Edge, Anti-Alias, or Feather (*see the previous page*).

4. Click the area you want to select. The marching ants indicate the selected area **⑱**.

TIP Tolerance controls how many colors the Magic Wand selects adjacent to the pixel you click. The lowest tolerance, 0, selects only one color, the exact color of the pixel you select with the tip of the Magic Wand. Increasing the tolerance up to a higher setting, to a maximum of 255, selects a greater range of colors.

After you finish working with a selection, you can deselect the selected area.

To deselect a selected area:

Click outside the selection with one of the Marquee or Lasso tools.

TIP You cannot deselect with the Magic Wand tool by clicking outside the selection. This only selects a different area.

or

Choose **Edit**>**Deselect**.

You may find that the Magic Wand tool has selected too little area, or you may find you need a different shape. You can change a selected area by using modifier keys with the selection tools.

To change the shape of selections:

With an area selected, use any of the selection tools.

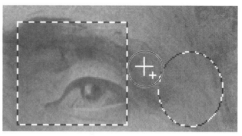

⓳ Hold the Shift key to **add to a selection.**

- Hold the Shift key to add to the selected area. A plus (+) sign indicates you are adding to the selection ⓳.

- Hold the Option/Alt key to delete from the selected area. A minus (–) sign indicates you are subtracting from the selection ⓴.

TIP You can switch tools at any time. For instance, if the original selection was created by the Magic Wand, you can use the Lasso to modify it.

TIP The additional selection does not have to touch the original. For instance, you can select the top and bottom of an image, leaving the middle untouched.

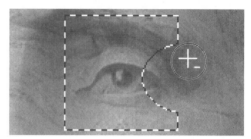

⓴ Hold the Option/Alt key to **delete** *from a selection.*

Rather than use marquee or lasso selection tools, you can also use the Edit menu commands for images.

To use the Selection commands:

- Choose **Edit** > **Select All** to select all the pixels in the image.

- Choose **Edit** > **Deselect** to deselect the pixels enclosed by the marching ants.

- Choose **Edit** > **Select Inverse** to swap the status of the selected pixels, that is, deselect the selected pixels and select everything else.

Selecting Pixels

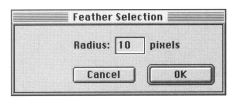

㉑ *The* Feather Selection *dialog box.*

Glow indicates feathering

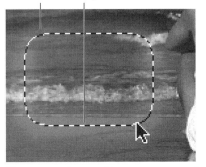

㉒ *Press on the marching ants to see a glow that indicates the area that is feathered.*

Once you have selected a certain area with the Magic Wand, you might not want to keep clicking to select similar colors.

To use the Similar command:

With an area selected, choose **Edit > Select Similar**. This selects all the areas of the entire image that have the same color.

TIP The Select Similar command uses the tolerance set for the Magic Wand.

TIP You can also use the Select Similar command on selections created by the Marquee or Lasso tools.

To feather an existing selection:

1. With the area selected, choose **Edit > Feather** to open the Feather Selection dialog box **㉑**.

2. Enter the number of pixels that you want to blur along the edge of the selection and then click OK.

TIP If you do not see the feathering, position the cursor over the marching ants and press the mouse button. The feathering is displayed as a glow in the image **㉒**.

Once you have made a selection, you can change the size or shape of the selection using the Modify Marquee commands:

To modify selections:

1. With an area selected, choose **Edit > Modify Marquee** and then choose one of the following commands:
   - Expand increases the size of the marquee area.
   - Contract decreases the size of the marquee area.
   - Border selects an area around the current marquee area.
   - Smooth reduces any small irregularities in the marquee area.

2. Set the size to change the marquee area.

3. Click OK to apply the change.

Selecting Pixels

Using the Pixel Tools

Most tools, such as the Paint Brush and Pencil, have both vector and pixel-based modes. The Rubber Stamp tool, however, works only on pixel images, not vector objects. The Rubber Stamp tool acts like a paintbrush, but instead of painting with a solid color, you paint with an image.

To set the Rubber Stamp options:

1. Choose the Rubber Stamp tool in the Toolbox **❷❸**.

2. In the Rubber Stamp Tool Options **❷❹**, use the source list to choose Aligned Source or Fixed Source.

TIP The source is the place in the image where the Rubber Stamp tool begins to sample the image.

TIP Use Aligned Source when you want to be able to release the mouse button but not lose the position of the area you are copying. This is useful when working on large images.

TIP Use Fixed Source when you want to make multiple copies of one image. Each time you release the mouse, the source is restored to the original position.

3. Use the Sample list to choose either of the following:
    *   Image allows the Rubber Stamp to sample only the area inside the image.
    *   Document allows the Rubber Stamp to sample anywhere inside the document.

TIP Document sampling lets you sample vector objects to paint them as pixels.

4. Use the Edge size control to specify the size of the Rubber Stamp brush.

5. Use the Edge softness control to change the softness of the Rubber Stamp edge.

❷❸ *The* **Rubber Stamp** *in the Toolbox.*

Brush preview   Edge softness control

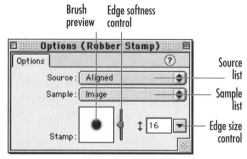

Source list

Sample list

Edge size control

❷❹ *The* **Rubber Stamp Options.**

How the Rubber Stamp Works

Digital rubber stamps (such as the ones found in Fireworks or Photoshop) simply copy the image from one area and paint it onto another. They do not recognize specific shapes or items. If you drag with the Rubber Stamp in a large enough area, you copy the image from one area to another.

Using the Pixel Tools

Area being sampled   Image being painted

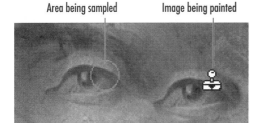

㉕ *Painting with the Rubber Stamp.*

To use the Rubber Stamp tool:

1. Position the Rubber Stamp tool over the image and click to define the source or the area that you want to copy. A circle indicates the source area.

2. Move the Rubber Stamp tool to the area where you want to copy the source.

3. Drag with the Rubber Stamp. The source circle follows your movements as the Rubber Stamp paints the image elsewhere **㉕**.

4. To change the source, hold the Option/Alt key and click a new area. Then paint with the Rubber Stamp tool with the new source area.

Using the Pixel Tools

Rather than cutting paths, the image-editing Eraser paints with a color or deletes pixels from an area.

To set the Eraser options:

1. Choose the Eraser in the Toolbox ㉖.

2. In the Eraser/Knife Tool Options ㉗, choose the round or square shape.

3. Use the edge size control to set the size of the Eraser.

4. Use the Edge softness control to change the appearance of the Eraser edge.

5. Use the Erase to list to control the effect of the Eraser.

   - Transparent removes the pixels.
   - Fill Color uses the Fill color set in the Toolbox.
   - Stroke Color uses the Stroke color set in the Toolbox.
   - Canvas Color uses the color of the canvas.

   TIP The Erase to: Transparent option removes the pixels from the image allowing the underlying image to show through ㉘.

The Eyedropper allows you to choose colors by sampling them from images.

To use the Eyedropper:

1. Choose the Eyedropper tool in the Toolbox ㉙.

2. Use the Eyedropper Options ㉚ to set the size of the area the Eyedropper uses to judge the color.

   - The 1 Pixel setting picks up the color from the single pixel directly underneath the Eyedropper.
   - The 3×3 Average setting picks up the color averaged from nine pixels within the 3×3 pixel area.
   - The 5×5 Average setting picks up the color averaged from the twenty-five pixels within the 5×5 pixel area.

㉖ *The* **Eraser** *in the Toolbox.*

Brush preview   Edge softness control

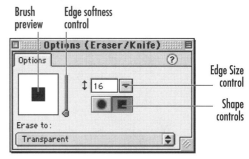

㉗ *The* **Eraser/Knife Tool Options.**

Edge Size control

Shape controls

㉘ *The effects of the* Erase to Transparent setting

㉙ *The* **Eyedropper** *in the Toolbox.*

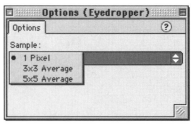

㉚ *The* **Eyedropper Options** *let you control the size of the area sampled by the Eyedropper.*

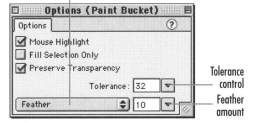

31 *The* **Paint Bucket** *in the Toolbox.*

Edge list

32 *The* **Paint Bucket Options.**

Tolerance control

Feather amount

50   100

33 *At a setting of 30, the Paint Bucket fills a small area of color. At a setting of 60, the Paint Bucket fills a larger area of color.*

34 *The Brush tool set to* **Preserve Transparency** *draws only on the image.*

With image objects, the Paint Bucket acts as a speedy way to fill an area with a color.

To set the Paint Bucket options:

1. Choose the Paint Bucket tool in the Toolbox **31**.

2. In the Paint Bucket Options **32**, use the Tolerance control to set how wide an area the Paint Bucket fills **33**.

3. Use the Edge list to set the edge of the area filled by the Paint Bucket to Hard Edge, Anti-Aliased, or Feather.

4. If the edge is set to Feather, use the Feather amount to set the width of the feathered border.

TIP The Fill Selection Only option causes the Paint Bucket to fill the selected area or object regardless of the tolerance.

TIP The Mouse Highlight option causes the Paint Bucket to highlight whatever object it is .

To use the Paint Bucket:

1. Choose the Paint Bucket tool in the Toolbox.

2. Click the Paint Bucket over the image. This fills the image with the currently selected Fill color.

TIP If the image has a selected area, the Paint Bucket fills only within the selected portion of the image **33**.

The Pencil, Brush, and Paint Bucket can be set so the tools do not affect the transparent areas of the image.

To work with the Preserve Transparency setting:

1. Open the options for the Brush, Pencil or Paint Bucket.

2. Choose Preserve Transparency.

3. Paint with the tool in the Image Editing mode. The tool will work only on the existing areas of the image, not in the transparent areas **34**.

Using the Pixel Tools

Applying Xtras

Some of the commands in the Effect panel *(see Chapter 9)* can also be applied to pixel images. When applied to pixel images, these effects are called Xtras **⑤**.

To apply Xtras to image objects:

1. Use any of the techniques to switch to the Image Editing mode *(see page 168)*.

2. Choose an Xtra from the Xtras menu.

3. If the Xtra has a dialog box, adjust the settings as desired. *(See Chapter 9, "Effects" for details as to use the settings for each of the Xtras.)*

3. Click OK to apply the settings.

To apply Xtras to vector objects:

1. Select one or more vector objects.

2. Choose an Xtra from the Xtras menu. A dialog box appears indicating that the image will be converted into a pixel image **⑥**.

3. Click OK. The object is converted and the Xtra is applied.

To reapply Xtras quickly:

With an object selected, choose **Xtras > Repeat [Name of Xtra]**.

TIP The Mac keystroke is Command-Option-Shift-X.

TIP The Win keystroke is Ctrl-Alt-Shift-X.

⑤ *The Gaussian Blur and Brightness/Contrast Xtras were able to blur only the selected area outside the image.*

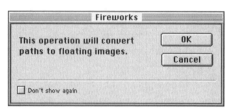

⑥ *The dialog box that appears when you want to apply an Xtra to a vector object.*

Using Xtras instead of effects?

Unlike effects, which can be edited or turned off, Xtras do not let you go back later to change the values or remove their effect. So why would anyone want to use Xtras?

Xtras allow you to apply an effect to only a portion of an image object.

They require less computer processing and do not have to be redrawn every time a document is opened or manipulated.

Some third party plug-ins work only as Xtras.

IMPORTING 13

As the poet John Donne wrote, "No man is an island, entire of itself." So although Fireworks boasts a wealth of tools, fills, and effects, it is not a software island unto itself. It is very likely that you will need to work with other programs along with Fireworks.

For instance, you probably have scanned images from pixel-based programs such as Adobe Photoshop. Or you may have used Photoshop to create artwork with a special text effect.

You might have logos and other artwork created in vector-drawing programs such as FreeHand or Illustrator.

Fortunately Fireworks makes it easy to bring all of these types of files into its program.

Working with Scanned Artwork

You can bring scans into Fireworks in several ways. The scans can be TIFF, GIF, JPEG, PNG, BMP, or PICT (Mac) files.

To scan an image directly into Fireworks:

1. Choose **File**>**Scan** and then use the TWAIN module or Photoshop Acquire plug-in that matches your scanner.

2. Follow the scanner software instructions to scan the image. The scanned image opens in Fireworks as a new document ready for image editing.

To open an existing scanned image:

1. Choose **File**>**Open** and then choose the scan you want to open.

2. Click OK. The scan opens ready for image editing **①**.

TIP The Fireworks document opens with the same resolution and size as the original scan.

Opening scans creates a new document. You can also import scans into existing Fireworks documents.

To import scans as image objects:

1. Choose **File**>**Import** and then find the scan you want to import. Click OK. A small corner symbol indicates the file is ready for placing on the currently selected Fireworks layer.

2. Drag the corner symbol to draw a rectangle that scales the image to fit.

   or

   Click to place the scanned image at the original size.

3. The scan appears as an image object on the currently selected object layer **②**. *(For more information on working with image objects, see Chapter 12, "Working with Pixels.")*

① *A scan opened in* **image-editing mode** *on the background layer of a Fireworks document.*

② *A scan imported as an* **image object on a layer** *of a Fireworks document.*

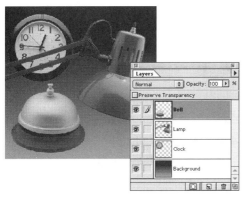

❸ *You can control how a* **Photoshop document** *with layers* *is imported into Fireworks.*

❹ *The* **Photoshop File Options** *controls how Photoshop documents are imported.*

❺ **Maintain Layers** *keeps Photoshop layers as individual Fireworks layers.*

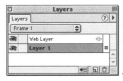

❻ **Use Flat Composite Image** *merges all the layers of the Photoshop file into one layer.*

Working with Photoshop Files

Fireworks lets you import and open Photoshop files. You can control how features such as layers, layer masks, and layer effects are imported into Fireworks.

To open Photoshop files with layers:

1. Choose **File** > **Open** and then open the Photoshop file ❸. The Photoshop File Options dialog box appears ❹.

2. Set the File Conversion to Maintain Layers.

TIP Do not select Use Flat Composite Image or all the layers will be flattened into one image.

3. Click OK. The file opens as a Fireworks document. Each layer in Photoshop will get its own layer in Fireworks ❺.

TIP If you always want the same settings for imported images, click the Don't Show Again box.

TIP You can also use the Import command to place Photoshop layers into existing Fireworks documents.

To open Photoshop files as one layer:

1. In the Photoshop File Options dialog box, select Use Flat Composite Image.

2. Click OK. The Photoshop layers are merged into one Fireworks layer ❻.

TIP You can also use the Import command to place a flattened version of a Photoshop file into an existing Fireworks document.

Photoshop layer effects allow you to add shadows, glows, and bevels to images. Fireworks lets you maintain those effects

To open Photoshop files with layer effects:

◆ In the Photoshop Options dialog box, choose Maintain Layers. Any layer effects that were applied in Photoshop ❼ are converted into the nearest Fireworks effect ❽.

TIP Some Photoshop features, such as Color or Inner Glow, do not have an equivalent in Fireworks and are discarded when imported. *(See the sidebar on the next page.)*

To open Photoshop files with text:

◆ In the Photoshop Options dialog box, choose one of the two Text options:
  • Editable converts the text into a Fireworks text block ❾.
  • Maintain Appearance converts the text into an image object that looks as it did in Photoshop ❾, however the text is no longer editable.

TIP Special effects such as Layer Masks are discarded when you choose Editable.

You can also import Photoshop layers as shared layers for working with animations. *(See Chapter 15, "Animations" for more information on working with shared layers.)*

To convert Photoshop layers into shared layers:

◆ In the Photoshop Options dialog box, choose Make Shared Layers for the Layers option.

You may also want to convert Photoshop layers into frames for animations.

To convert Photoshop layers into frames:

◆ In the Photoshop Options dialog box, choose Convert to Frames for the Layers option.

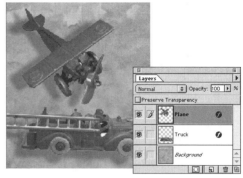

❼ *Fireworks lets you maintain* **Photoshop layer effects** *such as these drop shadows.*

❽ *Most Photoshop effects are converted into the nearest Fireworks effect.*

Editable

Maintain Appearance

❾ *The difference between text that has been set for* **Editable** *and* **Maintain Appearance.**

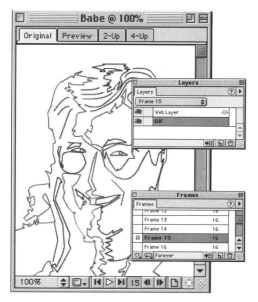

10 *GIF Animations import into Fireworks with each of the animation images on its own Fireworks frame.*

Importing GIF Animations

Fireworks can open and convert GIF animations into Fireworks frames. This makes it easy to convert existing GIF animations into new Fireworks animations. *(For more information on creating animations in Fireworks, see Chapter 15, "Animations.")*

To open Animated GIF files:

◆ Choose **File > Open** and then find the Animated GIF you want to open. Click OK. The animation opens with each image frame of the animation on its own Fireworks frame **10**.

TIP You can also use the Place command to import Animated GIF files with the same results.

Working with Photoshop

Fireworks 3 has made the transition from Photoshop to Fireworks as seamless as possible. However, there are some features which may not import correctly in Fireworks. For instance, if Fireworks does not have the equivalent of a particular Photoshop layer effect such as the inner glow, the effect will be discarded when the Photoshop file is imported into Fireworks.

Other effects may change their value when imported from Photoshop into Fireworks.

Similarly, although the text import has been set for Editable, the text may shift slightly when it is opened in Fireworks.

Importing Vector Objects

Fireworks can also open artwork created in vector-drawing programs such as Macromedia FreeHand, Adobe Illustrator or CorelDraw. This lets you use the more sophisticated tools in the vector-drawing programs and then add the artwork to your Fireworks document as editable objects.

To set the size of imported vector artwork:

1. Choose **File** > **Open** and navigate to choose the vector file. The Vector File Options dialog box appears ⓫.

2. Use the Scale control to import the art at a specific size compared to its original size.

    or

    Adjust the width or height field to change the size of the art to fit a space.

    or

    Set the resolution to something other than 72 pixels per inch to change the size of the art.

    TIP The same choices are available if you import vector files into existing Fireworks documents.

If your artwork has pages or layers, you can specify how the pages or layers are opened.

To set which pages of vector artwork to open:

◆ In the Vector File Options dialog box, use the page number list to choose which page is imported ⓬.

    or

    Choose Open Pages As Frames from the Open As list to open each of the pages as a Fireworks frame ⓬.

    TIP Opening multiple pages as frames makes it easy to convert vector artwork into animations.

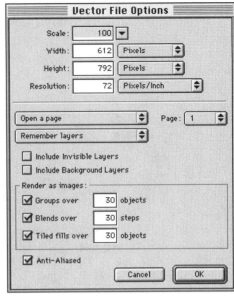

⓫ *The* **Vector File Options** *dialog box.*

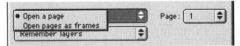

⓬ *The* **Page options** *for importing vector artwork from a program that lets you specify multiple pages.*

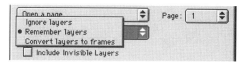

⑬ *The* **Layer options** *for importing vector artwork.*

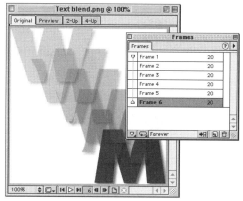

⑭ *Individual layers in vector artwork can be converted into individual frames in Fireworks.*

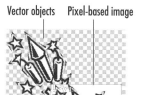

⑮ *The* **Render as images options** *controls whether objects are imported as vector objects or pixel-based images.*

Vector objects   Pixel-based image

⑯ *The difference between importing as vector objects or pixel-based images.*

To set the layers of opened vector artwork:

1. In the Vector File Options dialog box, choose the following layer options **⑬**:
   - Remember layers imports the layers as Fireworks layers.
   - Ignore layers imports the artwork onto one Fireworks layer.
   - Convert layers to frames opens each of the layers as a Fireworks frame **⑭**.

2. Check Include Invisible Layers to bring in artwork on the layers that are not visible in the vector program.

3. Check Include Background Layers to bring in artwork on the background layers in FreeHand.

Fireworks lets you convert some of the vector objects into pixel images.

To convert imported vector art into pixel images:

- In the Vector File Options dialog box, choose one of the following Render as Images options **⑮**:
  - Groups over controls how groups should be converted.
  - Blends over controls how blends are converted.
  - Tiled fills over controls how tiled fills or patterns are converted.

   TIP Rendering vectors as pixels turns all the objects into a single image object **⑯**.

You can choose how the edge of the vector artwork appears.

To control the edge of imported vector artwork:

- In the Vector File Options dialog box, check Anti-Aliased to import with the Fill edge set to Anti-Aliased.

   or

   Deselect Anti-Aliased to import the artwork with the Fill edge set to Hard Edge *(see page 172).*

Importing Text

You can also import text saved in the ASCII or RTF formats into Fireworks documents.

To import text into Fireworks files:

1. Choose **File > Place.** Navigate to find an RTF (Rich Text Format) or ASCII text file.

2. Click to place the text file in a text block the same width as the document 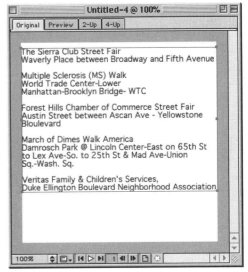.

   or

   Drag to set a specific width for the text block.

   TIP RTF text maintains all the font attributes that are in the Fireworks Text Editor. The character color comes from the first character color in the text file.

3. Use the Text Editor to make any changes to the text.

   TIP You can also open text files as their own Fireworks documents.

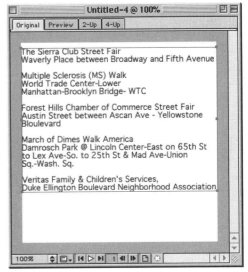

17 *RTF or ASCII text can be imported into Fireworks documents.*

Importing Text

OPTIMIZING 14

People who create Web graphics are obsessed, not necessarily with the look of the graphics (although that would be nice), but with file sizes. They can spend hours working to reduce the size of a graphic from 5.1 killobytes to 4.9 kilobytes.

Why the obsession? While two-tenths of a kilobyte may not seem like much to a single Web page, multiply it across the hundreds of graphics for a typical Web site and it adds up. That's a substantial amount of information that can take time to download—time that viewers don't want to waste sitting around waiting for a page to come into view.

Optimizing refers to making sure graphics are created in the proper format and in the smallest possible file size. It is often a juggling act to balance reducing the file size while at the same time keeping the appearance of the file.

Fireworks gives you specialized tools that that make it easy to reduce files while maintaining their appearance.

macromedia
FIREWORKS

Following the Optimizing Steps

There are several different parts to optimizing files. Use the steps below as a guide to optimizing files using the document window controls. *(For the equivalent steps using the special Export Preview controls, see page 202.)*

To optimize and export files:

1. Use the tab controls in the Document Window to control the onscreen preview of the file *(see the next page)*.

TIP The onscreen preview allows you to compare different optimization settings as well as judge how long it will take the file to download.

2. Use the Optimize panel to set the type of file, its compression, and other file characteristics *(see pages 192 and 197)*.

3. If you are optimizing a GIF file, control the colors in the file using the Color Table panel *(see page 194)*.

4. Set the transparency options *(see page 199)*.

5. Choose **File > Export** to export the file at the optimization settings. *(See Chapter 19, "Exporting".)*

The Optimize panel or Export Preview?

You can optimize images in two different places: in the document window using the Optimize panel or in the Export Preview dialog box. The document window makes it easier to modify the file as you optimize it. The Export Preview dialog box is used when optimizing Dreamweaver files.

This chapter uses the Optimize panel as the primary way to optimize files. The Export Preview dialog box is covered on *page 202*.

❶ *The **Preview** tab in the document window.*

Active panel

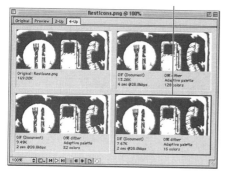

❷ *The **4-Up** tab lets you compare different optimization settings of the image.*

❸ *The Settings list in the Optimize panel lets you change the preview status of the preview sections.*

Controlling the Onscreen Preview

As you optimize images, they can change their appearance from the original artwork. The preview tabs allow you to see the effects of the optimization settings on the image.

To use the preview tabs:

◆ Click the Preview tab in the document window **❶** to see a full screen preview of the artwork.

or

Click the 2-Up tab to split the window into two sections so you can compare the original artwork to the artwork at the current optimization settings.

or

Click the 4-Up **❷** tab to split the window into four sections so you can compare the original artwork to the artwork at three different optimization settings.

TIP Use the zoom and magnification controls *(see pages 32–34)* to change the size or position of the preview.

To change in the preview sections:

◆ To see the original artwork within a preview section, choose Original–No Preview from the the Settings list in the Optimize panel **❸**.

or

◆ Choose Resume Preview to see the effects of the optimization settings.

To change the preview gamma display:

◆ Choose View > **Windows Gamma** or View > **Macintosh Gamma** to see how your image will appear using a different operating system. *(See the color insert for a display of this effect.)*

Optimizing GIF Files

One of the most popular types of Web files is the GIF (pronounced as either "gif" or "jif") format.

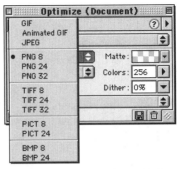

To choose GIF as the optimize format:

1. If the Optimize panel is not visible, choose **Window > Optimize**.

2. Choose GIF from the Format list. This changes the panel to the GIF options ❹.

3. Set the GIF options as described in the following exercises.

❹ *The* **Format list** *in the Optimize panel.*

GIF files are limited to a maximum of 256 colors. The GIF color palette determines which colors shall be used. *(See the color insert for a display of the different palettes.)*

To choose a GIF color palette:

◆ Choose one of the following from the Palette list ❺:

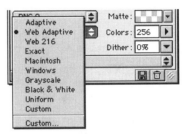

❺ *The* **Palette list** *in the Optimize panel.*

- Adaptive finds the Web-safe colors and then adds the non–Web-safe colors.
- Web Adaptive uses the Adaptive palette, however, if a color is within 7 units of a Web-safe color, then that color is shifted to the Web-safe color.
- Web 216 limits the colors to the Web-safe colors. If a color is not Web-safe, it will be replaced by a Web-safe color.
- Exact uses the Adaptive palette but limits itself to exactly the number of colors in the graphic.
- Macintosh or Windows limits the colors to those in either the Macintosh or Windows operating systems palettes.
- Grayscale shifts the colors to the range of grayscale values.
- Black and White limits the colors to either pure black or pure white.
- Uniform uses a mathematical palette based on RGB pixel values.
- Choose Custom to open a swatches palette saved from Fireworks *(see page 47)* or from Photoshop.

When should you use the GIF format?

Use the GIF format for images with flat or solid areas of color. Type, cartoons, and flat color logos usually look best when saved as GIF images.

You must use GIF images if you need the area around the image to be transparent or for animations. *(See the color insert for a display of the type of images that look best as a GIF.)*

Loss control

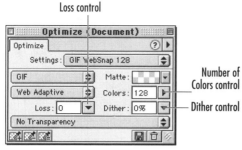

Number of Colors control

Dither control

➏ *The* **Optimize** *panel.*

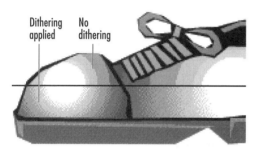

Dithering applied — No dithering

➐ Dithering *can help reduce banding, especially when using a reduced number of colors.*

Loss applied — No loss applied

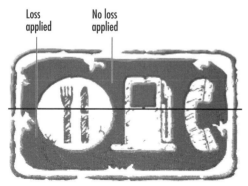

➑ Adding loss *lowers the size of a GIF file but can add distortion to the image.*

Most Web designers make GIF files smaller by reducing the number of colors in the color palette.

To reduce the number of colors in a file:

◆ Use the Number of Colors control to lower the number even further **➏**.

TIP Lowering the number of colors deletes colors based on how often the color appears in the image. You can use the Color Table panel to delete specific colors in the file *(see the next page)*.

Dithering is a technique that mixes a dot pattern of two colors to create the illusion of a third. Dithering helps maintain the look of GIF files when reducing colors.

To set the dithering of an image:

◆ Use the Dither control to change the how much dithering is applied **➐**.

Another way to lower the file size is to apply a Loss compression. This lowers the file size by throwing away some of details and distorting the image.

To apply Loss to a GIF image:

◆ Use the Loss control to increase the amount of Loss compression in the image **➑**. The higher the Loss values the more distortions will be created in the image.

Optimizing GIF Files

Adjusting the Color Table

In addition to lowering the number of colors for a GIF image, you can control each individual color in the file with the Color Table panel. *(See the color insert for how the Color Table changes images.)*

Selected color

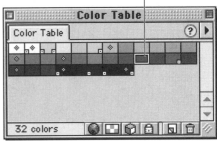

⑨ *The Color Table panel.*

To control the colors in the Color Table:

1. If the Color Table panel ⑨ is not visible, choose **Window > Color Table.**

2. Choose Rebuild Color Table from the Color Table panel menu to add the current colors to the panel.

TIP The word Rebuild appears at the top of the Color Table whenever the Color Table does not indicate the current optimization settings.

3. Click the color swatch in the Color Table to select the color. A highlight appears around the swatch.

4. Select additional colors by holding the Command/Ctrl key as you click the color swatch.

    or

    Hold the Shift key to select a range of colors.

5. Use the exercises that follow to change the colors in the table.

TIP Colors that have been locked or modified can be identified by the swatch feedback symbols **⑩** in the Color Table.

TIP Deselect Show Swatch Feedback in the Color Table panel menu to hide the swatch feedback symbols.

TIP Press a swatch in the Color Table to see where that swatch appears in the Preview image.

Locked and shifted to Web-safe   Locked to Web-safe

Shifted to Web-safe   Web-safe   Locked

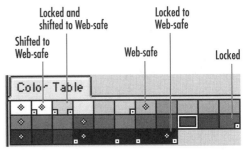

⑩ *The Swatch feedback in the Color Table gives you information about the status of the colors.*

Adjusting the Color Table

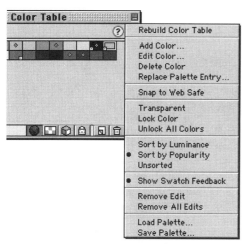

⓫ *The* **Color Table** *panel menu.*

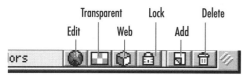

⓬ *The* **Swatch icons** *in the Optimize panel.*

To edit colors in the table:

◆ Choose Edit Color from the Color Table panel menu **⓫** or click the Edit icon at the bottom of the panel **⓬**. This opens the color picker.

To change the color to a Web-safe color:

◆ Choose Snap to Web Safe from the Color Table panel menu or click the Web icon **⓬**. This forces the color to the closest Web-safe color.

To delete colors from the table:

◆ Choose Delete Color from the Color Table panel menu or click the Delete icon at the bottom of the panel **⓬**.

To lock the color:

◆ Choose Lock Color from the Color Table panel menu or click the Lock icon at the bottom of the panel **⓬**.

TIP Apply the Lock color command again to unlock colors.

TIP Use the Unlock All Colors command from the panel menu to unlock all the colors in the table.

To add colors to the table:

◆ Choose Add Color from the Color Table panel menu or click the Add icon at the bottom of the panel **⓬**. This opens the color picker.

To remove changes to a color in the table:

◆ Choose Remove Edit from the Color Table panel menu. This restores the swatch to its original value.

TIP Use the Remove All Edits to restore all modified swatches to their original values.

You can also change the order in which colors appear in the Color Table.

To sort the colors in the Color Table:

◆ Choose one of the following from the Color Table panel menu:
- Sort by Luminance ⓭ arranges the colors from dark to light.
- Sort by Popularity ⓮ arranges the colors from most-used to least-used.

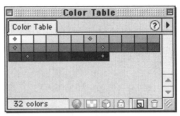

⓭ *Use the* **Sort by Luminance** *command to arrange colors from light to dark.*

If you have spent some time modifying a Color Table, you can save it for later use.

To save the colors in the Color Table:

1. Select Save Palette from the Color Table panel menu. This opens the standard Save As dialog box.

2. Use the Save As dialog box to name and save the palette to a location.

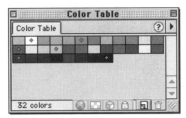

⓮ *Use the* **Sort by Popularity** *command to arrange colors in order of their use within the file.*

To load colors into the Color Table:

1. Select Load Palette from the Color Table panel menu.

2. Navigate to a saved palette. The palette replaces the swatches in the current Color Table.

TIP You can also load Color Table .act files created by Adobe Photoshop or Adobe ImageReady.

Adjusting the Color Table

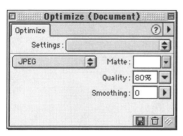

⑮ *The* JPEG settings *in the Optimize panel.*

80% Quality

20% Quality

⑯ Lowering the quality of a JPEG image *degrades the image by deleting details and creating square blocks in the image.*

With smoothing   Without smoothing

⑰ Adding Smoothing *to a JPEG can reduce the coarseness by adding a slight blur.*

When should you use the JPEG format?

JPEG images can contain up to 16.7 millions of colors. Use the JPEG format for photographic images or images with subtle blends. Also use JPEG images for illustrations that contain many blends and subtle gradients. *(See the color insert for a display of the type of images that look best as a JPEG.)*

Optimizing JPEG Files

JPEG files are reduced by *compressing* or throwing away some information in the image.*(See the color insert for an illustration of various compression settings.)*

To choose JPEG as the optimization format:

1. If the Optimize panel is not visible, choose **Window**>**Optimize**.

2. Choose JPEG from the Format list. This changes the panel to the JPEG options **⑮**.

3. Set the JPEG options as described in the following exercises.

To change the file size of the JPEG image:

◆ Use the Quality control to change the file size—the lower the quality, the smaller the file **⑯**.

TIP Lowering the file size can make the image look coarse or splotchy.

If you lower the JPEG quality, you may notice some coarse areas in the image. Smoothing can reduce the coarseness.

To smooth a JPEG image:

◆ Use the Smoothing control to slightly blur the image **⑰**. *(See the color insert for examples of the different JPEG settings.)*

Optimizing JPEG Files

The Sharpen JPEG Edges setting improves the appearance of flat colors in JPEG images ⑱.

To sharpen the edges of a JPEG image:

◆ Choose Sharpen JPEG Edges from the Optimize panel menu.

TIP Sharpen JPEG Edges does not sharpen the entire image, just where there is a flat area of color against a different colored background.

You have a choice as to how your graphics are revealed as they download. You can set the image to be revealed gradually ⑲. This lets visitors quickly decide whether or not the image is important enough to wait to see completely.

To create images that appear gradually:

◆ For GIF images, choose Interlaced.

or

◆ For JPEG images, choose Progressive.

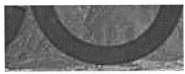

Sharpen JPEG Edges off

Sharpen JPEG Edges on

⑱ *The* **Sharpen JPEG Edges setting** *helps keep the flat areas of color, such as type, crisp against the background of an image.*

⑲ *How* **interlaced or progressive images** *appear as they are downloaded into a file.*

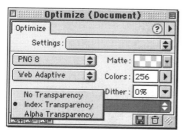

⑳ *The* Transparency list *lets you add transparency to GIF images.*

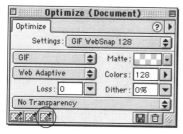

㉑ *The* Transparency Eyedropper *lets you select which colors should be made transparent.*

㉒ *The* Eyedropper *allows you to select colors in the image that should be transparent.*

Setting Transparency

One of the main advantages of the GIF format is that certain areas of an image can be made transparent. This allows you to have a Web graphic that blends into the background of the page.

To create transparency in a GIF image:

1. Choose GIF in the Optimize panel.
2. Choose Index Transparency from the Transparency list **⑳**.
3. Use the Transparency Eyedropper **㉑** to click the color in the image that you want to make transparent. The transparent area is indicated with a checkerboard grid.
4. Use the Eyedropper with the plus (+) sign **㉒** to select additional colors to make transparent.
5. Use the Eyedropper with the minus (–) sign to deselect colors.

TIP You can also select colors in the Color Table and click the Transparency icon to make those colors transparent.

A matte color changes the edges of transparent images so that they look better as they pass over background colors ㉓.

To choose a matte color:

1. Use the matte color well to open the pop-up swatches panel.

2. Choose the color closest to the backgrounds or images that you expect the file to be placed over.

TIP If you do not know the color of the background, use the None button in the Swatches panel ㉔ to specify no matte.

TIP Although there is no actual transparency for JPEG images, you can use the matte color to set the background color for JPEG images.

Optimizing Other Formats

Although Fireworks was designed for Web graphics, Fireworks does convert images for use in print and onscreen presentations.

To export other file formats:

1. Choose among the other file formats in the Optimize panel format list.

   • Animated GIF is used for animations. *(See Chapter 15, "Animations.")*
   • PNG is used for Web graphics that can be seen with specialized plug-ins. PNG is also used for onscreen presentations such as those created in Microsoft PowerPoint, Macromedia Director, or Macromedia Authorware.
   • TIFF is used for graphics to be inserted into page-layout programs such as QuarkXPress or Adobe PageMaker.
   • Choose PICT (Mac) or BMP (Win) for applications that cannot read any of the other formats.

2. Set the number of colors and matte color according to the previous exercises.

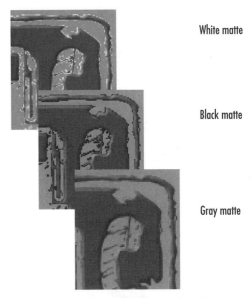

White matte

Black matte

Gray matte

㉓ **Different matte colors** *change how images appear over backgrounds. In this case the gray matte looks best over the gray background.*

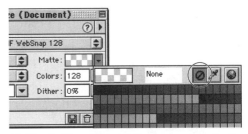

㉔ *Use the* **None button** *to set no matte color for a transparent GIF.*

㉕ *You can save the settings in the Optimize panel for later use.*

㉖ *The* **Settings** *list in the Optimize panel.*

㉗ *The* **Optimize to Size** *dialog box lets you set a target size that the optimization settings should be set to.*

Working with Optimization Settings

Fireworks has several techniques that make it easy to optimize images quickly.

You can save the settings in the Optimize panel so they can be easily applied to other documents.

To save optimization settings:

1. Set the Optimize panel to the settings you want to save.

2. Click the Save Settings icon or choose Save Settings from the Optimize panel menu **㉕**. A dialog box appears.

3. Give the settings a name and then click OK. This adds the settings to the Saved Settings list **㉖**.

TIP Saved settings automatically appear in the Settings list of the Optimize panel and can be accessed at any time.

To apply saved settings:

◆ Choose a saved setting from the the Settings list in the Optimize panel.

To delete saved settings:

◆ Saved settings can be removed from the list by removing the file from the Fireworks 3: Settings: Export Settings folder.

Fireworks lets you optimize files to a specific size.

To optimize a file to a target size:

1. Set the file type in the Optimize panel.

2. Choose Optimize to Size from the Optimize panel menu. A dialog box appears **㉗**.

3. Enter an amount in the Target Size field.

4. Click OK. Fireworks changes the optimization settings so that the file is smaller than the target size.

Working with Optimization Settings

Optimizing in the Export Preview

As mentioned earlier, you can also optimize images in the Export Preview dialog box. You can also export files directly from the Export Preview.

To optimize using the Export Preview:

1. Choose **File** > **Export Preview**. This opens the Export Preview dialog box **28**.

2. Use the Preview Window controls to split the preview area into sections **29**.

3. Use the Format list to choose the type of file format.

4. Set the format options.

5. Use the Transparency options to set any transparency for the file.

6. Click OK to set the optimization and return to the document window.

    or

    Click Export to export the file. (*See Chapter 19, "Exporting" for more information on exporting files.*)

To save settings using the Export Preview:

1. Click Save Current Settings **30** in the Export Preview.

2. Name the settings file.

3. Click OK. The setting appears in the Export Preview Saved Settings list as well as the Optimize panel settings.

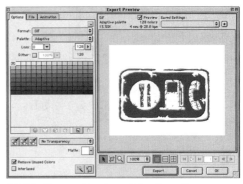

28 *The* **Export Preview** *dialog box allows you to optimize and export files.*

Preview window controls

29 *The* **Preview window controls** *in the Export Preview dialog box function like the 2-Up and 4-Up tabs in the document window.*

Save Current Settings

30 *The* **Save Current Settings button** *adds the current optimization settings to the Saved Settings list.*

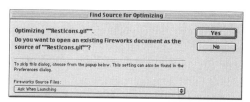

③ *Dreamweaver's* **Find Source for Optimizing** *dialog box lets you open the original Fireworks source file or the exported image.*

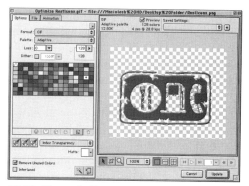

② *TheFireworks* **Export Preview** *appears as part of the process of optimizing Fireworks files from within Dreamweaver.*

Optimizing in Dreamweaver

One of the benefits of using both Fireworks and Dreamweaver is that you can make changes to Fireworks files while working in Dreamweaver.

To optimize in Dreamweaver:

1. In Dreamweaver, select the imported graphic.

2. Choose **Commands** > **Optimize Image in Fireworks.** This launches a special session of Fireworks.

3. A dialog box appears asking which file you want to open **③**.
   - Yes opens the original Fireworks PNG file. This is called the source file.
   - No opens the file that was exported from Fireworks and then inserted into Dreamweaver. This could be a GIF or JPEG file.

4. Use the Fireworks Export Preview dialog box **②** to make any changes to the file.

5. Click Update. The following happens:
   - Fireworks makes the changes to and saves the source file.
   - Fireworks re-exports the file.
   - Dreamweaver updates the inserted image on the page.

   TIP If you have made changes to the size of the file, click the Refresh button in the Dreamweaver Property Inspector to see those changes on the page.

ANIMATIONS 15

It's hard to believe that just a few years ago, there were very few Web pages with animated images. Today, it's hard to find a Web page that doesn't have some type of animated image. Words move up and down or from side to side. One picture turns into another. Images zoom in and out.

Any animation—cartoon, Web graphic, or motion picture—is basically a series of still images that appear in quick succession, giving the illusion of motion. Just like the flip books you played with as a child.

Fireworks gives you an extensive collection of tools and commands to create simple animations. (GIF animations created in Fireworks are called simple animations to distinguish them from the more sophisticated animations created by programs such as Flash or Dreamweaver.)

If this is the first web animation you've ever made, congratulations. You won't believe how thrilling it is to see your artwork come to life on the web. Enjoy the experience.

Working with Frames

Animations are created by putting artwork on sequential frames of a document.

To open the Frames panel:

◆ Choose **Windows** > **Frames**. The Frames panel appears **❶**.

Each document contains at least one frame. You can add more frames at any time.

To add individual frames:

1. Click the New/Duplicate icon in the Frames panel. A new frame appears in the Frames panel.

2. Click the name of the frame to make it the active frame. Any artwork created appears only on that frame.

To add multiple frames:

1. Choose Add Frames from the Frames panel menu. The Add Frames dialog box appears **❷**.

2. Use the number control to set how many frames to be added.

3. Click one of the four radio buttons to choose where to insert the new frames.

4. Click OK. The new frames appear.

To select and delete frames:

1. Click to select one frame.

2. Hold the Shift key and click another frame. All the frames between are selected.

   or

   Hold the Command/Ctrl key and click individual frames.

3. Click the Delete frame icon.

   or

   Choose Delete Frame from the Frames panel menu.

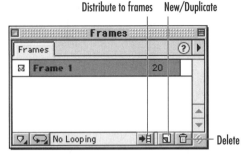

Distribute to frames   New/Duplicate

Delete

❶ *The* **Frames** *panel.* Every new Fireworks document has a single frame.

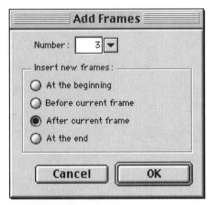

❷ *The* **Add Frames** *dialog box allows you to add many frames at once.*

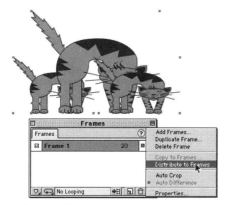

❸ *The* **Distribute to Frames** *command.*

❹ *Distribute to Frames sends each of the objects onto its own frame.*

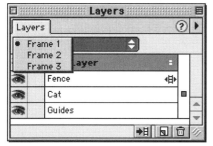

❺ *The* **Frames pop-up list** *in the Layers panel allows you to target a specific frame.*

You may find it easier to create objects on a single frame and then create new frames for each of the objects.

To distribute objects onto individual frames:

1. Create a file with all the objects on a single frame.

TIP Group objects that you want to stay together on a single frame. *(See pages 72–73 for more information on groups.)*

2. Select all the objects and choose Distribute to Frames from the Frames panel menu ❸. New frames are created with each of the objects in the selection on its own frame ❹.

   or

   Click the Distribute to Frames icon at the bottom of the Frames panel or Layers panel.

TIP The number of objects determines the number of frames.

TIP The Distribute to Frames command does not work if objects are on shared layers *(see the next page).*

Fireworks also gives you a shortcut in the Layers panel to move from frame to frame.

To control frames in the Layers panel:

1. Open the Layers panel.

2. Use the Frame pop-up list ❺ and choose the frame you want to move to.

TIP Use the animation controls to preview the animation *(see page 216).*

Working with Frames

When you create animations, you may want an image to appear on all the frames. One way to do this is to share a layer across the frames.

To share a layer across frames:

1. Select the layer that you want to share.

2. Choose Share Layer from the Layers panel menu. The Shared Layer icon appears next to the layer name ❻.

TIP You can also double-click the name of a layer to open the Layer Options dialog box to share a layer across frames.

TIP When a layer is shared across frames, editing the original object changes the object's appearance on all the frames.

You can also copy an object onto all the frames of a document.

To copy an object onto frames:

1. Create a file with multiple frames.

2. Create an object on one of the frames that you want to appear on all the frames.

3. With the object selected, choose Copy to Frames from the Frames panel menu. The Copy to Frames dialog box appears ❼.

4. Choose All Frames to copy the selected object onto all the frames of the image.

   or

   Use the other selections in the Copy to Frames dialog box to copy an object to a specific frame or a range of frames.

TIP After you copy an object to frames, editing the object changes its appearance only on the frame where you make the changes.

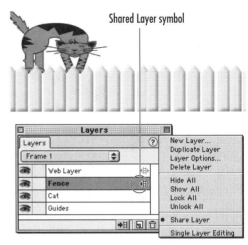

Shared Layer symbol

❻ *The Fence layer has been set to a* **shared layer.**

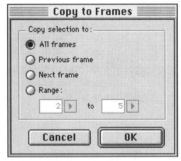

❼ *The* **Copy to Frames** *dialog box.*

❽ *A blend made in FreeHand can be imported into Fireworks to* **create an animation.**

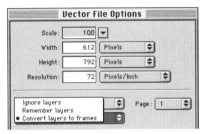

❾ *The* **Layers pop-up list** *lets you move objects in a vector file from layers to frames.*

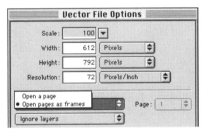

❿ *The* **Pages pop-up list** *lets you move objects from pages to frames.*

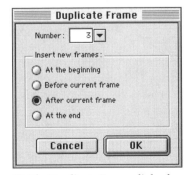

⓫ *The* **Duplicate Frame** *dialog box.*

Although Fireworks has a robust set of drawing tools, you may find it easier to create artwork in programs such as Macromedia FreeHand or Adobe Illustrator **❽** and then import the artwork onto frames in Fireworks.

TIP Use FreeHand's Release to Layers command to divide its blends onto individual layers.

To distribute vector layers onto frames:

1. Choose **File** >**Import** and find a vector file with objects on separate layers. The Vector File Options dialog box opens.

2. Use the Layers pop-up list **❾** to assign objects on each layer to frames and then click the OK button.

You can also use FreeHand's multiple pages to create animations in Fireworks.

To distribute pages onto frames:

1. Choose **File** >**Import** and find a vector file with objects on separate pages. This opens the Vector File Options dialog box.

2. Use the Pages pop-up list **❿** to assign objects on each page to frames and then click the OK button.

To duplicate frames:

1. Choose Duplicate Frames from the Frames panel menu. The Duplicate Frame dialog box appears **⓫**.

2. Use the number control to set how many times the frame is duplicated.

3. Click one of the four radio buttons to choose where to insert the new frames.

4. Click OK. The duplicate frames appear.

Working with Frames

Using Symbols and Instances

Symbols are objects or groups of objects that have been given the power to control copies of themselves. The copies are called *instances*. Whatever changes are made to a symbol are automatically applied to its instances. These are similar to the symbols and instances found in Macromedia Flash.

⑫ *The* **Symbol Properties** *dialog box lets you name and designate the type of symbol.*

To create a symbol:

1. Select the object or objects that you want to be the symbol.

2. Choose **Insert > Convert to Symbol**. The Symbol Properties dialog box appears ⑫.

3. Enter the name for the symbol.

4. Choose Graphic for symbols that are to be used in animations. *(For more information on working with Button symbols, see Chapter 18, "Behaviors.")*

4. Click OK. The object on the page is converted into an instance of the symbol ⑬.

⑬ *The* **corner arrow** *indicates the object is an instance of a symbol.*

TIP You can create additional instances of the symbol by duplicating the first instance.

TIP Use the Library to also create new instances of the symbol *(see page 212).*

TIP You can drag instances from one document into another. This automatically creates a symbol for the new document.

Other uses for symbols

Although graphic symbols are very helpful in creating animations, they are not limited to only animated images.

You can also use graphic symbols for elements that appear many times in your artwork. Since each instance is governed by the symbol, any changes to the symbol will change all the instances.

For instance, if you create a page with the name of the company duplicated many times, symbols let you change the typeface or color of the name and it will change throughout the document.

The **Symbol window** *allows you to edit a symbol.*

To edit a symbol:

1. Double-click an instance of the symbol. This opens the Symbol window ⓮.

   or

   With a symbol selected, choose **Modify > Symbol > Edit Symbol.** This opens the Symbol window.

   TIP You can also use the Library panel to edit a symbol *(see page 213).*

2. Make whatever changes you want to the symbol.

3. Close the window. All instances of the symbol are updated.

   TIP Notice that the Symbol window does not show the tabs for the Preview options. This makes it easy to tell if you are working on a symbol or the document.

To create a blank symbol window:

1. Choose **Insert > New Symbol.** This opens the Symbol Properties dialog box.

2. Name the symbol.

3. Choose Graphic for the type of symbol.

4. Click OK. A blank Symbol window appears.

5. Use any of the tools or commands to create a graphic within the Symbol window.

6. Close the window. This creates an instance of the symbol on the document page.

To break the link to a symbol:

1. Select the instance.

2. Choose **Modify > Symbol > Break Link.** This converts the instance into an ordinary object, no longer controlled by the symbol.

Save Outside the Symbol Window

The Save command does not work when you are working inside the Symbol window. You must close the window and then apply the Save command to save your work.

Using Symbols and Instances

Using the Library Panel

The Library panel allows you to store symbols that can be used in one file or between other files.

New Symbol   Symbol Properties

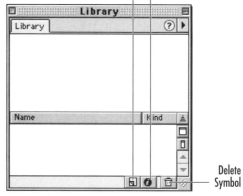

⓯ *The first time you open the Library panel for a new document, it has no symbols in it.*

Delete
Symbol

To create a symbol using the Library panel:

1. If the Library panel ⓯ is not visible, choose **Window** > **Library** or click the Library panel tab.

   TIP The Library panel for a new document is empty.

2. Click the New Symbol icon or choose New Symbol from the Library panel menu. The Symbol Properties dialog box appears.

3. Name the symbol and designate it as a graphic or button. *(For more information on working with buttons, see Chapter 18, "Behaviors.")*

4. In the Symbol window, draw artwork or drag artwork from the document.

5. Close the Symbol window. The artwork appears in the Library panel ⓰.

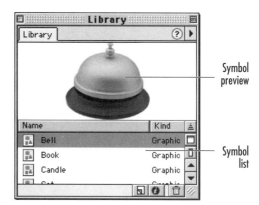

Symbol
preview

Symbol
list

⓰ **Symbols** *in the Library panel.*

To create instances from the Library panel:

◆ Drag the preview of the symbol from the Library onto the document page ⓱.

To delete a symbol from the Library panel:

◆ Select the symbol or symbols in the list and click the Delete icon.

   or

   Choose Delete from the Library panel menu.

   TIP If you try to delete a symbol that is in use, an alert box informs you that any instances of that symbol will be deleted.

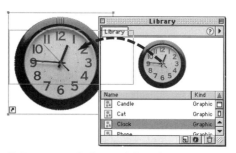

⓱ **Drag** a symbol out of the Library panel *to create an instance of that symbol.*

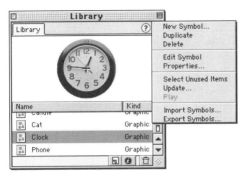

⑱ *The* **Library** *panel menu lets you edit, manage, import and export symbols.*

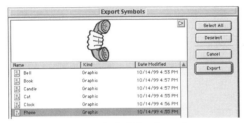

⑲ *The* **Export Symbol** *dialog box allows you to export specific symbols.*

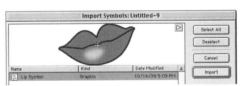

⑳ *The* **Import Symbols** *dialog box allows you to choose which symbols should be imported.*

To edit a symbol in the Library panel:

◆ Select the symbol in the list and choose Edit Symbol from the Library menu **⑱**.

or

Double-click the symbol preview in the Library panel.

To change the properties in the Library panel:

◆ Select the symbol in the list and choose Properties from the Library menu.

or

Double-click the name of the symbol in the symbol list.

To export symbols:

1. Choose Export Symbols from the Library menu. The Export Symbol dialog box appears **⑲**.
2. Select the symbols you want to export.
3. Click Export. The dialog box lets you name and store the symbol file.

To import symbols from other files:

1. Choose Import Symbols from the Library menu.
2. Navigate to find the file to import the symbols from.
3. Use the Import Symbols dialog box **⑳** to select the symbols to import.

TIP Symbols can be imported from any native Fireworks file.

If you import symbols from other files, you can automatically update them.

To update symbols:

1. Select the symbol you want to update.
2. Choose Update from the Library panel. Fireworks automatically updates the symbol. *(See Chapter 18, "Behaviors" for more information on importing symbols from one file to another.)*

Using the Library Panel

Tweening Instances

Instances allow you to create a series of steps so that one object changes over a series of frames. This is called *tweening*.

To animate instances by tweening:

1. Position an instance where you want the motion to start.

2. Position a second instance where you want the motion to end.

3. Make whatever changes you want to the first and second objects.

4. Select both instances, and choose **Modify** > **Symbol** > **Tween Instances**. The Tween Instances dialog box appears ㉑.

   TIP You can tween between more than two instances so that the animation moves in different directions.

5. Set the number of new instances in the Steps field.

6. Click Distribute to Frames to create new frames with each instance on its own frame.

7. Click OK. The new instances fill in the space between the original instances ㉒.

   TIP You can also use the Distribute to Frames command *(see page 207)* to distribute objects to frames later.

To tween effects:

1. Apply an effect to an instance of a symbol.

2. Apply the same effect to another instance of the same symbol.

   TIP You must apply the effect to both instances. To tween to no effect, set the values of the effect to zero.

3. Apply the Tween command. The effect changes across the intermediate steps of the tween ㉓.

㉑ *The* Tween Instances *dialog box.*

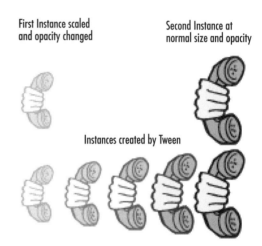

First Instance scaled and opacity changed

Second Instance at normal size and opacity

Instances created by Tween

㉒ **Tweening between two instances** *creates intermediate steps between the instances. In this case, the animation object appears to get bigger as it fades into view.*

㉓ *An example of a* **tweened drop shadow.**

㉔ *The* **Onion Skinning controls** *in the Frames panel.*

㉕ Onion skinning *shows dimmed representations of the objects on non-active frames.*

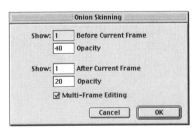

㉖ *The* **Onion Skinning** *dialog box.*

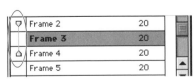

㉗ *The* **Onion Skinning icons** *(circled) show which frames are displayed.*

Editing Animation Frames

Fireworks uses a technique called *onion skinning* which allows you to see a dimmed version of objects on frames that are not selected.

To turn on onion skinning:

1. Open the Onion Skinning controls in the Frames panel **㉔**.

2. Choose one of the following options:
   - Show Next Frame displays the frame after the selected frame.
   - Before and After shows the frames before and after the selected frame.
   - Show All Frames displays all the frames in the document.
   - **TIP** The opacity of frames viewed through onion skinning is lowered so they are distinct from the selected frame **㉕**.

To customize onion skinning:

1. Choose Custom from the Onion Skinning controls menu. The Onion Skinning dialog box appears **㉖**.

2. Change the number of frames that should be visible.

3. Change the opacity of the visible frames.

   TIP Click to move the onion skinning icons to the frames you want displayed **㉗**.

Multi-frame editing allows you to work with objects that are on different frames.

To use multi-frame editing:

1. Choose Multi-Frame Editing from the Onion Skinning menu or the Onion Skinning dialog box.

2. Make sure Onion Skinning is active.

3. Use the various selection methods to select objects on either the active frame or the visible onion skinning frames.

Previewing Animations

As you create animations, you may want to see how the frames look in sequence. Fireworks lets you preview animations in the document window or in the Export Preview dialog box.

To preview animations in the document window:

◆ Use the animation controls at the bottom of the document window **28**.

- Click the next frame or previous frame buttons **29** to move one frame at a time.
- Click the first frame or last frame buttons **29** to jump to the beginning or end of the animation.
- Click the play button **29** to run the animation.
- Click the stop button **29** to stop playing the animation.

TIP If you want to see the animation using the Preview tab, make sure you have set the Optimization panel to Animated GIF. If not, the animation will play extremely slowly. *(For more information on using the Optimization panel and Preview tab, see Chapter 14, "Optimizing.")*

To preview animations in Export Preview:

1. Choose **File** > **Export Preview**.
2. Use the animation controls at the bottom of the preview area **30**.

28 *The* **Animation options** *of the Export Preview.*

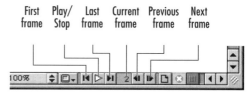

29 *The* **Animation Controls** *in the document window.*

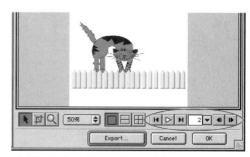

30 *The* **Animation options** *of the Export Preview.*

Previewing Animations

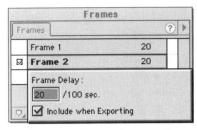

㉛ *The* **Frames Properties** *controls.*

Frame Delay field

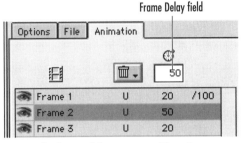

㉜ *Set the* **frame delay** *to control how long a frame is visible during an animation.*

Frame Controls

You can also control frame timing, or how long each frame remains visible.

To set the frame timing in the document window:

1. Double-click the name of the frame in the Frames panel. This opens the Frame Properties controls **㉛**.

   or

   Select the frame and choose Properties from the Frames panel menu.

   TIP Use the Shift key to select more than one frame at a time.

2. Enter a number in the Frame Delay field **㉛**. The higher the number, the longer the frame remains visible.

3. Press the Return/Enter key to apply the changes and close the Frame Properties control.

To set the frame timing in Export Preview:

1. Choose **File > Export Preview**.

2. Click the Animation tab to display the Frame list.

3. Enter a number in the Frame Delay field **㉜**.

Frame Controls

You can control how many times the animation plays using the *looping* controls.

TIP Some Web sites require banner ads to repeat only a certain number of times and then stop.

To set looping in the document window:

1. Click the Loop icon to open the Loop list ❸. Set the list as follows:
   - No Looping sets the animation to play once.
   - The numbers specify how how many times the animation repeats.
   - Forever plays the animation endlessly.
2. Press Return/Enter to apply the setting.

TIP The first time the animation plays is not counted in the Loop control. So to play the animation four times, set the loop number to three.

To set looping in the Export Preview:

1. Choose **File** > **Export Preview**.
2. Click the Animation tab to display the Loop controls at the bottom of the Animation Frames list ❸.
3. Click the Play once icon to have the animation play one time and then stop.
4. Click the Loop icon.
5. Use the control to open the Number of Times list and choose how many times the animation should play.

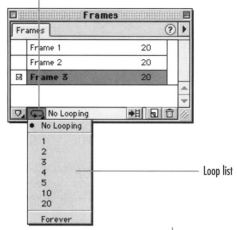

Loop icon

Loop list

❸ *The* **Loop controls** *in the document window.*

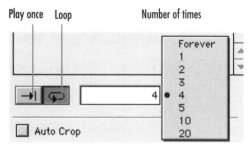

Play once Loop Number of times

❸ *The* **Loop controls** *at the bottom of the Export Preview Animation Frames list.*

Frame Controls

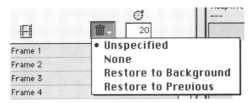

⑮ *The* **Disposal method** *list.*

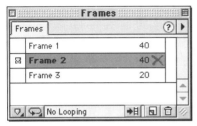

㊱ *A frame excluded from export* in the Frames panel.

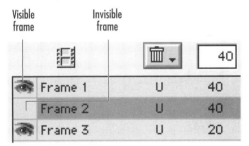

㊲ *The* **visibility settings for frames.** *In this example, frames 1 and 3 are set to export, but frame 2 is not set to export.*

You can also control how each frame blends between other frames and the background. Fireworks calls this Frame Disposal.

To set the transition of the frames:

1. Select a frame in the animation options panel of the Export Preview.

2. Use the Disposal method list **⑮** to control the blends between frames.dd

   - Choose Unspecified when the animation artwork is completely opaque. If you use Unspecified with art that is transparent, the frame is added to the previous one, instead of replacing it.
   - Choose None to add some of the image in the next frame to the previous one.
   - Choose Restore to Background when transparency is turned on so that each frame changes from one to another.
   - Choose Revert to Background when objects appear over a frame created earlier. Revert to Background is not supported by all browsers.

Even though you have created certain frames, you don't have to export them in the final animation.

To set the frames to export in the Frames panel:

1. Open the Frames properties control for the frame you want to control (*see page 217*).

2. Deselect Include When Exporting.

3. Close the control. A red X next to the frame **㊱** indicates that the frame will not export as part of the animation.

To set the frames to export in Export Preview:

1. Choose **File > Export Preview.**

2. Click the Animation tab to display the Frame list.

3. Click the Show/Hide icon in the Animation tab **㊲**. If the icon is visible, the frame exports. If the icon is not visible, the frame does not export.

Exporting Animations

After you have finished the frames of the animation, you use the Export controls to fine-tune the settings and export the file.

To set the animation export options:

1. Open the Optimize panel ③⑧.

   or

   Choose **File** > **Export** to open the Export Preview window.

2. Choose Animated GIF from the Format list ③⑨.

3. Set the GIF color and transparency options as desired *(see Chapter 19, "Exporting")*.

4. Use the Export commands to export the file *(see Chapter 19, "Exporting")*.

③⑧ *Choose* **Animated GIF** *from the Optimize panel to export a animation.*

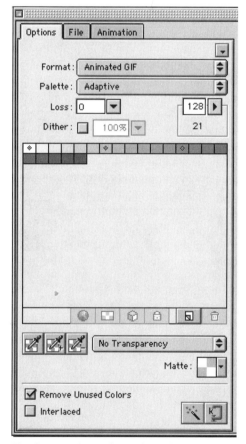

③⑨ *Choose* **Animated GIF** *from the Export Preview dialog box to export an animation.*

HOTSPOTS AND LINKS

Imagine you are creating a magical machine that transports people all over the world. How would you design the controls? One way might be to start with a map of the world. Your users would simply touch a certain part of the map and they would be instantly transported to where they wanted to go.

That's the idea behind image maps for web graphics. Different areas of an image hold information that send the viewer to different web pages or perform a certain action. All the viewer needs to do is click inside each area of the image and they are transported to a new web page.

The special areas on the image are created using the Fireworks hotspot tools. The information that sends you to a new web page or performs the action is called a link.

Creating Hotspots

You can draw hotspots directly on your image using one of the three hotspot tools.

TIP Hotspots are automatically drawn on the Web layer even if that layer is not the selected layer.

To draw a rectangular or circular hotspot object:

1. Choose the Rectangle or Circle hotspot tool in the Toolbox ❶.

2. Drag to create a rectangle or circle that defines the hotspot area ❷.

TIP Hold the Shift key to constrain the Rectangle to a square.

TIP Hold the Option/Alt key to drag from the center outward.

To draw a polygon hotspot object:

1. Choose the Polygon hotspot tool in the Toolbox ❶.

2. Click to set the first point of the polygon.

3. Click the next corner of the polygon to make the first line segment.

4. Click again to set the remaining segments.

5. Close the the hotspot object by clicking again on the first point.

Circle
hotspot tool

Rectangle
hotspot tool

Polygon
hotspot tool

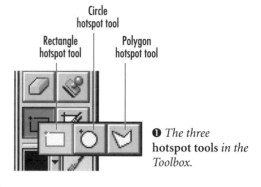

❶ *The three* **hotspot tools** *in the Toolbox.*

❷ **Hotspots** *can be rectangular, circular, or irregular polygons.*

Creating Hotspots

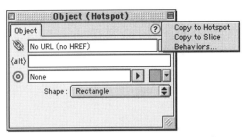

❸ *The Object panel menu lets you copy and convert regular paths into hotspot objects.*

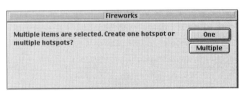

❹ *You can choose if one hotspot or multiple hotspots are created from multiple selected paths.*

❺ *Selected paths can be converted into hotspot objects.*

You can also copy and convert any Fireworks path into a hotspot object.

To convert a single object into a hotspot:

1. Choose the path you wish to convert.

2. Choose **Insert > Hotspot.**

   or

   Choose Copy to Hotspot from the Object panel menu ❸.

   or

   Drag the object square in the Layers panel from the object layer to the Web layer. *(For more information on working with the Layers panel, see page 96.)* This copies the shape of the selected object into a hotspot object.

   TIP When curved objects are converted to hotspots, they are converted to polygons with a series of small straight line segments.

You can also copy and convert multiple Fireworks paths into hotspots.

To convert a single object into a hotspot:

1. Choose the path you wish to convert.

2. Choose one of the choices for step 2 in the previous exercise. A dialog box appears asking how you want to convert the multiple objects ❹.

3. Click One to create one hotspot that covers all the selected paths.

   or

   Click Multiple to create individual hotspots that follow the shape of the selected paths ❺.

Creating Hospots

Modifying Hotspots

Once you have created hotspot objects, you can still modify them.

To move and modify hotspot objects:

1. Choose either the Selection or the Subselection tools in the Toolbox.
2. Drag inside a hotspot object to move it to a new positon.
3. Drag one of the anchor points of the hotspot object to change its shape ❻.

You can also change hotspot objects from one shape to another.

To change hotspot shapes:

1. Choose the hotspot object you want to convert.
2. Choose a shape from the hotspot panel shape list ❼.

The Web layer allows you to control the visibility of hotspots.

To show and hide hotspot objects:

1. To hide the hotspot objects, click the Eye icon for the Web layer ❽.
2. To show the hotspot objects, click the empty area in the Eye icon column for the Web layer.

    or

    Use any of the hotpsot tools on the image. The Web lay automatically becomes visible.

❻ *Use the Selection or Subselection tools to* **modify** *hotspot objects.*

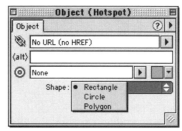

❼ *The* **Shape menu** *of the Hotspot Object panel.*

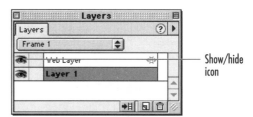

Show/hide icon

❽ *The* **Show/Hide icon** *for the Web layer.*

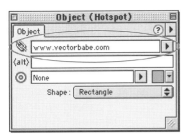

❾ The **Links field** *in the Hotspot Object panel.*

❿ *The* **history list** *in the Hotspot Object panel.*

Understanding URLs

URL stands for *uniform resource locator*. It contains information for the browser to perform an action. The most common URL links are http, mailto, and ftp.

http stands for HyperText Transfer Protocol. These are the links that send visitors to new Web pages.

mailto is used to send e-mail.

ftp stands for File Transfer Protocol. It directs the browser to download a file located in a specific location.

For more information on working with URLs, you can read *HTML 4.0: No Experience Required* by Stephen Mack and Janan Platt.

Creating URL Links

Once you have created hotspot objects, you can then apply URL links to them.

If you need to apply only one or two links, you can easily type them directly into the Hotspot Object panel.

To apply a single link:

1. Select the hotspot object.
2. Type the URL in the Links field in the Hotspot Object panel ❾.

As you apply or create URL links, a record of each link is retained as the history list. You can use the list to reapply a URL link without having to type it.

To work with the history list:

1. Select the hotspot object you want to apply a URL link to.
2. Press the pop-up history list next to the Links field in the Hotspot Object panel ❿.
3. Choose the link you want to apply to the hotspot.

TIP When you open a Fireworks file that has URL links, those links are automatically added to the history.

TIP The history list is only a temporary list and is deleted when you quit Fireworks. If you want a permanent record of all the URL links, you can add the list to a URL library *(see page 227).*

Hotspots do not have to have URL links. A hotspot can also be used as the trigger for a behavior. *(See Chapter 18, "Behaviors.")*

To remove the URL link from a hotspot:

1. Select the hotspot.
2. Choose No URL (no HREF) from the History list.

Assigning Hotspot Attributes

In addition to the URL links, there are other settings for hotspot objects.

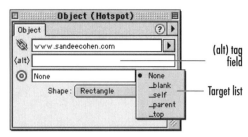

⊙ *The* Hotspot panel commands.

The (alt) tag contains the text that is displayed while the image is loading or if the image can not be found.

To set the (alt) tag:

◆ Type the text in the (alt) field **⊙**.

The Target field controls where the Web page requested by a link appears. Targets are usually used as part of framesets.

To set the target:

◆ Use the Target list or type in the field **⊙** the window or frame you want the link to open to.

- None and _self open the destination page in the same location that the button was in.
- _blank opens the destination page in a new browser window.
- _parent opens the destination page in the parent framset of the link.
- –top replaces all the frames in the current browser window and opens the destination page in that window.

⑩ *The* Hotspot color well *allows you to change the color of the overlay.*

Hotspots are displayed with a see-through overlay. You can change the overlay color to help organize different links.

To change the hotspot color:

◆ Use the hotspot color well **⑩** to set the color for different hotpsots.

TIP Darker colors make it easier to see through the overlay.

⓫ *The* **URL panel** *allows you to manage multiple URLs.*

⓬ *The* **URL panel menu.**

⓭ *The* **list of URLs** *in the URL panel.*

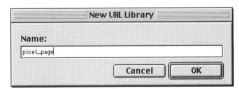

⓮ *The* **New URL Library** *dialog box.*

Managing Links

Typing URL links is fine if you only have a couple of links to add. However, complicated Web sites can have hundreds of links. Fireworks offers you many features for working with large numbers of links.

Rather than type links one by one, you can import URLs from any HTML file, Netscape Navigator bookmarks, or Internet Explorer favorites.

To import links:

1. If the URL panel **⓫** is not visible, choose **Window > URL Manager.**

2. Choose Import URLs from the panel menu **⓬**.

3. Navigate to select an HTML file, Navigator bookmarks file, or Internet Explorer favorites file. The URLs appear as a list in the panel **⓭**.

You can also create *libraries,* or groups of URLs. This allows you to group all the URLs for a certain Web site or client.

To create a URL library:

1. Choose New URL Library from the URL panel menu. This opens the New URL Library dialog box **⓮**.

2. Type the name of the library and click OK. This adds the library to the library list.

TIP Libraries can be used by multiple documents.

TIP To delete a library from the list, remove the library file located in the folder Fireworks: Settings: URL Libraries.

The URL panel keeps a history record of used URLs. This history is erased when you quit Fireworks. You can make the history permanent by adding the used URLs to a library.

Add URL   Delete URL

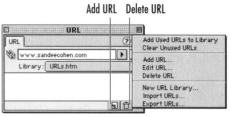

To add used URLs to a Library:

1. Create a new library or choose a library from the list.

2. Choose Add Used URLs to Library from the URL panel menu.

⓯ *Click the* **Add URL icon** *or choose Add URL from the menu to add URL links to a library.*

To add a new URL link to a Library:

1. Select the library that you want to add the URL link to.

2. Choose Add URL from the URL Manager menu or click the Add URL icon ⓯. This opens the New URL dialog box ⓰.

3. Type the URL in the field and then click OK. This adds the URL to the library.

⓰ *The* **New URL dialog box** *lets you type in new links for the selected library.*

To delete URL links:

1. Choose a link in the library.

2. Choose Delete Link from the URL panel menu or click the Delete URL icon.

URL links change continually. Fortunately, Fireworks provides a simple way to edit URL links in a document.

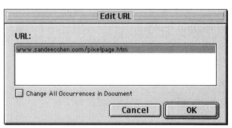

⓱ *The* **Edit URL dialog box** *lets you edit URLs and apply the changes to all occurrences of the URL in the document.*

To edit URL links:

1. Click the URL you want to edit.

2. Choose Edit URL from the URL panel menu. This opens the Edit URL dialog box ⓱.

3. Make whatever changes you want to the URL.

4. Check Change all Occurrences in Document to change all the objects that use that URL.

Managing Links

SLICES 17

Why would anyone spend hours creating an intricate Web graphic and then cut it up into different pieces? Well, that technique is called *slicing* and it allows you to define regions of an image that you can set to behave differently.

For instance, you might want to slice an image so that each slice has its own optimization settings. Or, you might want to slice an image into sections so that you can easily update each section of the image. You can also slice an image so that it contains plain HTML text, rather than an image.

Fireworks makes it easy to control where to put the slices and to apply special attributes to each slice region.

Using Ruler Guides to Slice

The easiest way to slice an image is to use ruler guides to define the slice area.

To slice using ruler guides:

1. Drag a guide from a ruler around the side of the area you want to slice.

2. Drag additional guides until you have defined all the slices for the image ❶.

3. When you export the file, set the Slicing to Slice Along Guides *(see Chapter 19, "Exporting.")*

TIP Fireworks opens Photoshop files with the Photoshop guides intact. They can then be used as slices in Fireworks.

TIP Use hotspot objects *(see Chapter 16, "Hotspots and Links")* to add links to slices created by guides.

❶ *Ruler guides can be used to define slices.*

❷ *The* **Rectangular Slice** tool *in the Toolbox.*

❸ *Drag the* **Slice tool** *to create a* **Slice** object.

❹ *The* **Polygon Slice tool** *in the Toolbox.*

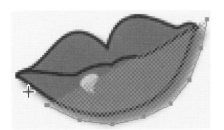

❺ *Click to create segments of a polygon slice.*

When should you use Polygon Slices?

Polygon slices are useful when you want to add behaviors or hotspots to intricate graphics or where rectangular slices would overlap.

Try to avoid too many polygon slices, as they require special Javascript code that can slow down the processing of your Web pages.

Creating Slice Objects

Ruler guides may not provide enough control to slice all the areas of the image accurately. For instance, a guide around one area may cut through an area that you don't want sliced. Slice objects let you select the areas to be sliced.

To use the Rectangular Slice tool:

1. Choose the Rectangular Slice tool from the Toolbox ❷. (Be careful, it is sharp.)
2. Drag a rectangle around the area that you want to slice ❸. This creates a rectangular slice object.

TIP If slice objects overlap, additional images will be created.

3. Use the Selection tools to move or modify slice objects.

TIP Slice objects can be copied, pasted and duplicated just like ordinary objects *(see Chapter 6, "Working with Objects.")*

To use the Polygon Slice tool:

1. Choose the Polygon Slice tool from the Toolbox ❹.
2. Click to create a point that defines each segment of the polygon that defines the slice ❺.
3. Use the Selection tools to move or modify slice objects.

To create slices from objects:

1. Select the object.
2. Choose **Insert** > **Slice**. This creates a rectangular slice object around the selected object.

Viewing Slice Objects and Guides

You may find it difficult to select or work with objects that have slices over them. You can control whether or not the slices or the slices guides are displayed.

To show and hide slice objects:

◆ Click the Show/Hide icon for the Web Layer in the Layers panel ❻.

or

Click the Show or Hide Web Layer icons at the bottom of the Toolbox ❼.

To show and hide slice guides:

◆ Choose View > **Slice Guides.** This hides and displays the slice guides.

Show/Hide icon

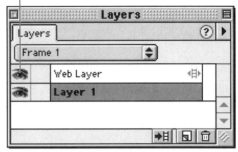

❻ *Use the* **Web Layer Show/Hide icon** *to control the display of slice objects.*

Hide Web   Show Web
Layer   Layer

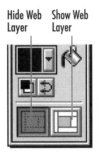

❼ *Use the* **Toolbox Show/ Hide Web Layer icons** *to control the display of slice objects.*

Why Slices? (Part Two)

Slicing also comes in handy when you need to use more than one export format for an image.

For instance, artwork that contains primarily flat colors should be exported as GIF files, but artwork with photographic images needs to be saved in the JPEG format.

You can also use slices so that GIF images contain their own unique color tables.

Viewing Slice Objects and Guides

Link list

❸ *The* **Slice object panel** *allows you to set the links and other attributes for slice objects.*

Setting the Slice Options

You set the options for slice objects using the Slice Object panel. Its controls are similar to the Hotspot options.

To set the slice options:

1. If the Object panel is not visible, choose **Window>Object.**

2. Select a slice object to display the slice object options **❸**.

To set the link for a slice object:

1. Use the link list to choose a link from either the current history or the current Library selected in the URL Manager. *(For more information working with the history, libraries, and the URL Manager, see Chapter 16, "Hotspots and Links.")*

2. To enter a link not in the list, type the link directly into the Link field.

   TIP The no URL (noHREF) setting lets you slice an image without a URL link.

Like hotspot objects, slice objects let you enter the (alt) text and target information. *(For a description of the (alt) text and target fields, see page 226.)*

To set the (alt) text and target:

1. Type the text for the Alt field.

2. Use the Target field or list to set a specific frame or window for the link.

You can also control the color of the slice object.

To set the slice object display color:

♦ Use the Color Well to set the display color for the Slice object.

Why Slices? (Part Three)

You also need to slice images to create the different Javascript behaviors such as Rollovers and Swap Images. *(For more information on working with behaviors, see Chapter 18, "Behaviors.")*

You can set a slice so that it displays ordinary HTML text in the sliced area. This makes it easy to update the information without creating new graphics.

To create a text slice:

1. Select the slice object and set the Export Settings to Text (No Image). The text settings appear **➒**.

2. Type whatever text you want in the image.

TIP Use whatever HTML codes you want to set the style, color, size, and other attributes of the text.

TIP The area inside a text cell is transparent and uses the canvas color as its background.

TIP You cannot see the text in a text slice in the Fireworks file. You need to export the image and view it in a Web browser before you can see the text **➓**.

Setting Slice Optimizations

You can also set a separate optimization for the area under each slice object. This allows you to mix different GIF palettes within an image or to mix GIF with JPEG files.

To optimize slices:

1. Select the slice object.

2. Use the Optimize panel to set the optimization for the area under the slice object **⓫**. *(For more information on working with the Opitimize panel, see Chapter 14, "Optimizing.")*

TIP You can select more than one slice object and use the Optimize panel to set the optimization for all the slice objects.

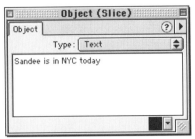

➒ *The slice object* **Text Settings.**

➓ *The information in a* **text slice** *as seen through a browser.*

⓫ *Select individual slices to then set the Optimize panel to create* **different optimization settings** *for slice objects.*

BEHAVIORS 18

People expect Web pages to be interactive. They want to click buttons to move to new pages. And they expect those buttons to provide feedback that they're in the off or on positions.

With Fireworks you can easily create interactive elements using behavior commands. For instance, a simple roll-over behavior allows users to click an object to move to a new Web page. A more complex behavior gives users several different looks as the user moves and clicks the button. Behaviors also let visitors move over one area to display pictures or animations in another.

Interface designers know that adding behaviors to Web pages is a great way to give visual feedback to the navigational elements. (They're also lots of fun!)

Understanding the Rollover States

Image maps *(see Chapter 16, "Hotspots and Links")* give visitors to your Web page only a subtle hint that they can click there ❶. Rollovers can have more obvious cues depending on the artwork you create ❷. Some behaviors only change the appearance of the area under the mouse cursor. Others can trigger actions anywhere on the page. There are four states that can be used in rollovers ❸:

- **Up** is the look when there is no mouse cursor inside the image area. This is the normal state of the rollover.

- **Over** is the look when the mouse cursor is moved over the rollover area.

- **Down** is the look after the mouse clicks.

- **Over While Down** is the look when the mouse cursor passes over a rollover that is in the Down state.

TIP The Down and Over While Down states are best used with framesets so that the rollover is seen in one frame while the new page appears in another.

Creating Symbol Buttons

The easiest way to create buttons is to use the Symbol command. *(For more information on Graphic Symbols, see Chapter 15, "Animations.")*

To create Symbol Buttons:

1. Choose **Insert** > **New Button.** This opens the Button Symbol window.

2. Click the tabs to create the artwork for each of the states *(see the next page).*

2. Click the Active Area tab to specify the trigger area.

3. Use the Link Wizard to set the following attributes for the button *(see page 242).*

❶ *When the mouse* **passes over an image map,** *it shows a simple hand cursor.*

❷ *When the mouse* **passes over a rollover,** *it shows the hand cursor and the image variation that was created for the Over state. In this case a glow was added to the silhouette.*

❸ *The* **four rollover states** *can be set for whatever looks you want. Each state gives a different response to the action of the mouse.*

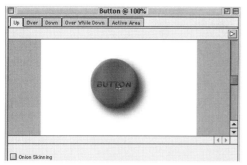

❹ *The Button Symbol window in the* **Up** *state.*

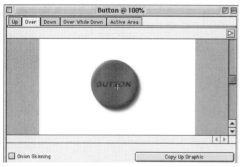

❺ *The Button Symbol window in the* **Over** *state.*

❻ *Buttons are displayed in the* **Library** *panel.*

Creating a Simple Rollover

A simple rollover is a button that has only two states: Up and Over.

To create a Simple Rollover:

1. Choose **Insert** > **New Button.** This opens the Button Symbol window.

2. Click the Up tab ❹ and use any of the Fireworks tools and commands to create the artwork for the Up or Normal state of the button.

3. Click the Over tab ❺ to switch to the window that controls the appearance of the Over state of the button.

4. Click the Copy Up Graphic to bring the artwork from the Up window into the Over window. You can then make any adjustments as desired.

   or

   Use any of the Fireworks tools and commands to create new artworks for the Over state of the button.

5. Close the Button Symbol window. An instance of the button appears on the page as well as in the Library panel ❻.

   TIP The Simple Rollover in the Behaviors panel is locked because the Behavior was created as part of the Symbol.

   TIP The Active Area tab sets the trigger area of the button as well as the slice area of the button.

   TIP To see if the button is working correctly, click the Preview tab.

Creating a Nav Bar

A Nav Bar is a set of buttons that work together. When you click one button in a Nav Bar, the other buttons change their state.

The first step to creating a Nav Bar is to create a Nav Bar Image. This is a button that uses all four states: Up, Over, Down, and Over While Down.

To create a Nav Bar Image:

1. Choose **Insert >New Button.** This opens the Button Symbol window.

2. Click the Up, Over, Down ❼, and Over While Down ❽ tabs to create the artwork for each of the button states.

TIP Use the Copy Over Graphic, and Copy Down Graphic buttons to copy the artwork from one state to the next.

3. Click the Show Down State Upon Load to make the Down state the initial appearance of the button.

4. Close the Button Symbol window. An instance of the button appears on the page. This instance can be deleted if you are creating a Nav Bar.

TIP The Behaviors panel displays the Set Nav Bar Image attribute. This is locked because the Behavior was created as part of the Symbol.

TIP Remember, you must close the Symbol window to save your work.

❼ *The Button Symbol window in the* **Down** state.

❽ *The Button Symbol window in the* **Over While Down state.**

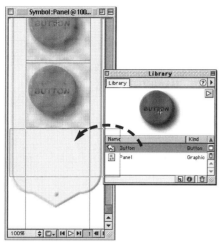

❾ **Drag buttons from the Library panel** *to create the buttons for a Nav Bar.*

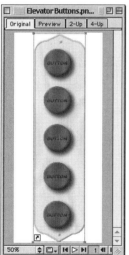

❿ **A finished Nav Bar** *appears in the document as an instance of the graphic symbol.*

Once you have created a Nav Bar Image, you can use that Symbol Button as part of a Nav Bar.

To create a Nav Bar:

1. Choose **Insert** >**New Symbol.** This opens the Symbol Properties dialog box.

2. Name the Symbol and click OK. This opens the Graphic Symbol document window.

3. Choose Share Layer from the Layers panel to set the current layer to be seen across all frames.

4. Use any of the tools to create the background artwork for the Nav Bar. For example, if your Nav Bar is supposed to look like elevator buttons, the background artwork would look like the metal plate surrounding the buttons.

5. Drag the Nav Bar Image button from the Library panel into the Nav Bar Symbol window ❾.

6. Drag any Nav Bar Image buttons into the Nav Bar document window.

7. Close the Symbol window. An instance of the Nav Bar appears on the page ❿.

TIP The Behaviors panel displays the Set Nav Bar Image attribute. This is locked because the Behavior was created as part of the Symbol.

TIP Remember, you must close the Symbol window to save your work.

TIP To see if the Nav Bar is working correctly, click the Preview tab.

Editing Buttons and Nav Bars

There are several special techniques you can use when working with Symbol Buttons or Nav Bars.

To edit a Symbol Button:

1. Double-click the instance of the button on the page ⓫.

   or

   Double-click the preview or name of the button in the Library panel ⓫. This opens the Symbol Button window.

2. Make any changes to the artwork for each of the states of the button.

3. Close the Symbol window to apply the changes to the symbol in the document.

   TIP Remember, you must close the Symbol window to save your work.

To edit a Nav Bar:

1. Double-click the instance of the Nav Bar on the page ⓬.

   or

   Double-click the preview of the Nav Bar in the Library panel ⓬. This opens the Symbol window.

3. Close the Symbol window to apply the changes to the Nav Bar in the document.

   TIP Double-click the instance of a button in a Nav Bar to edit that button..

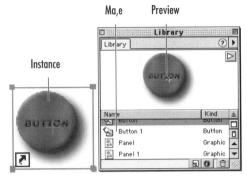

⓫ *Double-click button instances or Library entries to edit them.*

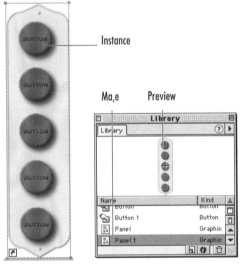

⓬ *Double-click Nav Bar instances or Library entries to edit them.*

⓭ *Use the* **Button Text field** *in the Object panel to change the text for all the states of a button.*

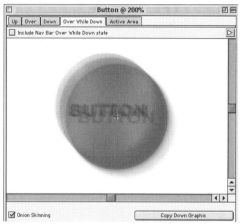

⓮ **Onion Skinning** *allows you to view and make changes to all the button states.*

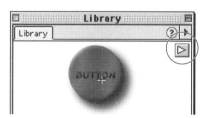

⓯ *The* **Play button** *in the Library window allows you to cycle through the button states.*

Fireworks keeps track of the text on a button. You can edit that text without having to open the Symbol Button window.

To edit the text on a button:

1. Select the instance of the button you want to edit.

2. With the Object panel open, change the text in the Button Text field ⓭.

3. Press Return to apply the change.

TIP The Button Text field changes the text on all the button states, even if they were not originally the same.

TIP If you edit the text within the Button Symbol window, a dialog box appears asking if you want to apply the changes to all the button states.

Onion Skinning allows you to see and edit objects on different frames *(see page 215).* You can also use Onion Skinning to edit all the button states.

To use Onion Skinning for Button Symbols:

1. Open the Button Symbol window.

2. Select Onion Skinning ⓮.

3. Use the selections tools or commands to select the objects on the button states.

4. Make any changes your want to the artwork.

5. Close the window to apply the changes.

TIP You can use any of the Alignment or Transformation tools or commands to change the objects in the button.

To display the Symbol Button states:

◆ Click the Play button in the Library Window ⓯. This cycles through all the button states.

TIP There is also a Play button in the Button Symbol window that cycles through the button states.

Using the Link Wizard

Despite its name, the Link Wizard does more than just set the links for a button. It also controls the export settings, links, target and file name. You can also use the Link Wizard to set the attributes for individual buttons.

To set the Link Wizard Export settings:

1. Click the Active Area tab for a button.
2. Click the Link Wizard. This opens the Link Wizard dialog box.
3. Click the Export Settings tab **16**.
4. Choose one of the Export Presets listed in the pop-up menu.

    or

    Click the Edit button. This opens the Export Preview dialog box.
5. Make whatever changes you want to the Export Preview and click OK. The settings are applied to the button.

TIP The Previous and Next buttons let you move between the Link Wizard tabs.

To set the Link Wizard Link settings:

1. Click the Link tab in the Link Wizard **17**.
2. Use the Link field to set the link.
3. Type the alt tag in the (alt) field.
4. Use the Status Bar field to type the message to be displayed in the Status Bar when the cursor passes over the button.

TIP The Status Bar text is optional but is considered a helpful addition to your Web site.

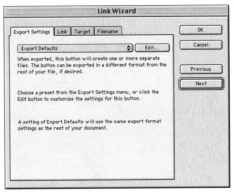

16 *The* **Link Wizard Export Settings** *lets you set the optimization for a Button Symbol.*

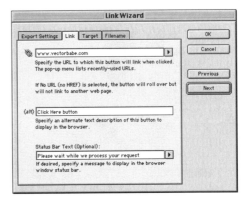

17 *The* **Link Wizard Link settings** *let you set the URL, (alt) tag, and Status Bar Text for a Button Symbol.*

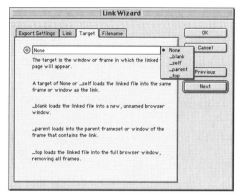

⑱ *The* **Link Wizard Target settings** *let you set where the destination page opens.*

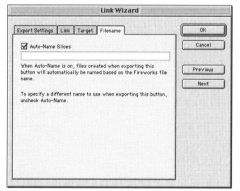

⑲ *The* **Link Wizard Filename settings** *let you customize the name when the button is exported.*

To set the Link Wizard Target:

1. Click the Target tab in the Link Wizard **⑱**.

2. Set the Target control as follows:
   - None and _self opens the destination page in the same location that the button was in.
   - _blank opens the destination page in a new browser window.
   - _parent opens the destination page in the parent framset of the link.
   - –top replaces all the frames in the current browser window and opens the destination page in that window.

   TIP You can type the frame name in the target field.

You can give your button a custom name. This makes it easier to identify the images exported for the button.

To set the Link Wizard Filename:

1. Click the Filename tab in the Link Wizard **⑲**.

2. Deselect Auto-Name Slices to open the Filename field.

3. Type the custom name to be used when the file is exported.

To use the Link Wizard for individual buttons:

1. Choose the button you want to edit.

2. Click Link Wizard in the Object panel.

3. In the dialog box that appears, choose Current to edit just that button.

4. Use the Link Wizard exercises described on these two pages.

5. Close the Link Wizard to apply the changes to that one button.

Importing Symbols

Once you have created a symbols in one
document, you can use that symbol in
other documents.

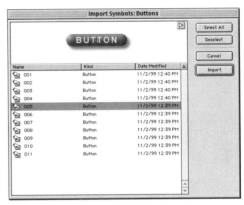

To drag a Symbol into a document:

1. Open the document containing the
    Symbol Button and the new document.

2. Drag and drop the Symbol Button from
    the Document Window or the Library
    panel into the new document.

To import a Symbol Button into a document:

1. Choose Insert > Libraries > Other and
    navigate to find the document that
    contains the Symbol Button.

2. Click OK. This opens the Import
    Symbols dialog box ❷.

3. Select the symbol or symbols you want
    to import.

4. Click Import to add the selected
    symbols to the document.

Fireworks ships with three libraries of
buttons, elements, and nav bars you can use
in your own documents.

To import the Fireworks library elements:

1. Choose Insert > Libraries and then
    choose one of the following:

    - Buttons contains a set of buttons.
    - Nav Bars contains a set of buttons
      and nav bars that use those buttons.
    - Themes contains a button and two
      graphic elements that can be used as
      part of a coordinated theme.

2. Use the Import dialog box to import
    any of the items from the libraries.

❷ *The* **Import Symbols dialog box** *lets you
select symbols used in other documents and
import them into the current document.*

Importing Symbols

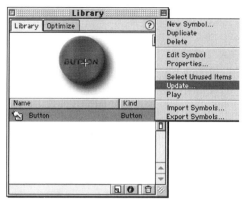

㉑ *Use the* **Update command in the Library panel** *to change an imported instance to its original symbol.*

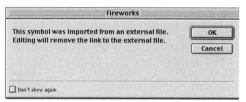

㉒ **Editing an imported instance** *breaks the link between the instance and the original symbol.*

Editing Imported Instances

Instances of symbols imported from other documents retain a link to the original symbol.

If you edit the symbol in the original document, you can then update the imported instance.

To update an imported instance:

1. Edit the symbol in the original document.

2. Select the imported instance in the second document.

3. Choose Update from the Library panel menu ㉑. A dialog box appears indicating that the object was updated.

TIP Imported instances of an edited symbol do not update unless you specifically apply the Update command. This allows you to edit the symbol in one document without affecting other documents.

You can break the link by editing the symbol.

To edit an imported symbol:

1. Double-click the symbol in the document window or Library. A document box appears asking if you want to break the link ㉒.

2. Click OK. This releases the symbol from the link to the original file.

3. Make any changes to the symbol.

Editing Imported Instances

Creating a Swap Image Behavior

Fireworks also lets you create a *swap-image* behavior. This means that moving the cursor over one area of the image triggers an action to show something elsewhere in the image ㉓–㉔.

You need to create certain elements in order to create a swap-image behavior. The order that you create these elements is important.

To create the elements of a swap-image behavior:

1. Create the frames with different images under the area to be changed.

   or

   Create an external file, such as a GIF animation, which can be set to display under the area to be changed. *(For more information on creating GIF animations, see Chapter 15, "Animations.")*

2. Create a slice object (but not a hotspot) to define the area to be changed by the behavior *(see the next page).*

3. Create a hotspot or slice object to define the area that triggers the behavior *(see the next page).*

4. Assign a swap-image behavior to the hotspot or slice object *(see page 248).*

To create the frames for the area to be changed:

1. Create a frame with the normal state for the image ㉕.

2. Duplicate this frame and create artwork for the changed area of the image ㉖.

3. If necessary, duplicate this frame and create artwork for any additional swap-image behaviors.

㉓ *When the cursor is outside an object, the image is displayed in its normal state.*

㉔ *When the cursor passes over the image, the* **Swap-image behavior** *changes the display of another part of the image.*

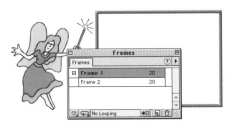

㉕ *Frame 1 displays the normal state of the image.*

㉖ *Frame 2 displays the second state of the image.*

㉗ *The area to be changed in a swap-image behavior must be covered with a slice object.*

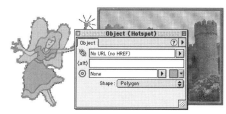

㉘ *The area that triggers the change can be defined with either a hotspot or a slice object.*

After you create the frames, you then need to add a slice object that defines the area to be changed.

To define the area to be changed:

1. Drag a slice object that completely covers the area to be changed **㉗**.

2. In the Slice Objects panel, set the Export Settings that for the area.

TIP Leave the Link to No URL (noHREF).

3. Give this slice a distinctive name.

TIP Although a distinctive name is not necessary, it will help as you assign the area for the Swap Image behavior.

You can use either a hotspot or slice object to define the area that triggers the swap-image behavior.

To define the area that triggers the change:

1. Select the path or object that triggers the change.

2. To create a hotspot area the same shape as the path, choose **Insert >Hotspot ㉘**.

   or

   Use any of the hotspot tools to define the area for the rollover.

TIP Using a hotspot object allows you to make a nonrectangular area.

   or

   To create a slice object that can trigger the change, choose **Insert >Slice.**

TIP Using a slice object to trigger the change allows you to have that area also change its appearance.

Creating a Swap Image Behavior

The final step in creating a swap-image behavior is to assign the behavior to the Hotspot or Slice that triggers the action.

To assign the swap-image behavior:

1. Select the hotspot or slice object that triggers the change.

2. Choose Swap Image from the Behaviors panel. The Swap Image dialog box appears.

3. Choose the name of the slice object that defines the area that triggers the change ㉙.

   or

   Click the slice object in the slice area diagram ㉙.

4. Choose the frame that is to be inserted into the area ㉚.

   or

   Designate an image file that is to be inserted into the area ㉚.

5. Choose Restore Image onMouseOut to change the area back to the original frame or image when the cursor leaves the trigger area.

6. Choose Preload Images to have the hidden images downloaded with the rest of the artwork. This makes the swap image revealed faster.

7. Click OK to return to the document. The swap image behavior appears in the Behaviors panel ㉛.

TIP To see if the swap image behavior is working correctly, click the Preview tab. However, you need to use the **File > Preview in Browser** command to see any external files used.

Slice object to be changed   **Slice area diagram**

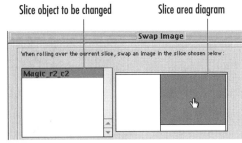

㉙ *The* **Swap Image dialog box** *lets you pick the area to be changed by the swap-image behavior.*

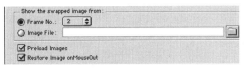

㉚ *Use the* **Show the swapped image from controls** *to choose the frame or external file that will display in the changed image area.*

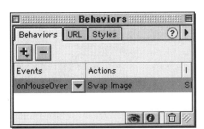

㉛ *The* **swap-image details** *are listed in the Behaviors panel.*

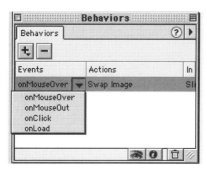

32 *The* **Events list** *allows you to modify the mouse action that triggers the behavior.*

33 *Use the* **Behaviors list** *to add behaviors to the object*

34 *The* **Swap Image Restore** *lets you customize how a swap-image behavior is restored to the normal state.*

There are modifications you can make to the Swap Image behavior. For instance, you may want the behavior to be activated by a mouse click rather than moving the mouse over the image.

To modify the swap-image behavior:

1. Select the hotspot or slice object that triggers the change.
2. Select the behavior in the Behaviors panel. A small triangle control appears in the Events column.
3. Click the Events triangle control. This opens the Events list **32**.
4. Choose the type of Mouse action that should trigger the behavior from the following:
   - onMouseOver triggers the action as the mouse moves inside the hotspot area.
   - onMouseOut triggers the action as the mouse leaves the hotspot area.
   - onClick triggers the action when the mouse button is clicked inside the hotspot area.
   - onLoad automatically triggers the action as the images are loaded.

You can also add a special control to how the swap-image behavior is restored.

To control the swap-image restore:

1. Select the hotspot or slice object that triggers the change.
2. Click the Plus (+) sign in the Behaviors panel. This opens the Behaviors list **33**.

TIP Click the Minus (−) sign in the to delete a selected behavior.

3. Choose Swap Image Restore **34**.
4. Use the Events control to change the mouse action for how the image is restored.

EXPORTING 19

Unlike print images, graphics created for the Web require special handling when it comes to exporting. Not only do you have to optimize to the proper file format *(see Chapter 14, "Optimizing")*, but you also have to make sure you create the HTML code necessary to create the image maps or reassemble sliced graphics.

Fortunately, Fireworks makes it easy to export your graphics together with the HTML code.

You also have some special export commands that make it easy to work with Macromedia Dreamwever 3.

Finally Fireworks lets you export files in formats that can be used by other applications such as Flash and Adobe Illustrator.

macromedia
FIREWORKS

Understanding Exporting

There are several steps to exporting files. Each of the steps controls different aspects of the final output.

To export files:

1. Set the optimization settings as desired.

2. Choose **File** > **Export**. This opens the Export dialog box.

3. If the file does not contain slices or image maps, you can do a basic export.

4. If the file contains slices, set the slicing controls *(see the next page)*.

5. If the file contains slices or image maps, set the HTML properties *(see the next page.*

6. If the file contains slices or image maps, set the location for the HTML file *(see page 254)*.

7. Name and export the files.

❶ *A graphic that does not contain slices or buttons can be handled as a basic export.*

Creating a Basic Export

If the file does not contain slices or image maps, it can be exported in one step. This is a basic export ❶.

To export without slices or image maps:

1. Choose **File** > **Export**. The Export dialog box appears.

2. Set the options for Slices and HTML to None ❷.

TIP If you do not have slices or image maps in the file, the Slices and HTML options should be automatically set to None.

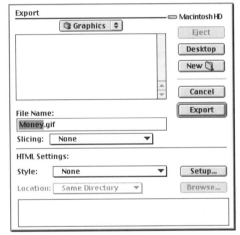

❷ *A plain graphic does not need any options for slicing or HTML.*

❸ *If you have slices in your graphic, you need to handle how those slices are handled.*

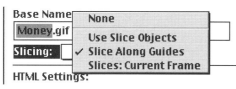

❹ *The Slicing list controls how the image is sliced.*

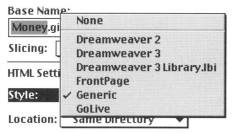

❺ *The HTML Style list controls the particular type of HTML code that is created.*

Exporting Slices

If you have added slices or rollover buttons to an image ❸, you need to set how those slices are exported.

The slice options control which elements should slice the image.

To set the slice options:

1. In the Export dialog box use the Slicing popup ❹ to choose how to slice the file:
   - Slice Objects slices along the slice objects.

   TIP Slice objects are automatically created when you create buttons or nav bars (*see Chapter 18, "Behaviors"*).

   - Slice Along Guides slices along the ruler guides.
   - Slices: Current Frame restricts the slices to the elements in the selected frame.

2. Set the HTML style and location options as described in the following exercises.

The HTML Style list lets you choose the specific type of HTML code.

To set the HTML Style:

1. In the Export dialog box use the HTML Style popup list to choose the type of HTML code ❺:
   - Dreamweaver 2 or Dreamweaver 3 exports to Macromedia Dreamweaver.
   - Dreamweaver 3 Library.lbi creates a library file for Dreamweaver 3.
   - Front Page exports to Microsoft FrontPage
   - GoLive exports to Adobe GoLive.
   - Generic is used for other programs or if you hand-code your web pages.

2. Set the HTML location as described in the following exercises.

The HTML Location list lets you choose where the file containing the HTML code is created.

To set the HTML Location:

1. In the Export dialog box choose the HTML Location ⑥:
   - Same Directory puts the HTML file in the same folder as the the exported images.
   - One Level Up puts the HTML file the the folder that contains the folder of the images.
   - Custom lets you select a folder.
   - Copy to Clipboard puts the HTML information in the computer's clipboard.

   TIP Copy to Clipboard allows you to switch to your page layout program and paste the HTML code directly onto a page.

2. Set the HTML properties as described on the next page.

Setting the HTML Properties

You can also control other aspects of the HTML code. These are called the HTML properties.

To access the HTML Properties:

1. If you are working in the document window, choose **File** > **HTML Properties**.

   or

   If you have opened the Export dialog box, click Setup. This opens the HTML Properties dialog box ⑦.

2. Set the HTML properties as described in the following exercises.

3. Click Set Defaults to make those settings the defaults for all documents.

   or

   Click OK to apply the settings to that file.

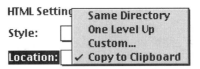

⑥ *The* **HTML Location list** *chooses where the HTML file should be located.*

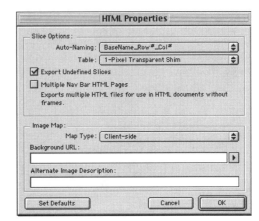

⑦ *The* **HTML Properties** *lets you customize the HTML code.*

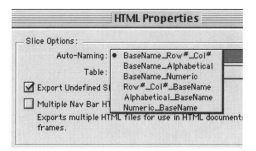

❽ *The* **HTML Auto-Naming list** *controls the names of the files generated from slices.*

HTML Properties

Slice Options:
Auto-Naming:
Table:
- Nested Tables – No Shims
- Single Table – No Shims
- 1-Pixel Transparent Shim
- Shims from Image Slices

☑ Export Undefined Slices

☐ Multiple Nav Bar HTML Pages
Exports multiple HTML files for use in HTML document frames.

❾ *The* **HTML Table list** *controls the tables that are created for sliced images.*

What are Shims?

In carpentry, shims are thin pieces of wood that you use to make things fit snugly. In Fireworks shims are 1-pixel images that are used inside tables to make sure the images align correctly.

Shims are named shim.gif and are located along with the rest of the images.

Do not choose the No Shims options unless you understand how they work and understand that they may not preview correctly in all browsers.

You can control how Fireworks names the sliced images.

To set the auto-naming conventions:

♦ Use the Auto-Naming list ❽ to set the choices as follows:

- BaseName_Row#_Col# adds suffixes indicating row and column position of the slice.
- BaseName_Alphabetical adds an alphabetical suffix.
- BaseName_Numeric adds a numbered suffix.
- Row#_Col#_BaseName adds a prefix indicating the row and column position of the slice.
- Alphabetical_BaseName adds an alphabetical prefix.
- Numeric_BaseName adds a numbered prefix.

To set the Table options:

♦ Use the Table list ❾ to set the choices as follows:

- Nested Table—No Shims creates tables within other table cells.
- Single Table—No Shims creates a single table without nesting. This option may not display properly in all browsers
- 1-Pixel Transparent Shims creates a transparent image that is used to align the table. This is the most common option.
- Shims from Image Slices creates shims from the color of the image inside the table. This helps ensure there are no gaps between objects on your page.

Setting the HTML Properties

To control the undefined slices:

◆ Deselect Export Undefined Slices ⑩ to only export those areas that are under a slice object.

TIP When Export Undefined Slices is unchecked, parts of the image create blank cells with the cell color set to the document's canvas color.

To export for documents without frames slices:

◆ Select Multiple Nav Bars HTML Pages ⑩ to create multiple HTML files that can be used with documents that do not have frames.

There are two types of code for image maps: client-side and server-side.

To control the type of Image map:

◆ Choose client-side ⑪ to have all the image map information downloaded along with the Web page.

or

Choose server-side ⑪ to have all the image map information kept on the server.

or

Choose both ⑪ to create the code for both types of image map.

You can also add a URL to the background image.

To set the background URL:

◆ Type the URL in the Background URL field ⑫.

You can also set the text that is displayed as the image downloads or if the image is not available.

To set the Alternate Image Description:

◆ Type the text in the Alternate Image field ⑫.

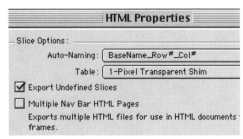

⑩ *The* Image Map Type list *lets you choose the type of image map code.*

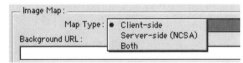

⑪ *The* Image Map Type list *lets you choose the type of image map code.*

Image Map:
Map Type : Client-side
Background URL :

Alternate Image Description :

⑫ *The* Background URL and Alternate Image Description *let you add the custom information for those attributes.*

Choosing the type of Image Map

The most common choice for image maps is a client-side. However, older browsers such as Internet Explorer 2 and Netscape 1 do not support client-side image maps.

Server-side image maps can be read by any browser but can take longer to download.

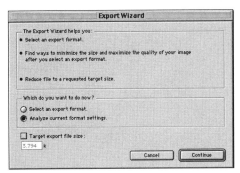

⓭ *The* **Export Wizard** *takes you through the steps necessary to export files.*

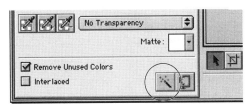

⓮ *The* **Export Wizard** *in the Export Preview dialog box.*

Using the Export Wizard

If you would like some help exporting files, Fireworks has an Export Wizard that can take you through the export steps.

To use the Export Wizard:

1. Choose **File > Export Wizard.** This opens the Export Wizard dialog box **⓭**.

   TIP You can also click the Export Wizard icon in the Export Preview dialog box **⓮**.

2. Click Select an Export Format to have the Export Wizard choose the format that is most appropriate for your image.

   TIP If you have opened the Export Wizard from the Export Preview dialog box you can choose Analyze Current Settings to have Fireworks determine whether or not the current format is appropriate for the image.

3. Check Target Export File Size to limit the size of the final exported file.

4. Click Continue for each of the Export Wizard screens to complete the process.

Using the Export Wizard

Exporting a Single Slices

You can export a single slice. This makes it easy to update a particular section of an image.

To export a single slice:

1. Select one or more slice objects.

2. Choose File > Export Special > Selected Slice. This opens the Export Preview dialog box.

   TIP If you have selected multiple slice objects, Fireworks skips the Export Preview dialog box.

3. Click Export. This opens the Export dialog box.

4. Name and export the file.

Exporting Other Formats

In addition to exporting ordinary HTML graphics, Fireworks lets you export files in formats for use in other applications.

To export layers or frames as individual files:

1. Choose File > Export Special > Layers/Frame to Files. This opens the Export dialog box **15**.

2. Use the Files From list **16** to choose one of the following:

   • Layers converts the artwork on each layer into its own file.
   • Slice Objects converts the artwork within each slice into its own file.
   • Frames converts the artwork on each frame into its own file.

3. If desired, select Trim Images to Crop so that only the live artwork is exported.

4. Click OK to export the artwork.

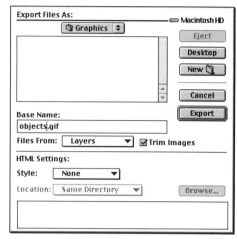

15 The **Export Files As** *dialog box lets you export files in different formats for use in other applications.*

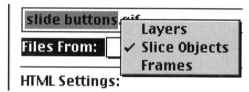

16 *Use the* **Files From list** *to choose which Fireworks elements should be exported.*

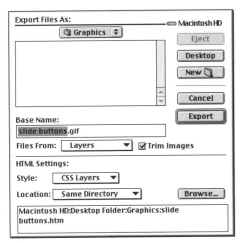

⑰ *Export as* **CSS Layers** *lets you use your artwork as part of cascading style sheets.*

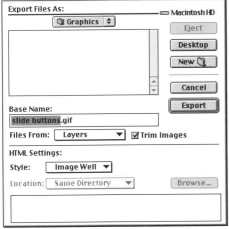

⑱ *Export as* **Image Well** *lets you use your artwork in Lotus Domino.*

You can save the document as cascading style sheets, which allow you to layer objects in web page layout programs such as Macromedia Dreamweaver.

To export as cascading style sheets:

1. Choose **File** > **Export Special** > **CSS Layers.** This opens the Export dialog box **⑰**.

2. Set the Files From list to Layers.

3. If desired, select Trim Images to Crop so that only the live artwork is exported.

4. Set the HTML Settings Style to CSS Layers.

5. Use the Location list to choose a location for the file.

6. Name and export the files.

You can save the document in the Lotus Domino Image Well format.

To export as Lotus Domino Image Well:

1. Choose **File** > **Export Special** > **Lotus Domino Image Well.** This opens the Export dialog box **⑱**.

2. Set the Files From list to Frames.

3. If desired, select Trim Images to crop so that only the actual artwork is exported.

4. Set the HTML Settings Style to Image Well.

6. Name and export the files.

You can export your images in the Flash SWF format. This lets you use your Fireworks images in Flash animations.

To export Flash SWF files:

1. Choose **File** > **Export Special** > **Flash SWF.** This opens the Export Special dialog box **⑲**.

2. Click Setup to open the Flash SWF Export Options.

3. Choose how objects are exported:
   - Maintain Paths converts Fireworks paths into editable Flash paths **⑳**.
   - Maintain Appearance converts paths into bitmapped images **㉑**.

4. Choose how text is exported:
   - Maintain Editability converts Fireworks text into Flash text which can be edited **⑳**.
   - Convert to Path converts Fireworks text into artwork **㉑**.

5. Set the JPEG quality for bitmapped images.

   TIP The lower the quality, the smaller the file size.

6. Use the Frame controls to choose which frames should be exported.

7. Choose a frame rate to control the speed of the animation.

8. Click OK to return to the Export Special dialog box.

9. Name and export the files.

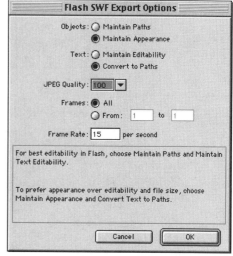

⑲ The **Flash SWF Export Options** controls how objects are converted into Flash SWF.

Fireworks image

Flash image

⑳ **Maintian Paths** and **Maintain Editability** creates Flash objects that can be edited, but lose Fireworks effects and transformations.

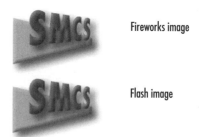

Fireworks image

Flash image

㉑ **Maintian Appearance** and **Convert to Paths** creates Flash objects that look the same as their original Fireworks artwork.

Exporting Other Formats

22 *The* **Illustrator Export Options dialog** *controls how Fireworks objects are converted into Illustrator files.*

Fireworks image

Illustrator image

23 *Fireworks effects and transformations are dropped when objects are converted into the Illustrator 7 format.*

You can also export your images as Adobe Illustrator files. These files can be opened by Illustrator or Macromedia FreeHand.

To export Flash SWF files:

1. Choose **File** > **Export Special** > **Illustrator 7**. This opens the Export Special dialog box **22**.

2. Click Setup to open the Illustrator Export Options dialog.

3. Choose Export Current Frame only which converts Fireworks layers into Illustrator layers.

   or

   Choose Convert Frames to Layers which converts each Fireworks frame into an Illustrator layer.

   TIP None of the Fireworks effects or text transformations are retained when the file is converted into the Illustrator format **23**.

4. Choose FreeHand 8 Compatible if you want the file to be opened in Macromedia FreeHand.

5. Click OK to return to the Export Special dialog box.

6. Name and export the files.

Cropping or Scaling Exported Images

Once you have created an image, you can scale the image or crop it to export just a certain area.

To scale an image in Export Preview:

1. Choose **File**>**Export Preview** to open the Export Preview dialog box.

2. Click the File tab. This opens the File Scale and Export Area options **㉔**.

2. Use the Percentage (%) slider or type in the field to scale the image to a percentage of its original size.

   or

   Enter an amount in the *W* (width) or *H* (height) fields to scale the image to an absolute measurement.

   TIP With Constrain selected, the width and height of the image keep the proportions of the original image.

You can also crop an image while you are working inside the Export Preview area.

To use the Export Area tool in Export Preview:

1. Choose **File**>**Export Preview**.

2. Click the Export Area tool **㉕** at the bottom the the preview area.

3. Adjust the handles **㉖** so the rectangle surrounds the area you want to export.

4. Use the Export Preview dialog box to export the image.

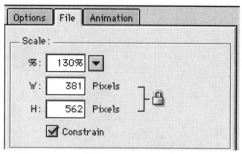

㉔ *The* **Scale controls** *of the File tab of the Export Preview dialog box.*

㉕ *The* **Export Area tool** *in the Export Preview dialog box.*

㉖ *Adjust the* **Export Area handles** *to set the area to be exported.*

②⑦ *The* **Export Area tool** *in the Toolbox.*

②⑧ *Use the* **Export Area tool** *to* **drag a rectangle around the area you want to export.**

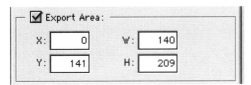

②⑨ *Use the* **Export Area controls** *to numerically adjust the size of the exported image.*

You can also use the Export Area tool to select and export a portion of the image.

To use the Export Area tool:

1. Choose the Export Area tool from the Toolbox **②⑦**.

2. Drag a rectangle around the area you want to export **②⑧**.

3. Adjust the handles so they are around the area you want to export.

4. Double-click inside the rectangle or click the Export button in the Tool Options panel. Only the selected area appears in the Export Preview window.

5. Use the Export Preview dialog box to export the image.

You can control the size of the export area numerically using the Export Area controls of the File tab.

To crop numerically in the Export Preview:

1. Choose **File** > **Export Preview**.

2. Choose the File tab **②⑨**.

3. Use the *X* and *Y* fields to set the upper left corner of the area to be exported.

4. Use the *W* and *H* fields to set the width and height of the exported area.

TIP When you set the export area numerically, you see the same handles as when you use the Export Area tool. You can drag the handles in the box that surrounds the selected portion to adjust the selection.

Updating HTML

You may find that you want to change the HTML code and images that have already been imported into a Web page along with other HTML text and graphics. If so, Fireworks gives you a powerful command that searches for specific HTML inside a Web page and updates it.

To update HTML inside an exsisting page:

1. Choose **File** > **Update HTML**. This opens a dialog box where you can navigate to find the HTML page you want to change.

2. Select the file.

3. A dialog box asks you where to put the graphics for the updated HTML.

TIP If Fireworks cannot find the proper HTML code to update, it adds the code for the selected image to the end of the document.

DEFAULTS A

As you have seen, Fireworks provides a great number of preset patterns, gradients, brushes, and effects that you can apply to objects. You can modify the default settings to create other effects. (Just remember the immortal words, "Defaults, dear Brutus, lie not in our stars, but in our software.")

This appendix shows the default settings for the textures, patterns, bevel effects, gradients, and brushes that you can apply to objects. It also shows the three libraries that are installed automatically with Fireworks.

In each case, consider these defaults as just the start for creating your own looks.

Textures

The 26 textures can be applied to either fills or strokes *(see page 105)*.

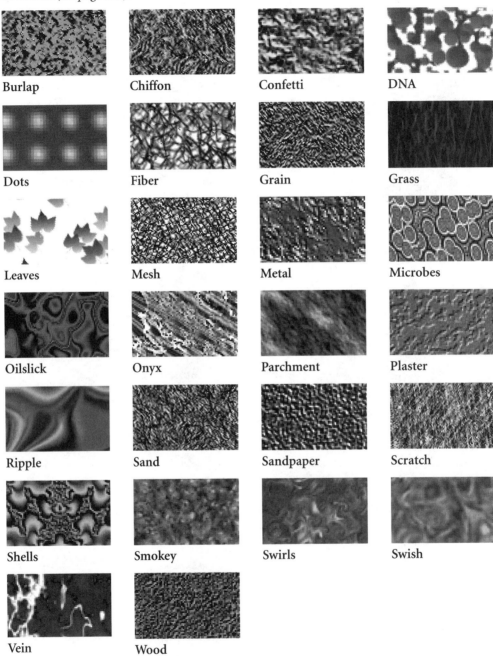

Burlap

Chiffon

Confetti

DNA

Dots

Fiber

Grain

Grass

Leaves

Mesh

Metal

Microbes

Oilslick

Onyx

Parchment

Plaster

Ripple

Sand

Sandpaper

Scratch

Shells

Smokey

Swirls

Swish

Vein

Wood

Patterns

The 14 patterns can be applied as fills *(see page 103)*.

| Aggregate | Bark | Berber Rug | Blue Wave |

| Bricks—Small | Grass—Tiny | Illusion | Impressionist—Red |

| Jeans | Leaves—Photinia | Red Goo | Tweed |

| Weave | Wood—Light |

Gradients

The 11 gradients can be applied as fills *(see page 100)*.

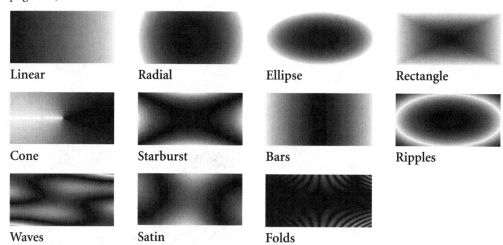

Linear	Radial	Ellipse	Rectangle
Cone	Starburst	Bars	Ripples
Waves	Satin	Folds	

Strokes

You can apply the 48 strokes to open or closed paths *(see page 113)*.

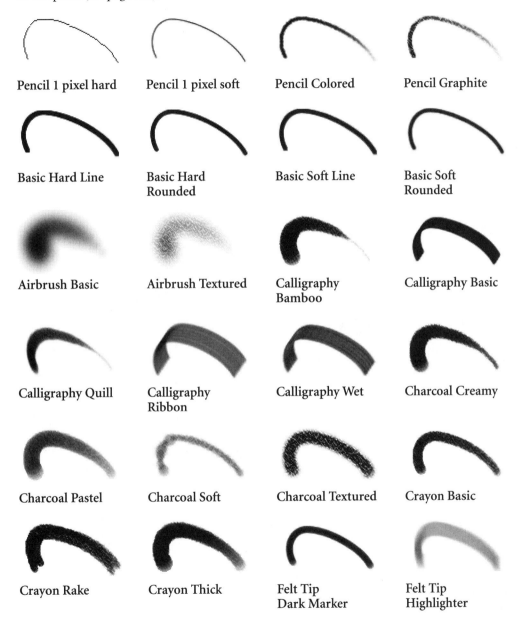

Pencil 1 pixel hard   Pencil 1 pixel soft   Pencil Colored   Pencil Graphite

Basic Hard Line   Basic Hard Rounded   Basic Soft Line   Basic Soft Rounded

Airbrush Basic   Airbrush Textured   Calligraphy Bamboo   Calligraphy Basic

Calligraphy Quill   Calligraphy Ribbon   Calligraphy Wet   Charcoal Creamy

Charcoal Pastel   Charcoal Soft   Charcoal Textured   Crayon Basic

Crayon Rake   Crayon Thick   Felt Tip Dark Marker   Felt Tip Highlighter

Strokes

Strokes *(continued)*

Strokes

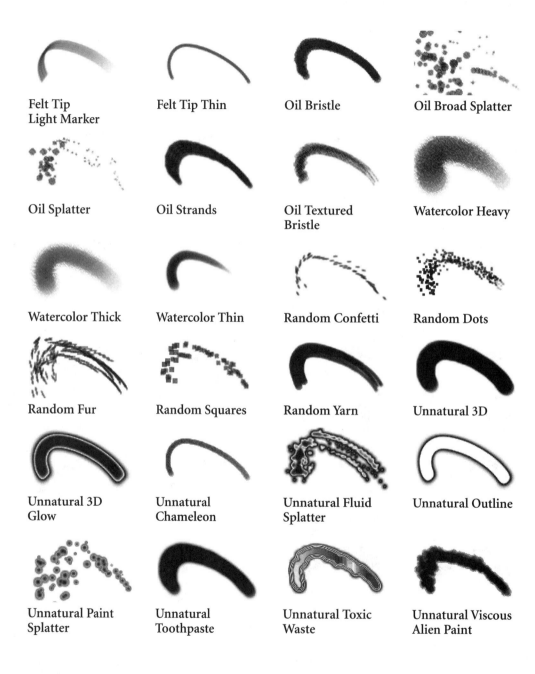

Felt Tip
Light Marker

Felt Tip Thin

Oil Bristle

Oil Broad Splatter

Oil Splatter

Oil Strands

Oil Textured
Bristle

Watercolor Heavy

Watercolor Thick

Watercolor Thin

Random Confetti

Random Dots

Random Fur

Random Squares

Random Yarn

Unnatural 3D

Unnatural 3D
Glow

Unnatural
Chameleon

Unnatural Fluid
Splatter

Unnatural Outline

Unnatural Paint
Splatter

Unnatural
Toothpaste

Unnatural Toxic
Waste

Unnatural Viscous
Alien Paint

Bevel Styles

There are seven different bevel styles that can be applied as either inner or outer bevels. Use the bevel controls to adjust the size, softness, and contrast *(see page 123)*.

Library Buttons

Fireworks installs libraries with elements that you can import into your own documents. These are the eleven buttons that are installed under the **Insert** > **Libraries** > **Buttons** command.

Inner Bevel Flat

Inner Bevel Smooth

Inner Bevel Sloped

Inner Bevel Frame 1

Inner Bevel Frame 2

Inner Bevel Ring

Inner Bevel Ruffle

001 button

003 button

005 button

BUTTON

007 button

009 button

011 button

002 button

004 button

006 button

008 button

010 button

Bevel Styles; Library Buttons

Library Themes

Fireworks installs libraries with elements that you can import into your own documents. These are the ten themes. Each theme consists of a horizontal divider, a bullet symbol, and a button. They are installed under the **Insert** >**Libraries** > **Buttons** command.

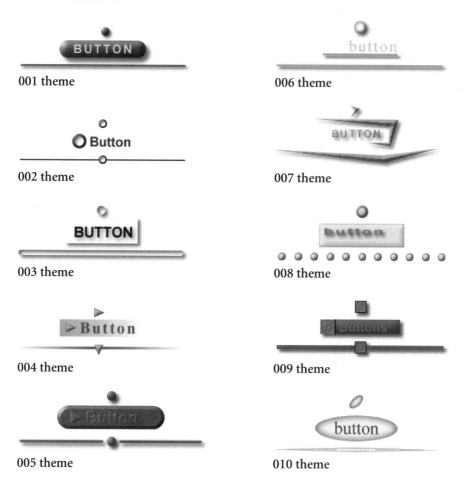

001 theme

002 theme

003 theme

004 theme

005 theme

006 theme

007 theme

008 theme

009 theme

010 theme

Library Nav Bars

Fireworks installs libraries with elements that you can import into your own documents. These are the six nav bars installed with Fireworks. Each has a button symbol as well as a nav bar graphic. They are installed under the **Insert** > **Libraries** > **Nav Bars** command.

001 nav bar

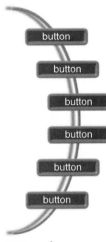

002 nav bar

005 nav bar

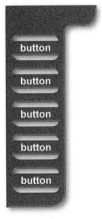

003 nav bar

004 nav bar

006 nav bar

KEYBOARD SHORTCUTS B

As you become more familiar with the various Fireworks features, you should begin to use the keyboard shortcuts for the commands you use most often. For instance, rather than use the mouse to choose **File>Export**, it is much faster and easier to use the keyboard shortcut.

This appendix lists the shortcuts for Fireworks menu commands. Most of these shortcuts are also listed on the menus. So you do not have to use this list to find the shortcut for the commands you use the most. However, this list can make it easy to find a certain shortcut or even to tell if a command has a shortcut assigned to it.

Windows Keyboard Shortcuts

The following are the keyboard shortcuts for the Windows platform. These are the abbreviations used for the keys.

Ctrl	Ctrl key
Alt	Alt key
Up	Up arrow key
Down	Down arrow key
Left	Left arrow key
Right	Right arrow key
Space	Spacebar

File Menu (Win)

New	Ctrl+N
Open	Ctrl+O
Open Multiple	Ctrl+Shift+O
Close	Ctrl+W, Ctrl+F4
Save	Ctrl+S
Save As	Ctrl+Shift+S
Import	Ctrl+R
Export	Ctrl+Shift+R
Export Preview	Ctrl+Shift+X
Preview in Primary Browser	F12
Preview in Secondary Browser	Shift+F12
Print	Ctrl+P
Exit/Quit	Alt+F4

Edit Menu (Win)

Undo	Ctrl+Z
Redo or Repeat	Ctrl+Shift+Z
Cut	Ctrl+X
Copy	Ctrl+C
Paste	Ctrl+V
Paste Inside	Ctrl+Shift+V
Paste Attributes	Ctrl+Alt+Shift+V
Select All	Ctrl+A
Deselect	Ctrl+D
Superselect	Ctrl+Up Arrow
Subselect	Ctrl+Down Arrow
Select Inverse	Ctrl+Shift+I
Duplicate	Ctrl+Alt+D
Clone	Ctrl+Shift+C
Crop Selected Image	Ctrl+Alt+C

View Menu (Win)

Zoom In	Ctrl++(plus), or Ctrl+Spacebar+drag
Zoom Out	Ctrl+- (minus)
Fit Selection	Ctrl+0 (zero)
Fit All	Ctrl+Alt+0 (zero)
Full Display	Ctrl+K
Hide Selection	Ctrl+M
Show All	Ctrl+Shift+M
Hide Edges	Ctrl+H
Hide Panels	Ctrl+Shift+H, or Tab
Rulers	Ctrl+Alt+R
Grid	Ctrl+' (apostrophe)
Guides	Ctrl+; (semicolon)
Slice Guides	Ctrl+Alt+Shift+;

Magnification Submenu (Win)

50%	Ctrl+5
100%	Ctrl+1
200%	Ctrl+2
400%	Ctrl+4
800%	Ctrl+8
3200%	Ctrl+3
6400%	Ctrl+6

Grid Options Submenu (Win)

Snap to Grid	Ctrl+Shift+' (apostrophe)
Edit Grid	Ctrl+Alt+G

Guide Options Submenu (Win)

Lock Guides	Ctrl+Alt+;
Snap to Guides	Ctrl+Shift+;
Edit Guides	Ctrl+Alt+Shift+G

Insert Menu (Win)

New Symbol	Ctrl+F8
Convert to Symbol	F8
Hotspot	Ctrl+Shift+U
Image	Ctrl+R
Empty Image	Control+Alt+Y

Modify Menu (Win)

Image Object . . . . Ctrl+E

Exit Image Edit . . . . Ctrl+Shift+D

Join . . . . Ctrl+J

Split . . . . Ctrl+Shift+J

Merge Images . . . . Ctrl+Shift+Alt+Z

Group . . . . Ctrl+G

Mask to Image . . . . Ctrl+Shift+G

Ungroup . . . . Ctrl+U

Symbol Submenu (Win)

Tween Instances. . . . . . Ctrl+Alt+Shift+T

Transform Submenu (Win)

Free Transform . . . . Ctrl+T

Numeric Transform . . . . . Ctrl+Shift+T

Rotate 90 degrees CW . . . . Ctrl+9

Rotate 90 degrees CCW . . . . Ctrl+7

Arrange Submenu (Win)

Bring to Front. . . . . Ctrl+F

Bring Forward . . . . Ctrl+Shift+F

Send Backward. . . . . Ctrl+Shift+B

Send to Back . . . . Ctrl+B

Align Submenu (Win)

Left. . . . . Ctrl+Alt+1

Center Vertical . . . . Ctrl+Alt+2

Right. . . . . Ctrl+Alt+3

Top. . . . . Ctrl+Alt+4

Center Horizontal . . . . Ctrl+Alt+5

Bottom . . . . Ctrl+Alt+6

Distribute Widths . . . . Ctrl+Alt+7

Distribute Heights. . . . . Ctrl+Alt+9

Text Menu (Win)

Editor. . . . . Ctrl+Shift+E

Attach to Path . . . . Ctrl+Shift+Y

Convert to Paths. . . . . Ctrl+Shift+P

Style submenu . . . . Windows

Plain . . . . Ctrl+Alt+Shift+P, or F5

Bold . . . . Ctrl+Alt+Shift+B, or F6

Italic. . . . . Ctrl+Alt+Shift+I, or F7

Underline. . . . . . Ctrl+Alt+Shift+U, or F8

Text Align Submenu(Win)

Left . . . . Ctrl+Alt+Shift+L

Center. . . . . Ctrl+Alt+Shift+C

Right. . . . . Ctrl+Alt+Shift+R

Justified . . . . Ctrl+Alt+Shift+J

Stretched . . . . Ctrl+Alt+Shift+S

Text Editor (Win)

Increase kerning. . . . . . Ctrl+Right Arrow

Decrease kerning . . . . Ctrl+Left Arrow

Increase leading. . . . . . . Ctrl+Up Arrow

Decrease leading . . . . . Ctrl+Down Arrow

Xtras (Win)

Repeat Xtra . . . . Ctrl+Alt+Shift+X

Window Menu (Win)

New Window. . . . . Ctrl+Alt+N

Toolbox. . . . . Ctrl+Alt+T

Object inspector . . . . Ctrl+I

Stroke panel. . . . . Ctrl+Alt+B

Fill panel . . . . Ctrl+Alt+F

Effect panel . . . . Ctrl+Alt+E

Swatches panel . . . . Ctrl+Alt+S

Color Mixer . . . . Ctrl+Alt+M

Tool Options panel . . . . Ctrl+Alt+O

Layers panel . . . . Ctrl+Alt+L

Frames panel . . . . Ctrl+Alt+K

Info panel. . . . . Ctrl+Alt+I

Behaviors inspector . . . . . . Ctrl+Alt+H

URL panel. . . . . Ctrl+Alt+U

Styles panel. . . . . Ctrl+Alt+J

Help Menu (Win)

Using Fireworks. . . . . . Ctrl+Alt+Shift+X

Miscellaneous (Win)

Default stroke and fill colors . . . . D

Swap stroke and fill colors X

Next frame . . . . Ctrl+Page Down

Previous frame . . . . Ctrl+Page Up

Windows Keyboard Shortcuts

Macintosh Keyboard Shortcuts

The following are the keyboard shortcuts for the Macintosh platform. These are the abbreviations used for the keys.

Cmd	Command key
Opt	Option key
Up	Up arrow key
Down	Down arrow key
Left	Left arrow key
Right	Right arrow key
Space	Spacebar

File Menu (Mac)

New	Cmd+N
Open	Cmd+O
Open Multiple	Cmd+Shift+O
Close	Cmd+W
Save	Cmd+S
Save As	Cmd+Shift+S
Import	Cmd+R
Export	Cmd+Shift+R
Export Preview	Cmd+Shift+X
Preview in Primary Browser	F12
Preview in Secondary Browser	Shift+F12
Print	Cmd+P
Quit	Cmd+Q

Edit Menu (Mac)

Undo	Cmd+Z
Redo or Repeat	Cmd+Shift+Z
Cut	Cmd+X
Copy	Cmd+C
Paste	Cmd+V
Paste Inside	Cmd+Shift+V
Paste Attributes	Cmd+Shift+Opt+V
Select All	Cmd+A
Deselect	Cmd+D
Superselect	Cmd+Up Arrow
Subselect	Cmd+Down Arrow
Select Inverse	Cmd+Shift+I
Duplicate	Cmd Opt+D
Clone	Cmd+Shift+C
Crop Selected Image	Cmd+Opt+V

View Menu (Mac)

Zoom In	Cmd++(plus), or Cmd+Spacebar+drag
Zoom Out	Cmd+- (minus)
Fit Selection	Cmd+0 (zero)
Fit All	Cmd+Opt+0 (zero)
Full Display	Cmd+K
Hide Selection	Cmd+M
Show All	Cmd+Shift+M
Hide Edges	Cmd+H
Hide Panels	Cmd+Shift+H, or Tab
Rulers	Cmd+Opt+R
Grid	Cmd+' (apostrophe)
Guides	Cmd+; (semicolon)
Slice Guides	Cmd+Shift+Opt+;

Magnification Submenu (Mac)

50%	Cmd+5
100%	Cmd+1
200%	Cmd+2
400%	Cmd+4
800%	Cmd+8
3200%	Cmd+3
6400%	Cmd+6

Grid Options Submenu (Mac)

Snap to Grid	Cmd+Shift+' (apostrophe)
Edit Grid	Cmd+Opt+G

Guide Options Submenu (Mac)

Lock Guides	Cmd+Opt+;
Snap to Guides	Cmd+Shift+;
Edit Guides	Cmd+Opt+Shift+G

Insert Menu (Mac)

New Symbol	Cmd+F8
Convert to Symbol	F8
Hotspot	Cmd+Shift+U
Image	Cmd+R
Empty Image	Cmd+Opt+Y

Modify Menu (Mac)

Tween Instances . . . . Cmd+Opt+Shift+T

Image Object . . . . Cmd+E

Exit Image Edit . . . . Cmd+Shift+D

Join . . . . Cmd+J

Split . . . . Cmd+Shift+J

Merge Images . . . . . . Cmd+Shift+Opt+Z

Group . . . . Cmd+G

Mask to Image . . . . Cmd+Shift+G

Ungroup . . . . Cmd+U

Transform Submenu (Mac)

Free Transform . . . . Cmd+T

Numeric Transform . . . . . Cmd+Shift+T

Rotate 90 degrees CW . . . . Cmd+9

Rotate 90 degrees CCW . . . . . . Cmd+7

Arrange Submenu(Mac)

Bring to Front . . . . Cmd+F

Bring Forward . . . . Cmd+Shift+F

Send Backward . . . . Cmd+Shift+B

Send to Back . . . . Cmd+B

Align Submenu (Mac)

Left . . . . Cmd+Opt+1

Center Vertical . . . . Cmd+Opt+2

Right . . . . Cmd+Opt+3

Top . . . . Cmd+Opt+4

Center Horizontal . . . . Cmd+Opt+5

Bottom . . . . Cmd+Opt+6

Distribute Widths . . . . Cmd+Opt+7

Distribute Heights . . . . . . Cmd+Opt+9

Text Menu (Mac)

Editor . . . . Cmd+Shift+E

Attach to Path . . . . Cmd+Shift+Y

Convert to Paths . . . . Cmd+Shift+P

Style Submenu (Mac)

Plain . . . . Cmd+Opt+Shift+P, or F5

Bold . . . . Cmd+Opt+Shift+B, or F6

Italic . . . . Cmd+Opt+Shift+I, or F7

Underline . . . . Cmd+Opt+Shift+U, or F8

Text Align Submenu (Mac)

Left . . . . Cmd+Opt+Shift+L

Center . . . . Cmd+Opt+Shift+C

Right . . . . Cmd+Opt+Shift+R

Justified . . . . Cmd+Opt+Shift+J

Stretched . . . . Cmd+Opt+Shift+S

Text Editor (Mac)

Increase kerning . . . . . Cmd+Right Arrow

Decrease kerning . . . . Cmd+Left Arrow

Increase leading . . . . . . Cmd+Up Arrow

Decrease leading . . . . Cmd+Down Arrow

Xtras (Mac)

Repeat Xtra . . . . Cmd+Opt+Shift+X

Window Menu (Mac)

New Window . . . . Cmd+Opt+N

Toolbox . . . . Cmd+Opt+T

Object inspector . . . . Cmd+I

Stroke panel . . . . Cmd+Opt+B

Fill panel . . . . Cmd+Opt+F

Effect panel . . . . Cmd+Opt+E

Swatches panel . . . . Cmd+Opt+S

Color Mixer . . . . Cmd+Opt+M

Tool Options panel . . . . . Cmd+Opt+O

Layers panel . . . . Cmd+Opt+L

Frames panel . . . . Cmd+Opt+K

Info panel . . . . Cmd+Opt+I

Behaviors inspector . . . . . Cmd+Opt+H

URL panel . . . . Cmd+Opt+U

Styles panel . . . . Cmd+Opt+J

Help Menu (Mac)

Using Fireworks . . . . Help

Miscellaneous (Mac)

Default stroke and fill colors . . . . D

Swap stroke and fill colors X

Next frame . . . . . Command+Page Down

Previous frame . . . . . Command+Page Up

Macintosh Keyboard Shortcuts

Toolbox Keyboard Shortcuts

The following are the keys that are used to access the tools in the toolbox (*see page 21*). These keys are pressed without using any modifier keys such as Command or Ctrl. For instance, to choose the Rectangle tool, you press only the *R* key. If a letter is used for more than one tool, such as the *B* for Brush and Reshape Brush, it means that pressing the key again toggles between the tools.

Toolbox

Pointer	V or 0 (zero)	Polygon	G
Select Behind	V or 0 (zero)	Text	T
Crop	C	Pencil	Y
Export Area	J	Brush	B
Subselect	A or L	Redraw Path	B
Marquee	M	Scale	Q
Ellipse Marquee	M	Skew	Q
Lasso	L	Distort	Q
Polygon Lasso	L	Freeform	F
Magic Wand	W	Reshape Area	F
Hand	Spacebar or H	Path Scrubber (+)	U
Magnify	Z	Path Scrubber (-)	U
Line	N	Eyedropper	I
Pen	P	Paint Bucket	K
Rectangle	P	Eraser	E
Ellipse	R	Rubber Stamp	S

REGULAR EXPRESSIONS C

The Find & Replace commands allow you to use Regular Expressions as part of the text and URL information. Regular expressions are special symbols that can be added to change how the Find & Replace commands work. They work like the special symbols and wildcard characters in word processing and page layout programs.

There are hundreds of different regular expressions—many more than could be covered in this book. If you are interested in working with regular expressions, a good reference is *The Dreamweaver 2 Bible* by Joseph Lowery, published by IDG Books.

You can also find information on regular expressions at *http://developer.netscape.com/docs/manuals/communicator/jsguide/regexp.htm.*

Regular Expressions

Character	Looks for	Example
^	The beginning of the input or line.	^H finds the **H** in **Help** but not **FreeHand**
$	The end of the input or line	s$ finds the **s** in **Fireworks** but not **wish**
*	The preceding characters that appears zero or more times	es* finds the **es** in **best** or the **ess** in **mess** or finds the **e** in **bet**
+	The preceding character that appears one or more times	es+ finds the **es** in **best** or the **ess** in **mess** but does not find the **e** in **bet**
?	The preceding character that appears zero or one times	st?on finds the **ston** in **Redstone** or the **son** in **Davidson** but does not find anything in **Littleton** or **Emerson**
.	Any single character except for the newsline character	.ealthy finds both **healthy** and **wealthy**
|	Either the characters before the | or the characters after the |	www|http finds both **www** or **http**
(n)	The preceding character when it occurs n number of times	e(2) finds **ee** in **sleep** or **keep** but not **kept**
(n,m)	The preceding character when it occurs at least n times but not more than m times	FF(2,4) finds **FF** in **FF0000**, **FFF000** or **FFFF00**
[abc]	Any of the characters in the brackets	[abc] finds **a, b,** or **c**
[a-c]	Any of the characters in the range of the characters between the hyphen	[a-e] finds **a, b, c, d,** or **e**
[^abc]	Any character not enclosed in the brackets	[^aeiou] finds the **d** in **adapt** and the **c** in **ouch**
[^a-c]	Any of the characters not in the range of characters between the hyphen	[a-s] finds the **t** in **text** or **u** in **ugly**, but not the **a** in **apple**
\d	Any numerical character from 0 to 9	\d finds the **2** in **H20** or the **7** in **7th Heaven**
\D	Any non-numerical character (same as [^0-9])	\D finds the **th** in **7th** or the **rd** in **3rd**
\f	Form feed character	
\n	Line feed character	
\r	Carriage return	
\s	Any white space character such as a tab, form feed or line feed	\spress finds the **press** in **Peachpit press** but not **depressed**
\S	Any single non–white-space character	\Spress finds the **press** in **depressed** but not **Peachpit press**
\t	A tab character	
\W	Any non-alphanumeric character	\W finds characters such as the **&** in **Big & Tall** or the **@** in **@mindspring.com**

INDEX

C

Index

Index

Index

P

Index

Index